Assessing Teacher Quality

Understanding Teacher Effects on Instruction and Achievement

Assessing Teacher Quality

Understanding Teacher Effects on Instruction and Achievement

EDITED BY

Sean Kelly

TEACHERS COLLEGE PRESS

Teachers College, Columbia University
New York and London

Published by Teachers College Press, 1234 Amsterdam Avenue, New York, NY 10027

Library of Congress Cataloging-in-Publication Data

Assessing teacher quality : understanding teacher effects on instruction and achievement / edited by Sean Kelly.
p. cm.
Includes bibliographical references and index.
ISBN 978-0-8077-5279-1 (pbk. : alk. paper)
ISBN 978-0-8077-5280-7 (hardcover : alk. paper)
1. Teachers–Rating of–United States. 2. Teacher effectiveness–United States. I. Kelly, Sean.
LB2838.A777 2012
371.100973–dc23 2011033302

ISBN 978-0-8077-5279-1 (paper)
ISBN 978-0-8077-5280-7 (hardcover)

Printed on acid-free paper
Manufactured in the United States of America

19 18 17 16 15 14 13 12 8 7 6 5 4 3 2 1

Contents

Acknowledgments

Many of the chapters in this volume were originally presented at the Understanding Teacher Effects on Student Outcomes Conference held at the University of Notre Dame in November 2008, hosted by the Center for Research on Educational Opportunity (CREO) and supported by the Institute for Educational Initiatives. As this volume goes to press, it now seems a long time ago! Yet also, the themes and perspectives seem even more relevant now than when I first envisioned this book project. I thank all the contributors for sticking with this project through the many rounds of revisions, and other contributors for enthusiastically joining the project along the way. Each of the authors in this volume was very gracious in working with me to craft such fine chapters, and it was a pleasure to see them develop as we worked.

I joined the CREO faculty and Department of Sociology in 2005. Throughout this time, I have been lucky to have had the support of great colleagues in Maureen Hallinan, William Carbonaro, Warren Kubitschek, and, more recently, Mark Berends. After our 2008 conference on teacher effects, I remember asking Bill Carbonaro what he thought about the possibility of my pursuing a book on this topic. His encouraging response gave me the confidence to get started right away. I've also had the chance to work with some really excellent current and former graduate researchers at CREO, including Heather Price, Richard Majerus, Elizabeth Covay, and Guillermo Montt. Although there are too many individuals to list, I've had a great deal of support from others in the Department of Sociology, at the Institute for Educational Initiatives, and throughout the University of Notre Dame. Moreover, I feel indebted to the community of scholars who have interacted with me over the years in the sociology of education and shown me not only what truly excellent research looks like but also much goodwill and support.

I would also like to thank my former colleagues at the Center for English Learning and Achievement (CELA) at the University of Wisconsin–Madison, among them Adam Gamoran, Martin Nystrand, Samantha Caughlan, and Mary Juzwik. Many of the ideas in chapter 1 can be traced back to our work at CELA, the new research projects we have worked on, and the many discussions we have had since I completed my PhD in sociology at UW-Madison.

Finally, I would like to thank Brian Ellerbeck at Teachers College Press for allowing me to edit a book on such an important and controversial topic, and Wendy Schwartz and the rest of the editorial team at Teachers College Press for working so diligently on our manuscript.

—Sean Kelly, Michigan State University

Introduction

Sean Kelly

This volume addresses a fundamental question in the educational sciences: What effect do teachers have on their students? In an era of test-based accountability, where educational reform efforts are moving rapidly to implement various programs of teacher accountability, questions of teacher effects are taking center stage in educational research, policy development, and program implementation. In 2008, the Center for Research on Educational Opportunity at the University of Notre Dame hosted a conference on understanding teacher effects that brought together a diverse group of educational scholars, including sociologists, psychologists, economists, teacher educators, and educational policy experts. This book is the result of that conference and subsequent research and discussion among the participants and others. In all, the authors in this volume present evidence that shows that teacher effects are important and highly variable and pertain to diverse aspects of students' educational lives. Moreover, a central tenet of this volume is that effective or ineffective instruction can seldom be traced solely to "good" and "bad" teachers, although it is useful to pose questions about the general principles of effective practice and the characteristics of teachers' training and service that lead to positive outcomes for students. Rather, effective instruction occurs at the intersection of students, teachers, and the school as a whole; schooling is a complex social experience with many interdependencies. As Hamilton argues in chapter 3, an understanding of "effective teaching" should not be confused with identifying "effective teachers," a term that seems to assume that effectiveness is a stable attribute of individual teachers.

In chapter 1, I set the stage for the rest of the volume by reviewing policy trends in the accountability movement and providing an overview of school and teacher effects research, which Konstantopoulos elaborates on in chapter 2. Next, I analyze the promises and pitfalls of teacher accountability. Like Hamilton in chapter 3, I see ways that teacher accountability programs might improve teaching and learning, as well as dangers ahead.

Even if most of these dangers can be avoided, I remain highly skeptical of the accountability movement because I do not believe it addresses the fundamental barriers to effective instruction in the classroom. In chapter 1, I argue that educational policies should tackle problems of instruction head-on by developing and implementing process models of reform. I outline, in abstract terms, several of the dimensions of instruction that educational reforms need to address.

In chapter 2, Konstantopoulos provides a thorough but succinct review of the quantitative literature on identifying how and why individual teachers affect student achievement growth. In recent decades, educational researchers have made great headway on this topic, developing novel statistical techniques and collecting and analyzing new data. In applied studies of educational performance, "value-added" modeling is transforming the way that schools, districts, and states think about teacher effects. In the past, student achievement was typically tested once a year at a few specific grade levels, such that examining changes over time meant comparing tests scores of 5th-grade students in one year to different students the next year. Value-added models shift the focus to examining longitudinal data; how much achievement growth students experience from when they arrive in the fall to when they complete a year of school in the spring. Yet Konstantopoulos makes clear that in spite of this progress, there is still a great deal we don't know about teacher effects. In using test data to identify teacher effects, the quality of the data and methods is critical.

In chapter 3, Hamilton provides a balanced assessment of how test-based accountability affects teachers' classroom instruction. Reviewing the findings of one of the few comprehensive studies of this topic, Hamilton finds both positive and negative effects of test-based accountability and discusses how such systems might be designed to maximize the intended outcomes and minimize unintended negative consequences. Her recommendations are linked to empirical findings, clearly stated, and provide a much needed framework for future research and policy development. Reading her recommendations, it is clear that the development of effective teacher accountability systems will be an iterative process of program implementation, research, and subsequent revision.

Are high-stakes tests, the cornerstone of the contemporary accountability movement, the best way to identify "good" teachers? Do teachers identified as highly effective on one test look equally effective on other tests? Does test performance come at the expense of students' social and behavioral development? In chapter 4 Jennings and Corcoran argue that identifying highly effective teachers is more complicated than it appears at first; whether a teacher is identified as high or low performing often depends on the specific domain of learning that is being examined.

Jennings and Corcoran worry that the inherently unreliable identification of effective teaching, and the effects of high-stakes tests on teacher practice in the classroom, make them a risky tool for evaluating teacher performance.

In chapter 5, Ingersoll discusses the unique organizational characteristics of schools and the teaching profession and challenges "teacher deficit" perspectives. Teachers, Ingersoll argues, occupy a challenging middle ground; we rightly hold them responsible for the quality of students' work, but in many ways, both as individuals and as a profession, they have very little control over important conditions of instruction and learning. Nevertheless, as a workforce, teachers are remarkably committed to the success of their students. The data presented in chapter 5 remind us that if a lack of accountability is sometimes problematic, so is a lack of teachers' control over their own work. While Ingersoll believes that schools and teachers should be accountable to the public, educational reforms should offer teachers more, not less, control over their own work.

In chapter 6, Cann examines the matching of teachers to high- and low-track classes in mathematics. She finds that because of widely held cultural norms about teaching and learning in mathematics, math teachers work especially hard to secure teaching assignments with high-track students and avoid having to teach remedial classes. Yet this is not always the case; some teachers hold ideals of inclusive teaching and explicitly request courses with low-track students. Moreover, math departments vary in the extent to which high- and low-track courses are evenly distributed across the faculty. Cann's findings reinforce previous studies of teacher tracking and raise serious questions about value-added models of teacher effectiveness in the presence of teacher tracking.

In chapter 7, Everitt reports the results of an in-depth study of beginning teachers. Everitt's study is part of a growing body of research that demonstrates the importance of teacher adaptation in the classroom. Effective teaching can be conceptualized, in part, as a series of both macro and micro instructional adaptations in the classroom (Corno & Snow, 1986). In this important study Everitt digs deep into the coursework and student teaching experience of prospective teachers and finds that the injunction to adapt is a core element of teacher training. As such, Everitt argues, there is a fundamental disconnect between what many reform perspectives define as effective and the norms of adaptation that teachers are trained to embrace, and which they come to appreciate firsthand in their student teaching experiences.

In chapter 8, Youngs, Frank, and Pogodzinski examine the next stage in teachers' career development, their critical first years of teaching. As Youngs et al.'s analysis shows, novice teachers' instructional approaches are affected both by direct feedback from mentors and other colleagues and informally, as they try to model the approaches taken in their colleagues' classrooms and interactions with students. Mentors clearly have an important role to play in helping transition new teachers into the classroom, but there is also a certain "inertia" to the overall instructional ethos in subject-matter departments and schools as a whole that affects new teachers. Again, we see that the nature of a teacher's instruction—which is nicely measured by Youngs et al. in this study of English and language arts teachers—is less individually determined than we might think at first. This lends support to Hamilton's policy recommendation to explore ways to balance individual- and group-level accountability measures.

Penuel, Frank, Sun, and Kim, in chapter 9, continue to stress the idea that "good teachers are made, not born." Penuel and his colleagues analyze unique data on teachers' implementation of instructional reforms from a set of 21 schools, all engaged in locally developed initiatives to promote high-quality instruction. Like Youngs et al., Penuel and his colleagues show that implementing instructional reform is a collective effort by the teaching workforce in a school; teachers' social networks and the social capital constituted by teachers' collective pedagogical knowledge and norms of practice have strong effects on reform implementation. A teacher's true "value-added," Penuel et al. argue, is not just how much her students learn during a given year, but also how that teacher positively affects her colleagues' capacity and commitment to teach.

As the author of the concluding chapter, Gamoran was given the opportunity to review each chapter and was asked to synthesize and comment on the themes, arguments, and evidence presented in this volume. Gamoran begins with an important observation: Many current teacher quality reform efforts can be viewed as a logical reaction by policy makers to the present state of knowledge on teacher effects. Educational researchers routinely emphasize how much high-quality instruction matters, but have had great difficulty identifying readily observable dimensions of teacher training that have a large and consistent impact on student achievement growth (see chapter 2). Thus, in light of existing knowledge on teacher effectiveness, we should perhaps view test-based accountability reforms as a reasoned response to a lack of alternatives. Yet, Gamoran argues, what is needed is more knowledge about how to support the process of teaching, not incentives alone. Gamoran reiterates many of the core arguments in the present volume concerning the fundamental aspects of teaching that make accountability alone likely to fail. This chapter also contains succinct summaries of the results of exciting new research not discussed elsewhere in the book, which is consistent with the recommendations from this volume. These new research efforts are especially noteworthy in the context of this volume, because they not only incorporate the latest developments in testing and teacher effects research but also entail a renewed commitment to studying the teaching process. Ultimately, Gamoran believes, substantial improvement in the quality of classroom instruction is possible when grounded in a solid understanding of teacher effectiveness.

As final thoughts in introducing this book, I would like to make a connection between the real-world business of schooling and models of teaching from popular culture. In researching fundamental questions of teacher effects, and in making inferences about how educational policy might be informed by a robust understanding of teacher effects, I am often struck by the parallels between the most popular Hollywood teacher narratives, *Stand and Deliver*, *Dead Poets Society*, *Mr. Holland's Opus*, or *Freedom Writers*, and the accountability movement (for further discussion of Hollywood teacher narratives, see Kelly & Caughlan, 2011). I worry that teacher accountability reforms operate from the assumption that we could accomplish our loftiest educational ambitions if we just had more Mr. Keatings, Erin Gruwells, or Jaime Escalantes in our nation's schools. But as the research in this volume shows, effective teaching is *not* primarily the result of individual inspiration, charisma, and willpower. Policies based on such models of reform are doomed to fail. On the other hand, I hope that the right uses of test-based measures of teacher effectiveness will make a real difference in the schools that face the greatest educational challenges. Certainly, carefully developed value-added models have a role to play in identifying and supporting effective instruction. For example, value-added models might be used to help identify teaching assignments that are a good fit for specific teachers, as part of programs to reward highly trained teachers for working in difficult-to-staff schools with challenging behavioral climates or to identify areas of curricular strength and weakness in subject-matter departments.

Test-based accountability has come to affect nearly every member of the educational community, from the students who take high-stakes tests, to school officials who monitor student performance, to parents who make important educational decisions. Increasingly, teachers themselves have been affected as student performance is linked to individual classrooms. For educational policy makers and school officials responsible for evaluating teacher performance, this volume speaks to the limits and possibilities of teacher accountability. Teacher accountability programs may be successful in some ways, but they shouldn't be relied on as the sole or even primary method of reform. For teachers themselves, this volume provides a conceptual framework, grounded in studies of real schools and teaching, for an alternative vision of educational reform that goes beyond test-based accountability. I hope this book serves as a resource for researchers and practitioners who are actively involved in formulating and carrying out educational reforms that directly support the process of teaching. For parents, indeed for everyone who cares about educational progress, this volume illustrates again and again the difficulty and complexity of teaching and the need for genuine investments in our schools.

REFERENCES

Corno, L., & Snow, R. E. (1986). Adapting teaching individual differences in learners. In M. C. Wittrock (Ed.), *Third handbook of research on teaching* (pp. 605–629). Washington, DC: American Educational Research Association.

Kelly, S., & Caughlan, S. (2011). The Hollywood teachers' perspective on authority. *Pedagogies, 6*, 46–65.

CHAPTER 1

Understanding Teacher Effects

Market Versus Process Models of Educational Improvement

Sean Kelly

During the 1990s and 2000s, market-based models of school reform—those based on the principles of accountability, competition, and choice—have flourished. In particular, the accountability movement has placed an unprecedented emphasis on achievement levels—as measured by standardized test scores—in our nations' schools and classrooms. Increasingly, educational policy makers are looking toward the teacher as the critical lever of educational improvement, applying the principles of accountability to individual teachers. How will such dramatic shifts in policy affect students, teachers, and schools in the years to come? In particular, what effect might these changes have on deeply ingrained patterns of educational inequality in our schools? Certainly, the accountability movement has shone a powerful light on educational inequality, defining success not as the number of star pupils a school can produce, but in whether or not they provide instruction that is effective for all students. Underlying market-based models of reform is an intrinsic commitment to equality of educational opportunity.

But can market-based models of school reform fulfill this promise? Will the accountability movement—in particular, the growing emphasis on teacher accountability—lead to significant declines in educational inequality? The use of standardized tests to identify high- and low-performing teachers offers a potential means to motivate teachers and address core challenges of the profession. Teacher accountability programs can also be designed to encourage the best teachers to take jobs in chronically low-performing schools. Yet, as I will argue in this chapter, the promises of teacher accountability are dwarfed by the many pitfalls of using standardized tests to label teachers as effective and ineffective. Can ineffective teachers really be reliably identified with a standardized test, and does such a system encourage best practice in the classroom? These are not ancillary issues, but rather, concern the policy core of any teacher accountability system.

Most important, even if teacher accountability programs work as intended, they simply will not be able to solve our most persistent educational problems, because they do not directly address the most common barriers, such as a lack of student engagement, to effective instruction. Instead, school reformers must make a serious investment in teachers' instructional capacity, an approach I term a "process model" of school reform. This perspective on the underlying sources of educational problems and their solutions should have a familiar feel to it, for it is this perspective that underlies much of the frustration concerning current educational policy; we have renewed our commitment to addressing educational inequality but are taking an exceedingly indirect approach to actually doing something about it. In choosing this specific terminology to talk about school reform, I mean to explicitly reference Duncan and Biddle's (1974) orientation to school improvement in *The Study of Teaching*. Whatever the lever of change applied to schools and classrooms, in order to be successful, it must have an impact on "what teachers and pupils do in the classroom" (p. 44).[1]

Fortunately, process models of school improvement are concretely expressed in many successful contemporary reform initiatives. Such initiatives, starting with a conceptual understanding of fundamental problems of classroom instruction, offer innovative ways for schools and teachers to meet these problems head-on. The real business of school reform will mean investments in existing process-models of reform, the development of new and better ones, and continued basic research into the nature of educational problems. As a first step in that direction, we as a community of educators first need to admit that a more genuine effort at school improvement is needed than current educational policy offers.

ENDURING EDUCATIONAL PROBLEMS

While the growth of the accountability movement coincided with reports of widespread underperformance in our nation's schools, it is the distribution of educational success, rather than the average level of school performance, that constitutes our most serious educational challenge. On international assessments of educational achievement, the United States does lag behind other industrialized countries in mathematics and science performance of high school–age students. However, in contrast, U.S. students score significantly higher than those of other countries on reading assessments and both math and science in the early grades.[2] If average achievement levels are not grave cause for concern, educational disparities within the United States are severe indeed. Our primary educational problem is not our nation's average performance level but that so many of our disadvantaged students do not meet basic proficiency standards.

The best evidence on inequality in educational achievement comes from the National Assessment of Educational Progress (NAEP). NAEP is a nationally representative study of achievement in a variety of subjects conducted on a semiannual basis by the U.S. Department of Education. Table 1.1 reports achievement inequality from NAEP in reading and mathematics for recent years. Students eligible for free lunch, that is, students living in families within 130% of the federal poverty threshold, score 24 points lower in reading and 28 points lower in math (a gap of about .7–.8 standard deviations, a common statistical unit of measurement that expresses score differences in terms of the total variability in test scores). In relative terms, the average student eligible for free lunch scores at the 20th percentile in reading, while non-free-lunch students have reading test scores at about the 57th percentile. Achievement gaps among race ethnic groups are nearly as large. Likewise, White students, and those students in families living above the free-lunch income threshold, meet the NAEP proficiency standards at over twice the rate of Black and Hispanic students and those eligible for free lunch. These statistics refer to NAEP data from the country as a whole and reflect average differences in student performance within and between schools. Yet within our nation's urban and suburban areas, because of high levels of school segregation, the most glaring instance of educational inequality is often the

Table 1.1. Inequality in Educational Achievement: 8th-Grade NAEP Data

	READING 2007		MATHEMATICS 2009	
Student Characteristics	**Average Scale Score***	**Percent Proficient/ Advanced**	**Average Scale Score***	**Percent Proficient/ Advanced**
Race/Ethnicity				
White	272 (31)	40%	293 (33)	44%
Black	245 (33)	13%	261 (33)	12%
Hispanic	247 (35)	15%	266 (34)	17%
Free-Lunch Status				
Yes	247 (34)	15%	266 (34)	17%
No	271 (32)	40%	294 (34)	45%

*Standard deviation in parentheses

concentration of low-performing students in segregated schools. As an example, consider the city of Milwaukee, where Paul Jargowsky (1997) has investigated the "concentration of poverty"; the increasing prevalence of neighborhoods where high proportions of the residents live in poverty. In the Milwaukee Public Schools (MPS) district, which encompasses primarily the urban core of the greater metropolitan area, 104 of MPS's 120 elementary and middle schools serve high-poverty neighborhoods in which an average of 89% of students are eligible for free/reduced-price lunch.[3] In these schools, only 60% of 8th graders are classified as proficient or advanced on Wisconsin's Knowledge and Concepts Exam in reading, and only 35% in mathematics (according to MPS school report cards of 2006–07).

RESEARCH ON SCHOOL AND TEACHER EFFECTS

Early efforts to solve educational problems, both those related to low academic performance and those concerned with systematic inequalities in educational outcomes, focused on identifying high- and low-performing schools. Educational failings, it was reasoned, were caused by underresourced and often segregated schools. As the example of Milwaukee illustrates, such an approach fits well with observed educational inequalities. But beginning with the landmark Equality of Educational Opportunity study (Coleman, 1990; Coleman et al., 1966) researchers have concluded that only a small proportion of the total variance in student achievement lies across schools, between 10% and 15% on average (Scheerens & Bosker, 1997). In other words, between-school differences in educational inequality are far surpassed by the much larger variation—from student to student—in performance within schools. Moreover, much of the observed between-school variation is actually the result of differences in the aggregate characteristics of the students who attend different schools and not to the schools per se. In our example from Milwaukee, we can surmise that the primary reason that the schools serving neighborhoods with high concentrations of poverty score lower on achievement tests is not caused by low-quality instruction, but rather, by the substantial influence of high-poverty home and neighborhood environments. To say that test scores are strongly associated with family background should not be taken as evidence of innate differences in capacity to learn. Rather, the important insight is that because students from disadvantaged backgrounds often begin school with lower levels of achievement, schools serving impoverished neighborhoods can easily be wrongly identified as less effective if one focuses only on average test scores. Similarly, the language arts teacher whose students begin 9th-grade reading at a 6th-grade level has a more difficult instructional task ahead of him or her than the teacher whose students begin the school with average or above-average proficiency levels.

Indeed, when researchers use longitudinal data to investigate learning *rates*, as opposed to point-in-time differences in levels of achievement, they find that disadvantaged students and schools look quite similar to their more advantaged counterparts. As part of a long-term study of educational inequality in Baltimore, Johns Hopkins University researchers Doris Entwisle, Karl Alexander, and Linda Olson (1997) tracked the early school experiences of a cohort of students who differed dramatically in their socioeconomic status (SES), carefully collecting student achievement data over a number of years at both the beginning and end of each school year. The research team found that achievement growth during the school year was nearly identical in high- and low-SES schools; it was only in the summer that high-SES students learned at faster rates than the low-SES students. This finding has been replicated using nationally representative data by researchers at the Ohio State University (Downey, von Hippel, & Hughes, 2008). When researchers carefully identify the contribution of schools to academic achievement, they generally find that schools are more similar than they are different.

If school-to-school differences in performance are small on average, the opposite is true of teacher-to-teacher differences in performance. As Konstantopoulos summarizes in chapter 2, the difference in rates of achievement growth for students that have "effective" versus "ineffective" teachers is quite large. Citing the literature on teacher effects, New York University teacher educator Daniel Fallon (2000) concluded that "the most important variable in improving student learning is the quality of the teacher" (p. 4).

In the next section, I briefly summarize recent developments in state- and districtwide approaches to accountability that are placing an unprecedented emphasis on using standardized test data to evaluate teacher performance. In large part, the accountability movement, which places a heavy emphasis on labeling entire schools as high and low performing, is simply incongruent with established understandings of school effects. Thus, identifying the teacher and classroom as a critical source of achievement growth, and incorporating this into accountability regimes, would appear to be an important first step in meeting our nation's educational challenges. Proponents of teacher accountability are quite correct in looking to the teacher as a major lever of educational improvement and, potentially, a key source of educational inequality. However, I will argue, merely identifying the effects of teachers on student achievement growth will not necessarily lead, in and of itself, to educational improvement. Instead, we must support classroom instruction.

THE ACCOUNTABILITY MOVEMENT: FROM SCHOOL TO TEACHER ACCOUNTABILITY

Standardized tests were used in America's schools for a variety of purposes throughout the 20th century: to determine a student's eligibility for educational services, to provide information about overall educational performance, to motivate progress, and to assess particular educational programs and initiatives (National Research Council, 1999). Since the 1990s, there has been a rapid growth in "high-stakes" testing to hold students, schools, and teachers accountable for educational performance. This chapter is concerned in particular with *teacher* accountability programs, which are an extension of school accountability practices.

Standardized test–based school accountability became institutionalized by the No Child Left Behind Act of 2001 (NCLB). Promoted by the then incoming administration of President George W. Bush, NCLB was modeled after testing and accountability practices implemented in Texas by then Governor Bush. NCLB ties Title I funding (which constitutes the bulk of federal government spending on education) to the satisfactory implementation of school accountability in each state. Under NCLB, states are required to identify each individual school's progress toward meeting state-mandated proficiency standards—their so-called adequate yearly progress (AYP). NCLB has been criticized on a variety of fronts. For example, soon after its passing, National Academy of Education member and educational measurement scholar Robert Linn (2003) argued that the AYP goals in most states simply could not be reached under any reasonable assumptions of school improvement; the NCLB's lofty goal of having all schools reach 100% proficiency by 2013 was, in essence, impossible.

Nevertheless, the overarching idea behind NCLB—that student achievement and subgroup differences in achievement should be closely monitored and that schools should be held accountable for meeting proficiency standards—was generally well received. Moreover, while it was landmark federal legislation and ushered in new practices in many states, other states and districts had been developing similar policies for years. While many complaints were leveled at the peripheral aspects of the law,[4] there was little widespread complaint about the policy core of the law: the labeling and sanctioning of schools.[5] Yet it was readily apparent that suburban schools with a socioeconomically advantaged student population had a much easier time meeting AYP requirements than did schools serving disadvantaged and minority student populations (Kim & Sunderman, 2005). Rather than see this as a fundamental barrier to test-based accountability, though, in the years following NCLB, many states turned their attention to developing more elaborated accountability systems that would better identify a school's true "value-added": the additional knowledge and skills acquired during the schooling process as opposed to a point-in-time level of proficiency. Value-added models, it is hoped, will level the playing field for schools.

When NCLB was first passed, the majority of state accountability programs were based on simple cross-sectional comparisons of different cohorts of students (for example, a comparison between one year's 4th-grade class and the scores of the previous years' 4th graders). If a higher proportion of students meet proficiency standards in subsequent years (or if the baseline level of proficiency was very high to begin with), a school is deemed successful. Value-added accountability models shift the focus to examining longitudinal data; how much achievement growth do students experience from the fall of their 4th-grade year to when the same students enroll as 5th graders the following year (or even better, how much do they learn from fall to spring). Although student mobility and attrition creates problems in such an analysis, the goal is, at least in principle, to compare apples to apples (i.e., the same students).

Nearly everyone agrees that value-added models are an improvement over simple cross-sectional comparisons of different cohorts of students. If we take standardized test–based accountability as a policy given, and we assume that states must adopt this reform in order to secure valuable federal funding, then value-added models will work much better than the initial conception of NCLB. More important, perhaps, is that value-added methods of accountability have become a stepping stone to extending accountability practices to individual teachers' classrooms. In the 1990s, several states and districts at the forefront of standardized testing-based accountability, including North Carolina, Tennessee, and Kentucky, began experimenting with teacher effectiveness measures. Since that time, improvement in the data collection and assessment capabilities in state departments of education has made possible the more widespread use of teacher accountability programs. In 2005, eight states applied to the federal government to experiment with value-added models as part of their accountability system. In all these experimental programs, test-based teacher effectiveness measures have been introduced.[6]

Teacher accountability is seen by many as the logical next step to school accountability. The individual teacher's classroom is the most proximal link to student learning, so it would seem to make sense to hold individual teachers accountable for learning in their classrooms. The identification of high- and low-performing teachers, then, is a crucial first step in putting the profession as a whole on a path toward greater effectiveness. Indeed, the identification of teachers' contribution to student learning also sets the stage for specific reform measures, such as linking teacher pay and other rewards to classroom performance or recruiting effective teachers to low-performing schools. Since the enactment of NCLB, districts in several states have implemented a variety of pay-for-performance programs. Educational policy initiatives enacted under the administration of President Barack Obama, such as the "Race to the Top" initiative, reinforce the use of standardized tests as the core determinants of teacher accountability programs.

THE PITFALLS OF SCHOOL ACCOUNTABILITY

The rhetoric on both sides of the accountability movement often presents an extreme view of educational accountability. For example, proponents described the early effects of accountability in Texas as an educational "miracle." Some argue that the recipe for such a miracle is simple: Pressure teachers to teach effectively (Greene, 2000). On the other side, opponents of accountability see the NCLB as no less than a plot to destroy the nation's confidence in our public school system, leading to widespread privatization.[7] Both these positions, although extreme, represent, I believe, genuine sentiments and concerns. The implementation of early accountability programs was accompanied by gains in achievement and improvements in high school graduation rates. Although some would argue that those gains were more illusory than real, NCLB was modeled after an approach that was widely perceived to be successful. As for fears of school privatization, the provision of choice for students who attend so-called failing schools, both public and private, is in fact a key element of NCLB. Although the transfer provision refers to the choice to move to another *public* school but not yet a private school, many worry we are on a slippery slope.

Nevertheless, balanced accounts, such as the recent Hamilton et al. (2007) report on the impact of accountability, show that the negative effects are not as severe as most feared, nor are the positive effects quite as powerful as many proponents would like to believe. For example, as a result of NCLB, teachers do report a decline in morale, but they also report positive changes in the academic rigor of the curriculum and that staff are focusing more on improving student achievement as a result of pressure to make AYP. In this section, I consider some of the potential pitfalls of school accountability. In large part, these are concerns with the unintended negative consequences of school accountability. Importantly, I focus on simple models of school accountability—NCLB as initially conceived—rather than more nuanced models of accountability based on carefully constructed estimates of value-added. Many of the problems of school accountability, I will argue, stem from erroneously labeling schools as "successes" and "failures." School-level accountability systems may have an unintended negative impact on (1) the social distribution of educational success, (2) public confidence in our nation's public schools, and (3) teachers' instructional practice.

The Social Distribution of Educational Success

A principal tenant of the accountability movement is the labeling of schools as successes and failures. Indeed, in recent years, NCLB has label ed large numbers of schools as low performing in any given year; in several states over 40% of schools are labeled as failing to meet AYP in any given year (Olson, 2006). How are parents and teachers likely to respond to such labeling? Hopefully, many will dismiss such assertions of failure outright. A more alarming possibility is that an accountability system that labels so many schools as failures will produce higher levels of school segregation, and greater disparities in teacher quality across schools, as students and teachers flee "failing" schools for what they think are higher-performing schools.

In 2003, 26% of parents indicated that they moved to their current neighborhood because of the perceived quality of the local schools (National Center for Education Statistics, 2005). The labeling of large numbers of schools as failures may amplify parents' existing preoccupation with seeking out the "best" educational environments for their children. Of course, as we have already seen, though, actual differences in school quality are far weaker than NCLB would lead parents to believe. Moreover, because high-SES parents are more mobile than low-SES parents, this situation is likely to lead to increased segregation of students by both SES and race/ethnicity.

In addition to negatively affecting parental perceptions of school quality, the accountability movement has provided teachers with strong incentives to seek out schools that are free from the danger of NCLB-related sanctions and where their teaching practices are not under the harsh microscope of the need to meet AYP each year. When teachers move from school to school, they are much more likely to move from schools with high proportions of poor and minority students to schools with lower proportions of disadvantaged students (Lankford, Loeb, & Wyckoff, 2002). The result of this process of teacher mobility is that schools serving the students with the most privilege have far higher levels of teacher quality. The accountability movement has given the most highly qualified teachers yet another reason to seek out positions in high-performing suburban schools, namely, greater autonomy.

Public Confidence in Schools

At the heart of the accountability movement is the assumption that we cannot hide from our educational problems. Unless we shine a light on the low academic performance of schools, and the troubling disparities in achievement within schools, how can we break from the status quo? Yet there is something troubling about the single-mindedness with which NCLB goes after schools with low test scores when decades of social science research clearly reveals that schools are not the sole determinants of student achievement. What does it mean to say that over 63% of schools in the state of Massachusetts failed to meet AYP in 2007–8 when next door, in Pennsylvania, only 28% of schools failed to meet AYP (Hoff, 2009)? Clearly, these labels are in large part driven by choices about the mechanics of the AYP process, rather than some real crisis of education in particular states. The widespread labeling of the public schools in our poorest communities as failures has the potential to undermine public investment in the schools that need the most support.

Teachers' Instructional Practice

Clearly, in schools that fail to meet AYP, a certain amount of "teaching to the test" is likely to occur. Proponents of accountability do not necessarily see this as a downside, however. If the standardized tests used by states are well constructed to test the knowledge and skills we want students to have and encourage teachers to align their instruction to relevant standards, what's the problem?[8] Teachers find standardized tests useful in identifying students' strength and weaknesses, and some studies have found that test-based accountability provides teachers with an incentive to work harder and place a greater emphasis on achievement (Hamilton et al., 2007). Moreover, as I will argue in the next section, there may actually be some intrinsic benefit to constraining teachers' choice of instructional content to some extent. Yet the emphasis of the accountability movement on specific content may cause teachers to ignore the important dimensions of instructional process that produce long-term educational success. An important goal of classroom instruction, especially in the early grades, is to engage students and set them on the path toward a lifelong love of learning. While producing a love of learning and realizing the acquisition of important academic skills in the short term are not mutually exclusive, only one of these goals is well measured by a standardized test. Moreover, studies of the effects of accountability have uncovered some alarming practices, such as tailoring instruction to meet the needs of the small group of students "on the bubble" of meeting proficiency standards (Jennings, 2005). Such findings are a warning sign that perhaps the accountability movement has dangerously narrowed teachers' perspective on classroom instruction.

PROMISES AND PITFALLS OF TEACHER ACCOUNTABILITY

Are market-based reforms that target individual teachers likely to suffer from the same unintended consequences as school-level accountability systems? As discussed, developing teacher accountability models are often based on sophisticated value-added growth models, rather than point-in-time measures of achievement. As such, they are likely to avoid many of the problems of simplistic school accountability models. For example, there is no reason that teacher accountability systems should necessarily increase disparities in teacher quality across schools. Indeed, just the opposite could occur, with value-added models of teacher accountability identifying many "effective" teachers in disadvantaged schools. Teachers could even be awarded specifically for teaching the most challenging students. Indeed, by 2009, 25 states already had policies in place to incentivize teaching in hard-to-staff schools (Hightower, 2010). Nor would, I believe, teacher accountability necessarily lead to a crisis of confidence in our nation's teachers. There is no reason, for example, that the great majority of teachers in a district or state could not be labeled "effective." In fact, I see two potential benefits of teacher accountability policies that will support the profession, and in so doing, have a positive effect on classroom instruction. Teacher accountability models are positioned to *reward excellence* and to *reduce uncertainty* in an unprecedented way. At the same time, however, teacher accountability programs may have negative effects as well. Actually implementing teacher accountability programs is turning out to be a challenging endeavor; it is not easy to develop a system of accountability that can *reliably and accurately identify teacher performance* and that the teaching workforce believes is fair and impartial. In other words, there are barriers to teacher accountability, which are at once both technical and political, that could undermine its ability to motivate teachers. Moreover, as with any program of school accountability, there is the danger that teacher accountability programs will emphasize *outcomes over process*, and thus favor short-run gains over long-term student development.

Promises

Teacher accountability programs have the potential to produce two related effects—namely, rewarding excellence and reducing uncertainty —that address core challenges to the teaching profession (Lortie, 1975).

First, teacher accountability programs clearly have the potential to reward effective teachers for their efforts in the classroom. Unlike the case in many other professions, what teachers produce is unclear and difficult to measure. While teachers readily distinguish between good lessons, days, or classes from bad ones, they often lack an objective indicator of success with their students. The rewards of teaching are often portrayed as intrinsically gratifying "in-the-moment" experiences of reaching previously disengaged students. Well-designed tests give teachers a tangible indicator of success. Since teacher accountability programs emphasize students' development over time rather than simply their average level of achievement, they may be particularly well equipped to reward excellent teaching in low-performing schools.

Second, teachers face a great deal of uncertainty over both what and how to teach. There is often very little reassurance for the teacher that they are doing the right things in the classroom. Teacher accountability programs have the potential both to reduce uncertainty about what content should be taught and to provide reassurance to effective teachers that they are making the right pedagogical choices in the classroom. Contentwise, this may be seen as prescriptive, reducing teachers' options in the classroom. However, such reassurance from an "outside authority" could actually provide the best teachers with the confidence they need to pursue innovative approaches to instruction. Moreover, accountability programs based on yearly gain scores lengthen the reward structure of teaching, giving teachers a way to assess the overall effect of the year's instruction. This might encourage teachers to pursue long-term intellectual growth and develop a curriculum that is highly coherent (i.e., builds skills logically from one unit to the next). Yet teacher accountability programs also face several likely pitfalls.

Pitfalls

Reliably and Accurately Identifying Teacher Performance. Unlike simpler models of accountability, teacher accountability programs are based on a more complex model of value-added, at a minimum, an estimate of how teachers impact students' achievement gains during the year. This raises the possibility that the intended audience of teacher accountability programs, the teachers themselves, may not believe the results attached to their performance. Several aspects of value-added modeling make teacher accountability programs vulnerable to skepticism among the participating teachers: regression to the mean, correlations between student background and growth, unreliability in estimates of teacher effects, individual histories, and choice of test content.

A common phenomenon in the analysis of gain scores is regression to the mean; low-scoring students tend to gain more during the school year than do students who score higher in the fall (Seltzer, Choi, & Thum, 2003). Nearly all testing situations will produce some amount of regression to the mean simply because some of the students who scored poorly in the fall did so for esoteric reasons, such as being distracted, hungry, or sleep deprived. Thus some low-scoring students will, through no necessary actions of their own or the teachers, appear to gain more than a student who scored high in the fall by chance. Statistically, with only two time points of data (i.e., fall and spring), there is no way to separate regression to the mean caused by random error, a very common phenomenon, from a legitimate difference in student gains produced by instruction. Regression to the mean will have a more substantial impact on individual student scores than on the mean performance in a given classroom, but tests need to be carefully designed to minimize ceiling effects: when high-performing students "max out" on the first testing occasion and have little room for growth, potentially increasing the chance of regression to the mean at the class level. While the typical teacher may not be acutely aware of regression to the mean, it won't take long for teachers of initially high-achieving students to realize they are at a disadvantage in being evaluated as teachers, and to ask themselves the question: "How can you label me ineffective when I am teaching the cream of the crop?"

If regression to the mean might, in some instances, cause teachers of high-achieving students to exhibit lower gains on some tests, the relationship between students' family background and achievement growth might put teachers of low-SES students at a disadvantage. Learning is not purely a school-year phenomenon but is highly sensitive to home and neighborhood contexts. Studies of child rearing show vast differences in parenting practices across families (Hart & Risley, 1995). Differences in the nature of discourse in the home, for example, have a profound effect on children's vocabulary growth, something that surely affects success in school. No test can completely differentiate between what is learned at home and what is learned in school.

Students' individual educational histories also play an important role in their level of success in any given year. Students enter school each year with varying levels of attachment toward school and other motivational determinants. When students have a low sense of academic competence, have poor approaches to learning, or are just generally disengaged or apathetic toward schooling, the teacher's task is inherently more challenging. Indeed, most teachers would agree that they are really facing two equally important challenges at once: how to teach content and skills in the short term, and how to put the disengaged student back on a motivational path toward success. While value-added models may control for students' initial level of achievement, they don't capture any of the affective and behavioral variables that affect learning and on which students vary greatly.

The test scores of 20 or so students represents a finite amount of information that even under the best circumstances is an imperfectly reliable estimate of the quality of instruction in that classroom. Konstantopoulos takes up this concern in more detail in chapter 2. Informally, we can simply say that as with any measurement task, the more information the analyst has at his or her disposal, the better. If a teacher had a large number of students (say, 45 or more), then we might have high confidence that the achievement growth of those students was representative of the quality of instruction in that classroom. But with only 20 students or so, we worry that much of the observed achievement growth had to do with those particular students, rather than the teacher's approach. Fortunately, this issue of the low reliability of class-mean achievement growth can be addressed by pooling data across years or classrooms.

Finally, the choice of test content for an accountability regime is highly politically charged. Clearly, the same test must be used for purposes of accountability among all teachers; it is impossible to equate achievement growth across qualitatively different scores. Thus, the same test must be used for any one group of teachers. Yet can agreement be reached about, for example, the academic skills that an 11th-grade English teacher should emphasize? If teachers believe that they are being held accountable for teaching the wrong material or academic skills, or even that the test contains only a subset of what they deem important to learn, then such a test will not motivate them to perform. Rather, the "flawed" test will alienate them from their work. Individuals are much less likely to put forth effort on tasks they do not believe in.

To summarize, it will be difficult to motivate teachers with sanctions or rewards based on standardized test performance if the teachers do not actually believe that the qualitative label (i.e., *effective*, *ineffective*) matches their performance in the classroom. For all the preceding reasons, teachers may be profoundly distrustful of a performance label based on standardized test data. Moreover, administrators and policy makers who would act on such labels should be equally apprehensive. Does the test data produce an accurate and reliable estimate of a teacher's performance? Can we be confident enough in the labels we have assigned to act on them, rewarding and sanctioning teachers accordingly?

Outcomes over Process. When teachers are asked about what they like about their job, they respond that it is first and foremost the process of working with students in the classroom. Moreover, the most rewarding experiences with students are only indirectly related to learning specific knowledge and skills. Instead, teachers are interested in instilling a love of learning in students, imbuing them with an excitement for learning and academic initiative. Whatever is learned in the short-term teachers' reason pales in importance to developing the internalized motivations, dispositions, and habits of mind that will lead to lifelong learning. It is less helpful to study vocabulary, for example, if students don't find learning to use new words fun and rewarding. Thus, teachers pay close attention to selecting materials and methods of instruction that students find engaging. Does test-based accountability give teachers an incentive to provide engaging instruction?

Recent studies show that even school-level accountability may reduce the emphasis teachers place on providing engaging instruction. In a review of 49 qualitative studies of teachers' response to high-stakes testing, Au (2007) found that in the majority of cases, teachers responded by narrowing the focus of the curriculum and relying on traditional, teacher-centered methods of instruction. As one 8th-grade teacher in Hamilton et al. (2007)'s study responded:

> I can see that there are interesting things I'd like to teach that I can't. I have a project I do every year in math estimating animal population, but it takes a couple of weeks. I'm just not doing it this year. I'm not doing it because I've got to get them ready for these tests. And it's a shame because they get a lot out of it. (p. 103)

In this example, an in-depth project, one that has a proven track record of being engaging and memorable for students, and that the teacher looks forward to every year, has been dropped in favor of test prep.

Science educators seem particularly concerned that test-based account ability may undermine teachers' efforts to engage in best practices for science education (Southerland, Smith, Sowell, & Kittleson, 2007). Science educators place an emphasis on using the elements of the scientific method during classroom instruction. The elements of scientific inquiry—observing, questioning, examining prior research, planning and conducting investigations, and so on—facilitate science learning, in part because students find the scientific process to be authentic and engaging (see e.g., Gamoran et al., 2003). Unfortunately, research shows that such engaging, student-centered instruction is rare in math and science classrooms (Borman & Associates, 2005). Although standardized testing may not be inherently incongruent with any particular instructional approach, teachers have to be supported, through rigorous professional development programs, in how to meet state standards without adopting a rote-learning style of instruction. There are too many examples of instances in which, without the proper support, standardized tests have driven teachers away from engaging methods of instruction. As Southerland et al. (2007) argue, the problem with test-based accountability is not that the particular test questions in any given state are the wrong questions, but that it does not in any specific way motivate teachers to adopt research-based best practices.

Summary. Teacher accountability programs have the potential to simplify and focus the teacher's task and to provide an objective measure of performance. Insofar as anyone would be motivated to keep his or her job or to receive better pay, accountability programs have the potential to motivate teachers to perform better. Yet generating reliable and accurate estimates of the value-added by specific teachers represents a major challenge; in many cases, I worry that it will simply not be possible. The consequences of inappropriately sanctioning a teacher or rewarding the wrong teachers could be devastating to teacher commitment and satisfaction. Moreover, test-based teacher accountability may refocus teachers' efforts away from instructional methods that generate student engagement and interest in school. This potential negative outcome hints at perhaps the biggest indictment of teacher accountability. Even if, on balance, teacher accountability programs increase teachers' extrinsic motivation to succeed, these programs will be unable to address the daunting disparities in educational success we face because they fail to directly support classroom instruction.

THE ALTERNATIVE: PROCESS MODELS OF INSTRUCTIONAL IMPROVEMENT

Fortunately, there are many examples of innovative educational reforms that result in more engaging and rigorous instruction. What these reforms have in common is that they emphasize the common barriers to effective instruction and how to overcome them. In this section, I discuss several dimensions of effective teaching and provide examples of educational reforms that support each dimension. It is not my aim to advocate for a particular method of reform, nor is this a definitive outline of all the elements of a process model of instruction. Rather, my goal is to remind educators and policy makers that alternatives to market-based models of reform exist. Unlike market-based approaches to reform, process models of reform have a common ingredient: genuine investment in improving classroom instruction.

Student Engagement

The accountability movement pays little attention to the most important mediating factor linking instruction to learning, namely, student engagement. For achievement growth to occur, students must be actively engaged in the learning process (National Research Council & Institute of Medicine, 2004). *Engagement* refers both to affective dimensions of classroom experience, such as a student's interest in school or appreciation of a particular task, and to behaviors, such as participating in classroom discourse or completing assignments.

Educational researchers conceptualize disengagement as an iterative process that unfolds over a student's schooling career. Student engagement is much more than an immediate reaction to a particular assignment or teacher; it is related to internalized student attitudes and alignments that develop over time. Disengagement in high school is prefaced by low levels of academic success and strained relationships with teachers in elementary and middle school. Importantly, though, disengagement is not a student problem per se: The nature of instruction in our nations' schools is implicated in problems of student engagement. While many of the sources of student engagement can be located outside the classroom, an effective model of reform must address the relationship between what goes on within the classroom, what educators can manipulate, and student engagement. Further, most reforms that take engagement seriously pay special attention to engagement among low-performing students.

While not the only reason that students become disengaged, models of engagement assume that engagement is fundamentally linked with school performance in a reciprocal relationship.[9] Poor performance in school, or even perceived poor performance, leads to low levels of engagement, which in turn has negative effects on future achievement outcomes (National Research Council & Institute of Medicine, 2004). That is, students who get off on the wrong foot academically and develop a low sense of academic efficacy are the ones most at risk of becoming disengaged. Succinctly put, disregard for schooling helps protect the self-worth of low-achieving students. Low levels of self-efficacy are associated with a host of factors predicting poor performance in the classroom, including increased test anxiety, reduced use of cognitive strategies on classroom assignments, and less self-regulating academic behavior (Zimmerman & Martinez-Pons, 1992).

Importantly, classroom experiences often serve as the impetus for students to enact strategies to protect their self-worth. Process models of engagement emphasize the dimensions of instruction that break down the link between low performance and engagement. How might school reforms approach this fundamental barrier to effective instruction? Next, I briefly review two constructs that reforms have targeted to improve the motivational climate for low-achieving students.

Mastery Orientation. In *Different by Design*, Metz (1986) describes three middle schools offering nontraditional curricula. Two of the schools Metz observed shared a common approach to improving student engagement; evaluation was designed to stress student effort by tracking students' progress carefully and grading them primarily on progress and improvement rather than point-in-time skill mastery relative to other students. Metz found that in these schools, especially when individual teachers embraced the school's model fully, low-achieving students exhibited high levels of engagement, because of the lack of emphasis put on initial levels of achievement (pp. 74, 125). Educational psychologists refer to the type of educational environment Metz observed as fostering a "mastery orientation," the belief that achievement is related to one's effort (Dweck, 1986). Classrooms that have a mastery orientation encourage students to focus on their own achievements rather than their ability level relative to others.

Multiple-Ability Orientation. Students are most likely to develop a low level of self-efficacy and subsequently put forth less effort when they believe that "being good at school" is a singular immutable trait one either possesses or does not (Wood & Bandura, 1989). Rosenholtz and Rosenholtz (1981) characterize the classroom learning environment as being either unidimensional (with negative effects on engagement among low-achieving students) or multidimensional (with positive effects). One of the characteristics separating multidimensional classrooms from unidimensional classrooms is whether evaluation of student performance is based on a wide or narrow set of criteria. Multidimensional classrooms encourage a multiple-ability orientation by having a diversity of classroom tasks at which students can succeed. Cultivating a multiple-ability orientation is one of the key elements of "complex instruction," a model of school reform developed by Elizabeth Cohen and colleagues at Stanford University to address problems of engagement in heterogeneous classrooms (Cohen & Lotan, 1997). The complex instruction method stresses the use of small-group work and the creation of diverse student roles and task interdependence within the context of group work.

Disciplined Inquiry in the Classroom

One positive effect of accountability programs is their emphasis on content coverage. *Content coverage* refers both to the amount of time teachers spend engaged in substantive instruction as opposed to procedural matters, discipline, and other noninstructional activities and to coverage of specific skills that are linked to grade-appropriate content standards. Yet standards of intellectual quality must also be considered. There is the danger that in response to content standards, teachers will emphasize quantity over quality. The concept of "disciplined inquiry" provides a framework for understanding the elements of a rich learning experience.

Newmann, Marks, and Gamoran's (1996) definition of disciplined inquiry has three features: "using a prior knowledge base from one or more fields, striving for in-depth understanding rather than superficial awareness, and expressing conclusions through elaborated communication." The first feature, using a prior knowledge base, refers to the coherence of instruction, as well as the presence of an analytic framework. Curricular coherence refers to the relatedness of the elements of the curriculum—texts, themes, and classroom activities—within the curriculum (Nystrand, 1997). Curricular coherence entails building connections both within and among lessons. Disciplined inquiry also involves explicit attention to the knowledge base in each subject-matter area: vocabulary, concepts, and theories that students familiarize themselves with and that become tools for analysis. The second feature, striving for in-depth understanding, refers to the application of an analytic framework to a novel task. For example, in English and language arts classrooms, disciplined inquiry involves going beyond simple recitation or reports of what happened in a text, toward performing analyses and making generalizations based on the text. The third feature, elaborated communication, refers to extended, detailed written and oral expositions rather than worksheet-type tasks.

In the fields of science and mathematics the teaching for understanding (TFU) framework, discussed, for example, by Gamoran et al. (2003), emphasizes disciplined inquiry. Under TFU, teachers encourage their students' development of "standards of explanation and argumentation that approach the rigor of scientific and mathematical standards" (11). Gamoran et al. present an example of TFU in which a middle school teacher organizes a classroom research project based on student interests. When students report they widely prefer the taste of the third-floor water fountain to others in the building, she suggests a blind taste test, which reveals students actually prefer water from the first-floor fountain. As a result of presenting this data, the students questioned their preconceived notions about the school's water quality and set out on a quest to reconcile the incongruence between their expectations and findings. Their subsequent experiments investigated everything from bacterial counts on water fountains to how the school's plumbing system may have played a role in water quality. In this example, TFU encompasses many of the elements of disciplined inquiry: a project based on students' prior interests and understandings; an in-depth, ongoing, and thorough analysis; and a continuous process of elaborated communication in which students iteratively develop new hypotheses and synthesize the results of their analyses. In this example, classroom instruction is driven not by the specific content students are learning (e.g., expressing data, in this case bacteria counts, as fractions, i.e., proportional thinking) but by a model of scientific inquiry that is both engaging and rigorous. In other words, how students encounter fractions may be more important than the quantity of fractions they are exposed to.

Teacher Efficacy and Commitment

A third shortcoming of market-based models of reform is that while they might provide rewards for teachers deemed effective, the past logic of the accountability movement suggests that only so many teachers will be so labeled. Teacher accountability programs will likely operate under the assumption that a great many teachers are ineffective, because such an approach can only "fix" a school if ineffective teachers can be identified and removed or remediated. What effect will this have on teachers' sense of efficacy in the classroom and their level of commitment to the profession?

This is a vitally important question. Just as levels of academic self-efficacy influence engagement among students, teachers' perceptions of their own professional efficacy are likely to mediate their efforts as teachers. When teachers feel that they cannot accomplish their goals in the classroom, effort may suffer. Efficacy, while perhaps less tangible than other teacher characteristics, is an important predictor of effective instruction (Rosenholtz, 1989).

The accountability movement, by emphasizing specific, measurable outcomes, may reduce uncertainty, and increase efficacy, at least for those teachers who are able to meet external standards. Rosenholtz (1989) found that external evaluation can increase efficacy.[10] Yet external evaluations are not the only source of feedback for teachers. Supportive relationships and collaborative activities among teachers can be an equally salient source of positive feedback. Reforms that strive to develop a team approach to teaching, both in shared goals and responsibilities, will increase teacher efficacy and commitment. Rosenholtz found higher levels of efficacy and commitment among teachers in collaborative schools than in isolated or moderately isolated schools settings. Importantly, creating a collaborative school environment requires substantial investments; teachers need time and space to share ideas, and schools need experienced teachers to serve as instructional leaders.

Opportunities for Professional Development

I am convinced that being a teacher is one of the most demanding of all careers. I believe that the reason that classroom instruction seldom lives up to our expectations is simply that they are so great, and the task is so very difficult. Market-based models of reform seem to operate under the assumption that if teachers just *tried harder* we could meet our loftiest of expectations. Rather I believe that change in the classroom is exceedingly difficult. What does it take to change instruction along the dimensions discussed here: to make instruction more engaging and rigorous and to generate the confidence and commitment teachers need to succeed? Research suggests instructional growth requires sustained investment in professional development opportunities. Studies conducted at the National Research Center on English Learning and Achievement (CELA) speak to both the difficulty of instructional change and the possibilities of professional development.

Numerous studies in a variety of disciplines suggest that the most engaging forms of instruction are also the rarest; the bulk of students' time is spent in noninteractive, "drill and skill" instruction. In English and language arts classrooms, for example, genuine discussions, that is, free exchanges of information about, and analysis of, a text by students and the teacher, are rare. In one study, Nystrand (1997) found that 8th-grade classrooms averaged less than 50 seconds of discussion per class, and even less in grade 9. One reason why classroom discourse is so teacher centered is simply that asking "test questions" and then evaluating students' responses is easy for teachers to do, whereas initiating and managing a productive discussion is tricky business.

In the Partnership for Literacy, CELA educators developed a program of intensive professional development, which, among other emphases, would help teachers facilitate student engagement and disciplined inquiry, and where, for example, genuine discussions were likely to arise.[11] In short, the Partnership for Literacy emphasized providing teachers with conceptual and pedagogical tools and cultivating reflective practice. The partnership began with a summer institute, where groups of teachers from participating middle schools were primed to explicitly address several core aspects of literacy instruction such as increasing the coherence of their curriculum, raising the level of engagement in higher-order talk and writing, and scaffolding student performance on new and difficult tasks. Over the next 2 years, the partnership operated as a professional development community where teachers worked to solve problems in their classrooms. CELA instructional facilitators worked with each school's partnership teachers: keeping the conceptual dimensions of effective instruction relevant, helping teachers develop and share pedagogical tools, encouraging reflective practice, and providing teachers with innovative ways to evaluate their classrooms (e.g., videotapes and summaries of instruction from the CLASS computer program).

Nearly all teachers responded positively to the professional development. When compared with a control group of classrooms who did not participate in CELA's professional development activities, the partnership teachers showed marked improvement on important indicators of effective instruction. For example, CELA researchers collected data on the cognitive level of questions asked by teachers: Did questions call for a simple reporting of information (recall), or did the questions call for generalization or analysis? In the control classrooms, the proportion of high-cognitive-level questions was about 7% in the fall, increasing to 12% of all teacher questions in the spring. Among the partnership teachers, who had the benefit of the summer institute and early planning activities with their colleagues and instructional facilitators, approximately 18% of questions in the fall were of high cognitive level. By the spring, the proportion of high-cognitive-level questions asked by partnership teachers had increased to 30%, nearly double what it was in the spring, and well beyond the proportion asked by the control teachers. This is just one example of the kind of significant change that a well-developed professional development program can result in.[12]

CONCLUSION

If the accountability movement can be criticized for offering too simple a paradigm of educational improvement, it is elegant in its approach. It offers a way to affect every student at relatively little expense. It is, at least potentially, a "big lever" of educational change. But thus far, the hypothesis that school accountability can dramatically change educators' motivation to perform, and thus remedy deeply entrenched educational inequalities, appears to be only partially true at best. Since the inception of NCLB, any positive educational change, such as an increase in test scores, has been relatively small (Fuller, Wright, Gesicki, & Kang, 2007).[13] This shouldn't be surprising. To address our most difficult educational challenges, we are going to need a major increase in instructional capacity. Might accountability indirectly improve the process of instruction? Yes, perhaps it might, but the problem is that school and teacher accountability programs don't emphasize any changes in particular. There is no guarantee that teachers won't respond to accountability pressures in negative ways. Accountability programs do not directly affect the process of instruction itself. Instead, process models of reform are needed that increase student engagement and disciplined inquiry in the classroom, improve teacher efficacy and commitment, and offer rich opportunities for professional development and collaboration.

NOTES

1. Sociologists and others have criticized so-called process-product educational studies, which, in an inductive fashion, seek to identify classroom practices that correlate with achievement growth by measuring practices and outcomes and searching for patterns without much of a conceptual understanding of learning (in particular, the social context of classrooms). Note that the process models of reform I discuss in this chapter are closely grounded in theories of learning and the social organization of classrooms and schools.

2. For example, in 8th-grade math, U.S. students scored higher than 37 of 48 countries participating in the Trends in International Mathematics and Science study and lower than only 5 countries (the remaining 5 were not measurably different). In science, the United States scored higher than 35 of 47 countries and lower than 9 countries (and about the same as the remaining 3). Democratically governed industrialized nations (e.g., England, Norway, etc.), which might be most comparable to the United States, are represented in both the higher- and lower-scoring nations (NCES, 2009).

3. High-poverty neighborhoods are defined here as census tracts where greater than 35% of families live at less than 185% of the federal poverty level.

4. For example, there was concern that schools neglect subjects that are not part of the AYP calculation, such as the arts, foreign languages, and physical education, and that states were not provided with adequate funds to implement accountability systems (Hamilton et al., 2007).

5. Although this is my own qualitative assessment of reaction to NCLB, the general acceptance of the law at the time of its passing has been noted elsewhere (Olson, 2002).

6. Some states have also experimented with alternative metrics that might be used in lieu of or in conjunction with standardized tests, such as in-class assessments, national board certification, or student portfolios.

7. See for example a 2003 report by the People for the American Way Foundation, "The Voucher Veneer: The Deeper Agenda to Privatize Public Education" (2003).

8. Since 2002, states' use of multiple-choice test questions has increased, while use of open/constructed questions has decreased (Sawchuk, 2010).

9. In this section I have emphasized how the classroom motivational climate, in particular the nature of classroom evaluation, affects the engagement of low-performing students, but this just scratches the surface of the many important determinants of engagement. See the excellent book *Engaging Schools* (National Research Council & Institute of Medicine, 2004).

10. Rosenholtz's analysis focused on teacher "certainty," a construct that was closely aligned with a teacher's sense of efficacy (see p. 47).

11. The theoretical underpinnings, the research base, and the features of the professional development are detailed in Langer, Applebee, and Nystrand, 2005.

12. Author's calculations from the partnership data. Langer et al. (2005, pp. 91–99) provide a thorough comparison of instructional change experienced by the partnership and control classrooms.

13. The National Assessment of Educational Progress (NAEP) data is the only data well suited to measuring time trends in educational outcomes in the United States over short intervals. Unlike state test data in most cases, scores on the NAEP exam can be compared across time. The NAEP is administered to students in the 4th, 8th, and 12th grades. While 4th graders have shown substantial improvement in reading and math during the period of NCLB, there has been no improvement in the later grades, and little or no decrease in achievement gaps.

REFERENCES

Au, W. (2007). High-stakes testing and curricular control: A qualitative metasynthesis. *Educational Researcher, 36,* 258–267.

Borman, K. M., & Associates. (2005). *Meaningful urban education reform: Confronting the learning crisis in mathematics and science.* Albany: State University of New York Press.

Cohen, E. G., & Lotan, R. (1997). *Working for equity in heterogeneous classrooms.* New York: Teachers College Press.

Coleman, J. S., Campbell, E. Q., Hobson, C. J., McPartland, J., Mood, A. M., Weinfeld, F. D., et al. (1966). *Equality of educational opportunity.* Washington, DC: U.S. Government Printing Office.

Coleman, J. S. (1990). *Equality and achievement in education.* Boulder, CO: Westview Press.

Downey, D. B., von Hippel, P. T., & Hughes, M. (2008). Are "failing" schools really failing? Removing the influence of nonschool factors from measures of school quality. *Sociology of Education, 81,* 242–270.

Duncan, M. J., & Biddle, B. J. (1974). *The study of teaching.* Lanham, MD: University Press of America.

Dweck, C. S. (1986). Motivational processes affecting learning. *American Psychologist, 41,* 1040–1048.

Entwisle, D. R., Alexander, K. L., & Olson, L. S. (1997). *Children, schools, and inequality.* Boulder, CO: Westview Press.

Fallon, D. (2000, November 2). Teacher quality and our responsibility. A speech to the New York Association of Colleges for Teacher Education. Latham, NY.

Fuller, B., Wright, J., Gesicki, K., & Kang, E. (2007). Gauging growth: How to judge No Child Left Behind. *Educational Researcher, 36,* 268–278.

Gamoran, A., Anderson, C. W., Quiroz, P. A., Secada, W. G., Williams, T., & Ashmann, S. (2003). *Transforming teaching in math and science: How schools and districts can support change.* New York: Teachers College Press.

Greene, J. P. (2000). The Texas school miracle is for real. *City Journal, 10,* 3.

Hamilton, L. S., et al. (2007). *Standards-based accountability under No Child Left Behind.* Santa Monica, CA: Rand Corporation.

Hart, B., & Risley, T. R. (1995). *Meaningful differences in the everyday experience of young American children*. Baltimore, MD: Brookes.
Hightower, A. M. (2010, January 14). Holding all states to high standards. *Education Week: Quality Counts 2010, 29*(17), 33–35.
Hoff, D. (2009, January 7). Schools struggling to meet key goal on accountability. *Education Week, 28*(16), 1, 14-15.
Jargowsky, P. A. (1997). *Poverty and place: Ghettos, barrios, and the American city*. New York: Russell Sage Foundation.
Jennings, J. (2005). Below the bubble: "Educational triage" and the Texas accountability system. *American Educational Research Journal, 42*, 231–268.
Kim, J. S., & Sunderman, G. L. (2005). Measuring academic proficiency under the No Child Left Behind Act: Implications for educational equity. *Educational Researcher, 34*, 3–13.
Langer, J. A., Applebee, A. N., & Nystrand, M. (2005). *Final report*. National Research Center on English Learning and Achievement. Albany: State University of New York–Albany.
Lankford, H., Loeb, S., & Wyckoff, J. (2002). Teacher sorting and the plight of urban schools: A descriptive analysis. *Educational Evaluation and Policy Analysis, 24*, 37–62.
Linn, R. L. (2003). Accountability: Responsibility and reasonable expectations. *Educational Researcher, 32*(7), 3–13.
Lortie, D. C. (1975). *Schoolteacher:* A sociological study. Chicago: University of Chicago Press.
Metz, M. H. (1986 [2003]). *Different by design: The context and character of three magnet schools*. New York: Teachers College Press.
National Center for Education Statistics (NCES). (2005). *Parent and family involvement in education: 2002-03* (NCES 2005-043). Washington, DC: U.S. Government Printing Office.
National Center for Education Statistics (NCES). (2009). *The condition of education 2009* (NCES 2009-081). Washington, DC: U.S. Government Printing Office.
National Research Council. (1999). *High stakes: Testing for tracking, promotion, and graduation* (J. P. Heubert & R. M. Hauser, Eds.). Washington, DC: National Academy Press.
National Research Council & Institute of Medicine. (2004). *Engaging schools: Fostering high school students' motivation to learn*. Washington, DC: The National Academies Press.
Newmann, F. M., Marks, H. M., & Gamoran, A. (1996). Authentic pedagogy and student performance. *American Journal of Education, 104*, 280–312.
Nystrand, M. (1997). *Opening dialogue: Understanding the dynamics of language and learning in the English classroom*. New York: Teachers College Press.
Olson, L. (2002, January 16). States gear up for new federal law. *Education Week, 21*(18), 1, 24–25.
Olson, L. (2006, September 20). As AYP bar rises, more schools fail. *Education Week, 26*(4), 1, 20.
People for the American Way Foundation. (2003). *The voucher veneer: The deeper agenda to privatize public education*. Washington, DC: Author.
Rosenholtz, S. J. (1989). Teachers' workplace: The social organization of schools.

Research in Training Monograph Series. New York: Longman.

Rosenholtz, S. J., & Rosenholtz, S. H. (1981). Classroom organization and the perception of ability. *Sociology of Education, 54*, 132–140.

Sawchuk, S. (2010, January 27). Quality of questions on common tests at issue. *Education Week, 29*(19), 1, 11.

Scheerens, J., & Bosker, R. (1997). *The foundations of educational effectiveness*. Oxford, UK: Pergamon.

Seltzer, M., Choi, K., & Thum, Y. M. (2003). Examining relationships between where students start and how rapidly they progress: Using new developments in growth modeling to gain insight into the distribution of achievement within schools. *Educational Evaluation and Policy Analysis, 25*, 263–286.

Southerland, S. A., Smith, L. K., Sowell, S. P., & Kittleson, J. M. (2007). Resisting unlearning: Understanding science education's response to the United States' national accountability movement. *Review of Research in Education, 31*, 45–77.

Wood, R., & Bandura, A. (1989). Impact of conceptions of ability on self-regulatory mechanisms and complex decision-making. *Journal of Personality and Social Psychology, 56*, 407–415.

Zimmerman, B. J., & Martinez-Pons, M. (1992). Perceptions of efficacy and strategy use in the self-regulation of learning. In D. H. Schunk & J. L. Meece (Eds.), *Student perceptions in the classroom* (pp. 185–207). Hillsdale, NJ: Lawrence Erlbaum.

CHAPTER 2

Teacher Effects

Past, Present, and Future

Spyros Konstantopoulos

A fundamental educational objective is to provide high-quality instructional experiences that facilitate academic growth for all students. Much educational research has focused on identifying important school-related factors that affect student achievement and many school policy initiatives have attempted to ensure that valuable school resources are allocated adequately across schools. At the center of this line of research is the notion that school resources *do matter*; that is, they can affect student achievement positively. Teachers are considered one of the most important school resources. It is widely believed by educational researchers that teachers can affect student achievement positively, and a fundamental goal of teacher effects research is to examine how teachers help improve academic achievement for all students. Currently, with the passage of the No Child Left Behind Act (NCLB), test scores are widely used to hold schools and teachers accountable for student learning. One way to increase student achievement is through teachers, and NCLB has mandated state plans to improve the effectiveness of teachers. The underlying belief is that highly effective teachers can make a difference in promoting student achievement.

Previous research over the past 30 years has suggested that the effects teachers have on students' academic achievement vary considerably (Hanushek, 1971; Nye, Konstantopoulos, & Hedges, 2004; Rivkin, Hanushek, & Kain, 2005; Rowan, Correnti, & Miller, 2002). That is, student achievement depends at least partly on the teachers that students are assigned to. Folk knowledge has also suggested that differences in teacher effectiveness can be considerable, individual students report a profound and lasting impact of particular teachers. It is common to attribute academic success to particular teachers we have had and speak of them as "great teachers." Still, the research evidence about the effects of teacher characteristics on student achievement is mixed. Some research seems to suggest that teacher effects are negligible while other evidence suggests that they are important.

Notwithstanding the research work thus far, the factors that define effective teachers have not been identified explicitly. In addition, the aspects of classroom practices that result in effective instruction need to be studied further. It is essential to continue conducting research about teacher effects and determine what works best for students because the findings of these efforts can help policy makers, as well as district and school administrators, promote student progress through the cultivation of effective teachers. Research findings can also be useful to teachers themselves and can facilitate their professional growth and their effectiveness in the classroom.

In this chapter I first review key results from the main traditions of research about teacher effects on student achievement, including the more recent endeavors of value-added research. Second, I discuss the limitations of existing findings and stress the importance of conducting experiments to study teacher effects. Third, I summarize findings from the literature about the effects of teachers on minority and disadvantaged students. Finally, I conclude with some thoughts about the future of teacher effects research.

RESEARCH TRADITIONS IN TEACHER EFFECTS RESEARCH

Education Production Studies

The first tradition of research includes studies that measure the association between teacher characteristics and student achievement. Some of them are known as "education production function studies": They attempt to determine the relation between specific measured teacher characteristics such as teacher experience or teacher education and student achievement. However, because some parents may be able to choose the neighborhoods in which to live as well as the schools their children attend while other parents may not, student and family backgrounds are confounded with naturally occurring teacher characteristics (Tiebout, 1956). Education production function studies (e.g., Coleman et al., 1966) attempt to control for this confounding effect by using student and family background characteristics as covariates in regression models, a family of statistical models used to analyze naturally occurring variation in teachers and student achievement. A particularly important covariate to account for is prior achievement, because it can be seen as summarizing the effects of individual background (including prior educational experiences) and family background up to that time. However, even this covariate may leave important characteristics of the student, such as motivation, unmeasured.

The results produced from this research strand have been mixed. Some reviewers of the production function literature argue that measured teacher characteristics such as educational preparation, experience, or salary are only slightly related to student achievement (Hanushek, 1986). Other reviewers argue that there are more substantial positive effects from some of the resource characteristics (such as teacher experience and teacher education) on student achievement (Greenwald, Hedges, & Laine, 1996). More recently, researchers have demonstrated a positive association between teacher experience and student achievement (Clotfelter, Ladd, & Vigdor, 2006). In addition, National Board–certified teachers have been shown to be more effective than other teachers (Goldhaber & Anthony, 2007). Still, the relationship between observed teacher characteristics and student achievement is not always strong or evident.

It is important to recognize that failure to find that a set of observed teacher characteristics is associated with student achievement does not mean that all teachers have the same effectiveness in increasing student achievement. It is possible that the wrong characteristics were measured (e.g., ones that were convenient, but unrelated to achievement) but other characteristics that remain unobserved *would* be related to achievement (e.g., teacher motivation and commitment). Even when researchers attempt to measure the "right" teacher characteristics, it is possible that the measurement is so poor that the association between teacher characteristics and achievement is attenuated to the point of being negligible. In other words, in the bivariate case, measurement error can make teacher characteristics appear to be more weakly related to student achievement than they really are. In the multivariate case the effects of measurement error are less clear and thus may present challenges in interpreting education production function research.

Variation in Teacher Effects Studies

Another analytic strategy that leads to evidence about teacher effects does not attempt to estimate the relation between specific measured characteristics of teachers, but examines the *variation between classrooms* in achievement controlling for student background. That is, these studies are interested in the proportion of the variation in achievement that is attributed to (or explained by) teacher effects. Such analyses typically use prior achievement as a covariate so they can be interpreted as measuring differences in student achievement gain across classrooms net of prior achievement. It is important in these models to adjust for differences in student achievement that are caused by school-level factors (e.g., principal leadership and curricular organization). In other words, the teacher effects should not be confounded with either student background or school effects. Then, the observed differences in achievement gains across classrooms are hypothesized to be caused by differences in teacher effectiveness. The underlying assumption is that the between-classroom variation in achievement is caused by teacher differences in effectiveness. The advantage of this design is that it does not require the researcher to identify in advance, and measure adequately, the aspects of teacher behavior or other teacher characteristics that are related to achievement. On the other hand, this design cannot identify the specific teacher characteristics that are responsible for differences in teacher effectiveness.

Nye et al. (2004) summarized the findings from several studies on the magnitude of teacher effects and reported that typically a 1 standard deviation increase in teacher effectiveness should increase student achievement gains by about 1/3 of a standard deviation. Reporting results in the standard deviation metric allows researchers to compare the magnitude of teacher effects from study to study and to compare the size of teacher effects to other common approaches to educational improvement, such as class-size reduction. Nye et al.'s own results using data from Project STAR also pointed to teacher effects estimates that were nearly 1/3 of a standard deviation. The Project STAR results reported by Nye et al. likely captured "true" teacher effects because teachers and students were randomly assigned to classrooms within schools. As a result, potential confounding between teacher effects and student background should have been minimized. Project STAR, also known as the Tennessee class size experiment, was a large-scale 4-year cohort experiment that followed kindergarteners through 3rd grade. In kindergarten, the 1st year of the study, students and teachers were randomly assigned to small (15 students on average) and regular-size classrooms (22 students on average) within schools. Random assignment was repeated for students who participated in the study in the 1st, 2nd, or 3rd grades. In summary, evidence produced from observational studies and from large-scale experiments pointed to a similar magnitude of teacher effects.

A more recent study summarized estimates of teacher effects from several studies and allowed researchers to form a more complete picture about the range of the teacher effects (Hanushek & Rivkin, 2010). For example, in reading and language arts the estimates ranged approximately from 1/10th to 1/5th of a standard deviation and in mathematics from 1/10th to 1/3rd of a standard deviation (Hanushek & Rivkin, 2010). By way of comparison, the effect of 1 year in small classes as opposed to large classes on achievement gains estimated from Project STAR is only about 0.10 standard deviations. The teacher effects estimates reported in Nye et al. (2004) and Hanushek and Rivkin (2010) are typically larger than 0.1 standard deviations and therefore considerable. Stated in terms of observed achievement growth, effective teachers appear to increase student achievement by nearly an additional 1/4th of a year's growth in the early grades (Hill, Bloom, Black, & Lipsey, 2008).

Product-Process Studies

The third tradition of research discusses what constitutes good teaching practice and examines the association between teaching practice and student achievement. This line of work has provided evidence about the link between teacher behavior (i.e., what teachers do in the classroom) and student learning (Good & Brophy, 1987). In their pioneering work, Good and Grouws (1977) and Good (1979) discussed teacher effects as the teacher's ability to increase student performance on standardized tests. For example, Good (1979) reviewed findings on teacher effects from process-product studies and concluded that effective teachers substantially influenced academic achievement for all students. Process-product studies identify classroom processes (i.e., observed teacher characteristics) that are associated with student outcomes (i.e., products) such as achievement. Some of these teacher characteristics include teachers' confidence in teaching students successfully, efficient allocation of classroom time to instruction and academic tasks, effective classroom organization and group management, and active/engaging teaching that emphasizes understanding of concepts (Good & Brophy, 1987). Other reviewers reached similar conclusions and argued that teachers varied in their effectiveness in increasing student achievement (Brophy, 1986, 1988). Within this tradition, recent work has documented significant correlations between teacher evaluation scores and value-added teacher effects, as well as significant associations between teacher evaluation scores and student achievement (Gallagher, 2004). Teacher evaluation scores were derived from systematic observations of teachers teaching (Gallagher, 2004). The observations focused on exemplary teaching in reading and mathematics with emphasis on phonics instruction and higher-order thinking skills in reading and algebra, statistics and probability, and math reasoning in mathematics. Another recent study found that teachers with higher evaluation scores helped close, on average, the achievement gap between advantaged and disadvantaged students (Borman & Kimball, 2005).

Overall, all three lines of research have been equally important in informing the literature about the effects of teachers on student achievement regardless of the definition of teacher effects. There is consensus in the literature that the effects of teachers on student achievement vary considerably. That is, the variation in achievement across classrooms is important. However, in examinations of the association between specific teacher characteristics and achievement, the findings have been mixed. Some studies have demonstrated the importance of teachers in promoting student achievement, while others have found trivial or no relationships between teacher characteristics and student achievement. In addition, observed teacher characteristics do not explain much of the variability in teacher effectiveness. For example, evidence from Project STAR, where substantial variability in teacher effectiveness was observed, indicates that teacher experience and education explain only about 1% of the variation in teacher effectiveness. What can explain this difficulty in identifying what makes some teachers more effective than average? One possibility is that the teacher characteristics that are typically observed or measured do not represent accurately the complexity of teaching practices in the classroom that are most likely responsible for most of the variation in teacher effectiveness. That is, the challenge for researchers is to find ways to capture and quantify the teaching that takes place in the classroom.

Value-Added Research

The term *value-added* is used frequently with applied research conducted by states in the context of accountability or other educational programs. Value-added studies are similar to school and teacher effects studies, but different from studies that use simple cross-sectional analyses of school performance. However, value-added studies are also subject to some of the same concerns as cross-sectional studies.

Value-added models have gained considerable attention in the past 10 years because of the urgency of using achievement scores to determine teacher effects on student outcomes. The underlying goal of value-added models is to examine the effects of teachers on students' learning gains net of factors such as student background. These models intend to estimate the *unique* contribution or "value-added" of teachers to students' change or gain in learning. In that sense, value-added research is not a new idea; regression models that examine teacher and schools effects net of student background date back to the famous Coleman (1966) report.

Meyer (1997) argues the key objective in value-added research is to assess, for example, teacher effects on student achievement net of the effects of other sources that may affect student achievement. It is common practice in value-added research to gauge teacher effects via regression models that control for covariates hypothesized to influence student learning such as previous achievement. Often the outcome in such regression models is a post-test measure of student achievement on standardized tests, while the main predictor variable(s) represents teacher effects and other variables such as pre-test measures of student achievement are included as covariates to adjust for previous knowledge or ability (Ballou, Sanders, & Wright, 2004; McCaffrey, Lockwood, Koretz, Louis, & Hamilton, 2004). These are often called "residualized change models." Other times the outcome is simply a change score between two time points, assuming the scales are equated, in which case including pre-test scores as a covariate is less important.

A fundamental underlying assumption in value-added models is that the observed gains in student achievement are mainly caused by teacher effects (e.g., instruction, teacher characteristics) and not to other student-related factors that are unobserved and hence not controlled for (Schmidt, Houang, & McKnight, 2005). In principle, value-added models are hypothesized to provide more accurate estimates of teacher effectiveness than studies that do not take into account previous information about student background such as previous achievement or family socioeconomic status (SES). Because value-added models include previous achievement as a covariate they facilitate causal inferences about teacher effects more than models that do not include previous achievement. However, it is noteworthy that value-added models don't necessarily eliminate possible confounding effects completely, because of possible effects of other, unobserved factors (Braun, 2005). Along those lines more recent work has shown via validation and falsification analyses that common assumptions in value-added models don't always hold and that teacher effects estimates can't be interpreted as causal, at least in some cases (Rothstein, 2010). Similar points have been made by Rubin, Stuart, and Zanutto (2004), who provided a thoughtful discussion about causal inferences of teacher and school effects. In their discussion, Rubin et al. argue that causal estimates of teacher effects are difficult to conceptualize even in well-done randomized experiments, and that value-added models don't necessarily provide causal estimates, but should more likely be conceptualized as descriptive measures of teacher effects.

Education production function studies, as well as studies about the variation of teacher effects, can be thought of as value-added models, since they typically adjust for student background factors such as prior achievement and SES. Thus, as with those bodies of research, the critical question is whether value-added modeling can eliminate the confounding or selection problem that results from how students and teachers are assigned to classes. If selection is still evident, then interpreting teacher effects estimates as casual may not be warranted.

LIMITATIONS IN TEACHER EFFECTS RESEARCH

Within schools students are frequently placed into classrooms or assigned to teachers based on student characteristics such as achievement. In turn, teachers are not randomly assigned to classrooms either. This creates problems when inferring the relation between characteristics of teachers and student achievement. For instance, suppose that more experienced teachers are assigned to classes composed of higher achieving students as a privilege of seniority or to lower achieving students as a compensatory strategy. In such cases, the causal direction in the relation between teacher experience and student achievement is not that teacher experience causes achievement but the reverse. This ambiguity of causal direction is a major problem for production function studies of the effects of teacher characteristics on student achievement. In fact, a recent study by Clotfelter and colleagues (2006) reported that advantaged students are more likely to receive highly qualified teachers, and that this biases the association between teacher characteristics and achievement. The same caveat holds for teacher effects estimates that are defined as variability in achievement across classes. In particular, these teacher effects estimates could also be biased because they may not be properly adjusted by student background and omitted variable bias is likely.

Valid interpretation of results requires that covariates adequately control for pre-existing differences, including unobservable differences that are related to achievement growth among students assigned to different classrooms. Another requirement is that teachers are not assigned to classrooms on the basis of student characteristics, which may be known to the school but unavailable for use as covariates in the statistical analysis, and which might produce exaggerated or attenuated differences between classrooms in achievement or achievement gains when omitted. For example, schools might assign a particularly effective teacher to students believed to be entering a difficult period as a compensatory resource allocation strategy. Alternatively, schools might assign a particularly effective teacher to students believed to have promise for unusually large achievement gains as a work reward or as a meritocratic resource allocation strategy. Schools have many sources of information suitable for identifying students poised for unusually large gains or losses. They include essentially everything known about the child beyond test scores and easily recorded factors such as SES, gender, and family structure. Some examples are an impending divorce, change of residence, delinquency problems, problems with siblings, unemployment of parents, or adjustment problems in school, which may all signal potential difficulties in the next school year. Alternatively, improvements in student motivation, compliance, adjustment, or parental involvement may all signal unusually good prospects for the next school year. Even important covariates such as prior achievement do not completely control for unobserved student characteristics.

Even after controlling for previous achievement and student background, it is still difficult to interpret the estimates of teacher effects on student achievement, because the teacher effects may still be confounded with unobserved individual, family, school, and neighborhood factors. Nonetheless, when modeling data to estimate teacher effects it is absolutely crucial to adjust for important student covariates such as family background and previous achievement. However, researchers need to be cautious when making causal inferences because causality assumptions are not always warranted in teacher effects studies unless all relevant covariates are adjusted for in the model.

Strengthening the Internal Validity of Teacher Effects Estimates

One way to decrease the confounding problem discussed above is to design a study in which both students and teachers are randomly assigned (for research purposes and within the limits of sound educational practice) to classes within schools. Random assignment of students would ensure that all observable and unobservable differences between students in different classes would be, on average, no larger than would be expected by chance. While there is always some chance that the treatment and control groups will differ on some factor that affects school performance, this chance can be held to statistically acceptable levels (5% or even lower). In other words, because of random assignment one would not expect systematic differences between treatment and control groups on average. Importantly, random assignment ensures similar treatment and control groups in *unobserved* as well as observed characteristics. Random assignment of teachers to classes would ensure that teacher characteristics do not determine teacher assignment to classes. In addition, random assignment of teachers to classes guarantees that teacher assignment to classes is unrelated to classroom-level variables as well, such as compositional factors that might affect students' attention or motivation. That is, in principle teacher characteristics are uncorrelated with predictors of classroom achievement. As a result, well-designed experiments can provide useful knowledge about "true" teacher effects.

Experiments like Project STAR satisfy both conditions, since within schools and grades teacher and students were randomly assigned to classrooms. Hence one could argue that teacher effects estimates produced from Project STAR data are less likely to be biased as a result of confounding. One important aspect of random assignment, however, is that random assignment works best with larger samples. That is, random assignment of small samples of students, or of a few teachers to classes within a school, does not guarantee successful elimination of preexisting differences among students or teachers. In Project STAR it seemed that random assignment for teachers was successful, but the evaluation of successful randomization was not conducted within schools; rather it was done across schools, which may not be the best way to check whether randomization was successful. It is also noteworthy that there is no absolute way to check via post hoc methods how successful random assignment is. The tests about randomization are always performed on observed measures and do not provide any information about unobserved characteristics. At best the tests show whether there are preexisting differences in some observed measures. Hence, even with randomized study designs, making inferences entails a certain leap of faith. In a well-designed and executed experiment there is a higher likelihood that treatment conditions are equal on average than in other studies. However, even with data from randomized experiments careful statistical modeling may be necessary to reduce potential biases.

However, studies such as Project STAR are unique and are conducted sporadically. The findings produced from such experiments are informative in that they can effectively demonstrate the importance of teachers in promoting student achievement. In practice, however, random assignment of students and teachers to classrooms is rarely possible. Instead, decisions made about the assignment of students and teachers to classrooms should be aligned with the objectives set by the school districts (e.g., to increase achievement of lower-performing students).

In the same vein, researchers often have to work with data that are collected in natural settings such as schools and classrooms. In such cases teacher effects estimates are typically adjusted by covariates using post hoc approaches. One approach is to employ regression models and control statistically for important covariates that are hypothesized to affect the relationship between teacher effectiveness and student outcomes. The most important covariates include student background, such as prior achievement and family SES. Another approach is to create similar classrooms using student characteristics via propensity score matching, a statistical technique used by social scientists, medical researchers, and others to identify the best possible comparison groups when random assignment is not possible. The idea is to use relevant student variables that have been measured to equate, as nearly as possible, seemingly nonequivalent groups of students and get more accurate estimates of teacher effects (see Luellen, Shadish, & Clark, 2005). However, either approach relies heavily on the use of observed variables, which implies that much thought must occur in the design phase of the study about what should be measured.

Differential Effects of Teachers

The U.S. educational system is, in principle, designed to provide equal access to school resources and to reduce inequality in achievement. Thus, it is important to determine whether minority and disadvantaged students benefit more from having effective teachers. It is appealing to think that effective teachers will increase academic achievement for all students *and* simultaneously close the achievement gap between male and female, minority and white, and low- and high-SES students. One focus of NCLB is to close the achievement gap and to make certain that low achievers from disadvantaged backgrounds attain academic proficiency. An important mechanism through which this can be accomplished is the teaching workforce and the degree to which they are effective in improving student achievement. NCLB has mandated state plans to improve teacher effectiveness with the underlying belief that highly effective teachers can improve achievement, especially that of disadvantaged students.

There is some evidence from nonexperimental data that Black and White students benefit equally from teacher effectiveness (Sanders & Rivers, 1996). Other studies, however, have reported somewhat mixed findings. For example, some researchers have demonstrated that teacher characteristics such as experience are positively and significantly linked to the achievement of Black students (Murnane & Philips, 1981), whereas other studies have shown that teacher characteristics are not associated with the achievement of Black or Mexican students (Hanushek, 1971, 1992). A more recent study analyzed data from Project STAR and found that minority and disadvantaged students benefit from effective teachers as much as other students (Konstantopoulos, 2009). However, it is noteworthy that it is often difficult to find statistically significant interactions between teacher effects and student groups, because these coefficients are typically underpowered; that is, the probability of being detected by the statistical test is low. The main reason for this is that the sample size of an interaction is typically small and thus the interaction effect is measured with less precision. It's easier to be confident about a teacher's average impact on students than his or her impact on a specific subgroup of students.

Another challenge in assessing teachers' impact on subgroups of students is that teachers are not randomly allocated to schools, so some selection typically takes place. Research on teacher allocation to schools has documented that schools with high proportions of low-income or minority students often have difficulty recruiting and retaining high-quality teachers (Darling-Hammond, 1995). Ferguson (1998) documented that in districts, and therefore in schools, with higher proportions of minority students, teachers' test scores on basic tests of literacy skills (e.g., Texas Examination of Current Administrators and Teachers) were lower. He argued that teachers who scored higher on the basic tests (a hypothesized observed characteristic of effective teachers) were more likely to help their students do well in achievement tests. Hence, in districts with higher proportions of minority students, teachers were less effective in increasing their students' test scores. Ferguson also suggested that less effective teachers were more likely to teach in districts (and schools) with higher proportions of minority students. Two other studies have provided evidence that low-income students are more likely to be exposed to less effective teachers. First, Krei (1998) argued that low-income urban students are more likely to be exposed to less effective teachers than are other students. Similarly, Lankford, Loeb, and Wyckoff (2002) concluded that low-achieving, minority, and low-income students in urban settings attend schools with less qualified teachers. As a result, in the state of New York students in urban schools are about four times more likely to perform below the basic proficiency level than students in suburban schools (see Lankford et al., 2002). A recent study tested this hypothesis empirically using data from Project STAR and found that there was larger variability in teacher effectiveness in lower-SES schools (Nye et al., 2004). NCLB targets such low-SES schools and urges school systems to staff these schools with more effective teachers in order to improve student achievement, but that has been a major challenge.

The origins and exact nature of the differences in teacher effectiveness between lower- and higher-income schools are unclear. One plausible mechanism that might result in lower-income schools having teachers of lower-average quality is a "creaming" process. Specifically, once their effectiveness has been demonstrated it is plausible that higher-income schools lure these teachers away from lower-income schools using incentives such as better working conditions. Alternatively, effective teachers may choose to move to higher-income schools because of the work environment. In these schools the task of teaching is easier, while in many urban, predominantly Black schools, teachers may struggle more because of the poor behavioral climate (Kelly, 2010). Regardless of the mechanism of selection of effective teachers to higher-income schools, one would expect more consistent teacher effects in higher-income schools and more inconsistent teacher effects in lower-income schools. Teacher effects are likely more inconsistent in lower-income schools because such schools have a mix of more and less effective teachers.

CONCLUSION

Teachers are the "engines" of the U.S. education system and their effects on student achievement have been studied extensively the past 40 years. The findings in the teacher effects literature have consistently indicated that teachers differ considerably in their effectiveness in increasing student achievement. The evidence from both experimental and observational data has suggested that there are substantial differences among teachers in their ability to produce achievement gains in their students. However, the teacher characteristics that are typically observed, such as education, experience, licensure, or salary, have not been consistently related to student achievement. The findings in the literature are mixed and inconclusive. In addition, the observed teacher characteristics do not explain much of the variation in teacher effectiveness. For example, in Project STAR teacher education and experience explained only about 1% of the variation in teacher effectiveness, measured as the value-added in achievement at the classroom level. This indicates that the most important teacher characteristics are usually not observed, perhaps because they are difficult to measure.

In order to become more successful in estimating teacher effects, both in terms of long-term research studies of teacher effects and in applied programs and policies related to teacher effectiveness, several things need to be done in the near future. One of the major tasks of teacher effects research is to identify the factors that are likely to be accountable for most of the variation in teacher effectiveness. This can be accomplished by systematically observing classrooms and by interviewing teachers who are identified as effective as well as their colleagues. For example, teachers can speak to the most effective aspects of their instruction and what they think makes a difference in the classroom. The idea is to construct a synthetic profile of an effective teacher and then try to measure the characteristics of an effective teacher as reliably as possible. It is also important to identify effective instructional practices that take place in the classroom and measure them (see chapter 1). In other words, it is essential to define explicitly what teacher effectiveness is, construct reliable measures of the factors that constitute teacher effectiveness, and finally, collect high-quality data that will allow researchers to examine empirically what works best for students.

Another important aspect in planning teacher effects research is to design large-scale studies that will sort out the most important criteria for effective classroom instruction. The findings of these studies would be useful for policy makers because they could use them in targeted initiatives that capitalize on identifying teacher effects. More careful thinking has to be incorporated in designing studies to examine teacher effects. These designs could be carefully planned experiments that will eliminate preexisting differences in students and teachers. Of course, monitoring experimental studies as they are conducted and striving to minimize threats to the validity of the experiments are essential. The design of quasi-experiments and observational studies should also be well thought out. Matching techniques could be incorporated in the designs of such studies to facilitate the creation of similar classrooms.

Finally, data analysis is also an important part of teacher effects research. Estimating teacher effects is not a simple task and both methods and careful analysis can facilitate that objective. Although there have been advances in value-added methodology in the past 10 years, more work is needed, especially for longitudinal designs. In addition, analysts should be more careful and sophisticated when specifying their models and should strive to reduce bias in teacher effects estimates as much as possible. More rigorous analysis will result in more valid estimates and findings that will inform research as well as policy making.

In terms of "leveraging" teacher effects research in targeted initiatives, it seems that the knowledge produced from research thus far is not as advanced as one would like. Although there is confidence that teachers affect students, and that teacher-to-teacher differences in effectiveness are both real and substantial, identifying the variables that readily distinguish an effective teacher has been a challenge. In addition, it is unclear that teachers are equally effective in any classroom or school. For example, it is possible that the characteristics of an effective teacher may interact with school context and composition. Nonetheless, in order to ensure equitable allocation of resources in schools, it is important to provide incentives to effective teachers that will motivate them to teach in urban, disadvantaged schools.

REFERENCES

Ballou, D., Sanders, W., & Wright, P. (2004). Controlling for student background in value-added assessment of teachers. *Journal of Educational and Behavioral Statistics, 29*, 37–65.

Borman, G. D., & Kimball, S. M. (2005). Teacher quality and educational equality: Do teachers with higher standards-based evaluation ratings close student achievement gaps? *Elementary School Journal, 106*, 3–20.

Braun, H. (2005).Value-added modeling: What does due diligence require? In R. Lissitz (Ed.), *Value-added models in education: Theory and applications* (pp. 19–38). Maple Grove, MN: JAM Press.

Brophy, J. (1986). Teacher influences on student achievement. *American Psychologist, 41*, 1069–1077.

Brophy, J. (1988). Research linking teacher behavior to student achievement: Potential implications for instruction of Chapter 1 students. *Educational Psychologist, 23,* 235–286.

Clotfelter, C. T., Ladd, H. F., & Vigdor, J. L. (2006). Teacher-student matching and the assessment of teacher effectiveness. *Journal of Human Resources, 41,* 778–820.

Coleman, J. S., Campbell, E. Q., Hobson, C. J., McPartland, J., Mood, A. M., Weinfeld, F. D., et al. (1966). *Equality of educational opportunity.* Washington, DC: U.S. Government Printing Office.

Darling-Hammond, L. (1995). Inequality and access to knowledge. In J. A. Banks (Ed.), *Handbook of research on multicultural education* (pp. 465–483). New York: Macmillan.

Ferguson, R. F. (1998). Can schools narrow the Black-White test score gap? In C. Jenks & M. Phillips (Eds.), *The black-white test score gap* (pp. 318–374). Washington, DC: Brookings.

Gallagher, H. A. (2004). Vaughn Elementary's innovative teacher evaluation system: Are teacher evaluation scores related to growth in student achievement? *Peabody Journal of Education, 79,* 79–107.

Goldhaber, D., & Anthony, E. (2007). Can teacher quality be effectively assessed? National board certification as a signal of effective teaching. *Review of Economics and Statistics, 89,* 134–150.

Good, T. (1979). Teacher effectiveness in the elementary school. *Journal of Teacher Education, 30,* 52–64.

Good, T., & Brophy, J. (1987). *Looking in classrooms.* New York: Harper & Row.

Good, T., & Grouws, D. (1977). Teaching effects: A process-product study in fourth-grade mathematics classrooms. *Journal of Teacher Education, 28,* 49–54.

Greenwald, R., Hedges, L. V., & Laine, R. D. (1996). The effect of school resources on student achievement. *Review of Educational Research, 66,* 361–396.

Hanushek, E. A. (1971). Teacher characteristics and gains in student achievement: Estimation using micro data. *American Economic Review, 61,* 280–288.

Hanushek, E. A. (1986). The economics of schooling: Production and efficiency in public schools. *Journal of Economic Literature, 24,* 1141–1177.

Hanushek, E. A. (1992). The tradeoff between child quantity and quality: Some empirical evidence. *Journal of Political Economy, 100,* 84–117.

Hanushek, E. A., & Rivkin, S. G. (2010). Generalizations about using value-added measures of teacher quality. *American Economic Review: Papers and Proceedings, 100,* 267–271.

Hill, C. J., Bloom, H. S., Black, A. R., & Lipsey, M. W. (2008). Empirical benchmarks for interpreting effect sizes in research. *Child Development Perspectives, 2,* 172–177.

Kelly, S. (2010). A crisis of authority in predominantly Black schools? *Teachers College Record, 112,* 1247–1274.

Konstantopoulos, S. (2009). Effects of teachers on minority and disadvantaged students' achievement in the early grades. *Elementary School Journal, 110,* 92–113.

Krei, M. S. (1998). Intensifying the barriers: The problem of inequitable teacher allocation in low-income urban schools. *Urban Education, 33,* 71–94.

Lankford, H., Loeb, S., & Wyckoff, J. (2002). Teacher sorting and the plight of urban schools: A descriptive analysis. *Educational Evaluation and Policy Analysis, 24,* 37–62.

Luellen, J. K., Shadish, W. R., & Clark, M. H. (2005). Propensity scores: A introduction and experimental test. *Evaluation Review, 29*, 530–558.

McCaffrey, D. F., Lockwood, J. R., Koretz, D., Louis, T. A., & Hamilton, L. (2004). Models for value-added modeling of teacher effects. *Journal of Educational and Behavioral Statistics, 29*, 67–101.

Meyer, R. H. (1997). Value-added indicators of school performance: A primer. *Economics of Education Review, 16*, 283–301.

Murnane, R. J., & Phillips, B. R. (1981). What do effective teachers of inner-city children have in common? *Social Science Research, 10*, 83–100.

Nye, B., Konstantopoulos, S., & Hedges, L. V. (2004). How large are teacher effects? *Educational Evaluation and Policy Analysis, 26*, 237–257.

Rivkin, S. G., Hanushek, E. A., & Kain, J. F. (2005). Teachers, schools, and academic achievement. *Econometrica, 73*, 417–458.

Rothstein, J. (2010). Teacher quality in educational production: tracking, decay, and student achievement. *Quarterly Journal of Economics, 125*, 165-214.

Rowan, B., Correnti, R., & Miller, R. J. (2002). What large-scale, survey research tells us about teacher effects on student achievement: Insights from the Prospects Study of elementary schools. *Teachers College Record, 104*, 1525–1567.

Rubin, D. B., Stuart, E. A., & Zanutto, E. L. (2004). A potential outcomes view of value-added assessment in education. *Journal of Educational and Behavioral Statistics, 29*, 103–116.

Sanders, W. L., & Rivers, J. C. (1996). *Cumulative and residual effects of teachers on future student academic achievement.* Knoxville: University of Tennessee Value-Added Research and Assessment Center.

Schmidt, W. H., Houang, R. T., & McKnight, C. C. (2005). Value-added research: Right idea but wrong solution? In R. Lissitz (Ed.), *Value-added models in education: Theory and applications* (pp. 145–165). Maple Grove, MN: JAM Press.

Tiebout, C. M. (1956). A pure theory of local expenditures. *Journal of Political Economy, 64*, 416–424.

CHAPTER 3

Measuring Teaching Quality Using Student Achievement Tests

Lessons from Educators' Responses to No Child Left Behind

Laura S. Hamilton

Standardized testing of students' academic achievement has played a prominent role in education policy and practice for several decades, and this role continues to expand to encompass new uses for test results. Efforts to incorporate student test scores into teacher evaluations or teacher-level accountability measures can be considered the next logical step in a gradual expansion of large-scale testing from a tool that served primarily a monitoring function (Koretz, 1992) to the adoption of high-stakes systems designed to shape instruction while promoting accountability for small groups (e.g., school staff) and individuals (e.g., teachers or principals). The idea that teachers should be held responsible for promoting student learning, and that learning can be measured adequately through standardized tests, has a certain amount of commonsense appeal that has generated broad support from various stakeholder groups, including members of both major political parties. However, efforts to implement this idea are hampered by a number of factors, including problems inherent in the use of standardized achievement tests for multiple purposes. Most new and proposed teacher evaluation systems explicitly or implicitly rely on tests to serve multiple purposes, including creating incentives for teachers to cover specific material, providing information to guide decision making, and informing decisions about which teachers need assistance. Whether or not the new policies lead to the desired outcome of improved student learning will depend in large part on how policy makers and practitioners address these various uses of tests and what steps they take to promote appropriate uses of test score data.

Responsible use of student achievement tests or other educational tests requires a careful investigation of the validity of scores on those tests for the intended purposes (American Educational Research Association, American Psychological Association, & National Council on Measurement in Education, 1999; Kane, 2006). Advocates of test-based teacher evaluation often claim that it will improve student learning by motivating teachers and by providing information they can use to adjust their instruction, and that tests will provide accurate information for decision makers to use in placing, supporting, and rewarding teachers (for discussions of arguments for adopting evaluation systems that focus on student achievement, see, e.g., several chapters in Goldhaber & Hannaway, 2010). It is critical, therefore, for those who mandate the use of tests in teacher evaluation systems, as well as those who implement these systems, to consider what we know about the kinds of decisions that these systems can support and about the consequences they are likely to promote.

Because the widespread use of achievement tests for teacher evaluations is a recent phenomenon, we have relatively little evidence to support strong conclusions about what will happen when these systems are adopted on a large scale. However, policies that use high-stakes tests for school-level accountability have been in place long enough that we can identify some lessons that should inform the design of teacher accountability policies. A key question that can help inform the debate is the following: How do teachers and other educators respond to test-based accountability policies? In this chapter I draw on a recent study of responses to test-based accountability under No Child Left Behind (Hamilton et al., 2007; Stecher et al., 2008) as well as on the broader literature on high-stakes testing to explore the ways in which some of the changes to accountability policies that are currently being debated may be expected to influence instructional practice and student learning. The chapter will examine efforts to adopt accountability or evaluation policies at the individual teacher level, with a focus on the implications of relying heavily on standardized achievement tests. It will also address two related reforms: the development of data systems to support teacher-level accountability and to promote data-driven decision making, and the construction of measures of "teacher effectiveness" that influence personnel decisions. All these proposed reforms are evident in recent policy and funding initiatives such as the U.S. Department of Education's Race to the Top program (U.S. Department of Education, 2009).

The chapter begins with some brief background information on the Implementing Standards Based Accountability study and then discusses findings that are relevant to the use of student achievement tests in high-stakes accountability or evaluation systems. It concludes with a brief discussion of recommendations for promoting better use of tests in accountability systems. It should be noted that this chapter does not address all the potential limitations of relying on standardized achievement tests to evaluate teachers. In particular, it does not examine technical issues stemming from the use of value-added models to estimate teacher effectiveness or to award bonuses; these have been addressed extensively by other authors (e.g., Braun, 2005; McCaffrey, Han, & Lockwood, 2008; Rivkin, 2010).

THE IMPLEMENTING STANDARDS-BASED ACCOUNTABILITY STUDY

The Implementing Standards Based Accountability (ISBA) study examined how educators and administrators at all levels of the system, from the state to the classroom, have responded to the test-based accountability provisions of the No Child Left Behind Act (NCLB), with a focus on mathematics and science. The research team gathered survey and interview data over 3 years (school years 2003–4 through 2005–6) in California, Georgia, and Pennsylvania. Representative samples of districts in each of the three states were selected to participate, and within each of these districts, a representative sample of schools that served students in the elementary or middle grades or both was selected. All principals and all teachers who taught mathematics or science in grades 3, 4, 5, 7, or 8 were asked to respond to questionnaires, and a subset of schools in each district participated in site visits at which the principal, teachers, and parents were interviewed. Sample sizes and response rates for the principal and teacher surveys used in this chapter are provided in Table 3.1.

Table 3.1. Principal and Teacher Survey Responses, 2006

Respondents	California	Georgia	Pennsylvania	Total
Cooperating schools	91	111	97	299
Principal survey responses (N)	75	96	88	259
Principal response rate (%)	82.4	86.5	90.7	86.6
Teacher sample	972	1574	1059	3605
Teacher survey responses (N)	670	1366	931	2967
Teacher response rate (%)	68.9	86.8	87.9	82.3

Both the surveys and the interviews were designed to gather information on educators' practices and about their perceptions regarding the effects of NCLB on their schools and students. The teacher surveys and interviews included, among other topics, questions about teachers' instructional practices in mathematics and science; their perceptions regarding how their practices are affected by state standards, assessments, and accountability policies; their use of data for decision making; and their opinions about various aspects of the state accountability system. Principals responded to questions about their instructional leadership practices and school improvement strategies, as well as their opinions about the accountability policies. Additional information about the study design, data collection instruments, and analytic approach can be found in Stecher et al. (2008) and Hamilton et al. (2007).

The ISBA study examined a range of topics, including district-level reform strategies, capacity, school improvement efforts, instruction, and school climate. This chapter is not intended to provide a comprehensive overview of the study but instead draws selectively on ISBA findings to illustrate key points. In particular, it summarizes key findings related to the ways in which educators respond to high-stakes testing systems as a means of identifying lessons that may be relevant to the development of test-based teacher evaluation systems.

THE ADOPTION OF TEST-BASED EVALUATION POLICIES

The rationale for incorporating measures of student achievement into teacher evaluation systems is discussed elsewhere in this volume (see, e.g., Kelly, chapter 1), but it is useful to consider the specific ways in which the use of tests is intended to support efforts to improve teaching quality. While the theory of change underlying most teacher evaluation and pay-for-performance systems (Podgursky & Springer, 2007) is not identical to the theory that has informed the development of school-level accountability policies such as NCLB (Stecher et al., 2008), there are some commonalities in the mechanisms that are expected to promote change. First, test-based evaluation is intended to create *incentives* for teachers to teach in a certain way or to cover certain content, thereby presumably improving the quality of instruction provided by existing teachers. It is important to point out that most test-based accountability systems are not designed simply to convince educators to work harder, but are intended to encourage educators to redirect their efforts toward material that is deemed important enough to include on state or district tests. Second, tests provide *information*, both to help teachers improve their instruction (e.g., by identifying which students need extra assistance or which topics could benefit from greater coverage) and to help administrators and others, including parents, identify which teachers or schools appear to be promoting the desired outcomes. This information, in turn, can be used by administrators to make personnel decisions that are intended to improve the overall quality of the teaching force or by parents to inform school choice. Third, most school- and teacher-level accountability or evaluation systems have some sort of *assistance* component that is intended to provide extra guidance and support to low performers. While it is difficult if not impossible in practice to separate the effects of these three mechanisms, an understanding of how they operate within any specific system can help identify ways in which the system is and is not functioning as intended.

Whether change in teaching occurs as a function of incentives, information, or assistance, the use of tests has the potential to exert a strong influence on the nature of that change, in particular by encouraging teachers to reallocate time and resources away from content that is not on the test and toward tested material (Hamilton, 2003; Stecher, 2002). These changes in practice, in turn, can potentially lead to a narrowing of curriculum and instruction that results in improved scores on the high-stakes tests, without improving the underlying achievement that the tests were designed to measure—a phenomenon known as score inflation (Koretz, 2008; Linn, 2000). These related effects, narrowing of instruction that results in students missing opportunities to learn important content, and score inflation that results in a loss of useful information from test scores, need to be considered as new test-based evaluation systems are rolled out.

Although the debates surrounding test-based evaluation sometimes focus on the views of the most ardent supporters and critics, the effects on instruction are likely to be mixed in most cases. Possible responses of teachers to high-stakes tests can take a number of forms, ranging from some that may be considered beneficial (e.g., taking steps to improve one's instruction) to some that are clearly harmful (e.g., cheating). These responses are likely to vary in the extent to which they produce score inflation, with the risk of inflation increasing as practices become more tailored to a specific test rather than focused on the broader subject matter that teachers are expected to cover (for a description of a framework that describes forms of test preparation and their relationship to the validity of scores, see Koretz & Hamilton, 2006). The next section summarizes some key findings from ISBA related to changes in what and how teachers teach.

TEST-BASED ACCOUNTABILITY AND INSTRUCTIONAL CHANGE

Teachers in the ISBA study reported responding to test-based accountability policies in a variety of ways that included desirable and less desirable instructional activities (with the exception of cheating, which was not covered on the survey because of the difficulty of eliciting accurate reports). When asked about changes in the allocation of time across different subjects, teachers were more likely to report increases in time spent on tested subjects than to report decreases, whereas the opposite was true for nontested subjects. This pattern is consistent with findings from national studies (e.g., Center on Education Policy, 2006). Similar responses were observed in each of the three study years, suggesting small but consistent trends toward more mathematics and reading instruction and toward reductions in other areas. Although science tests were administered in both California and Georgia during the years of this study, teachers were less likely to report increases in time devoted to science, perhaps in part because science did not count toward schools' adequate yearly progress (AYP) status. Case studies suggest that the survey results regarding shifts in instructional time probably understate the actual change because in many schools, teachers of other subjects have been asked to integrate math and reading instruction into those subjects in ways that lead to reduced time for content in those subjects.

Teachers as well as parents in case study schools pointed to a number of changes that they believed would ultimately have negative effects on students; they included the elimination of arts and physical education programs as well as other activities such as field trips. Whether or not these changes are considered desirable depends on one's views on the relative importance of various subjects and activities. It is also worth noting that school policies that lead to changes in the amount of instructional time offered to students in various subjects were not consistent across students within a school or classroom; many schools have adopted policies of mandating extra instruction in math or reading for students not scoring at the proficient level, which results in these students having less exposure to material in other subjects than their higher-performing counterparts. It is also important to keep in mind that many of these changes were driven by decisions made by school or district administrators rather than the teachers themselves.

Teachers also reported changes in their instruction within specific subject areas. One set of items on the survey addressed various ways in which teachers might respond to high-stakes testing. The responses of elementary mathematics and science teachers in 2006 are summarized in Table 3.2. As with the findings regarding allocation of time across subjects, these responses

Table 3.2. Percentage of Elementary School Teachers Reporting Their Instruction Is Different as a Result of State Assessments, 2006

	California		Georgia		Pennsylvania
Instructional Practices	*Math*	*Science*	*Math*	*Science*	*Math*
Assign more homework	31 (4)	11 (2)	32 (3)	20 (3)	30 (3)
Spend more time teaching content	51 (5)	26 (3)	58 (3)	46 (4)	55 (4)
Offer more assistance outside school for students who are not proficient	27 (4)	10 (3)	33 (4)	15 (2)	21 (3)
Search for more effective teaching methods	62 (5)	39 (4)	76 (3)	67 (3)	60 (3)
Focus more on standards	68 (5)	48 (3)	76 (3)	72 (4)	78 (3)
Focus more on topics emphasized in assessment	64 (4)	28 (3)	71 (4)	62 (5)	71 (4)
Emphasize assessment styles and formats of problems	56 (5)	23 (3)	75 (3)	63 (4)	81 (3)
Spend more time teaching test-taking strategies	53 (5)	27 (3)	59 (3)	47 (5)	56 (3)
Focus more on students who are close to proficient	41 (4)	14 (2)	39 (3)	31 (3)	30 (3)
Rely more heavily on multiple-choice tests	29 (5)	23 (3)	37 (3)	40 (4)	23 (2)
Rely more heavily on open-ended tests	21 (3)	19 (3)	27 (2)	30 (3)	46 (3)

Standard errors are provided in parentheses.

Response options were "not at all," "a small amount," "a moderate amount," and "a great deal."

Cell entries are percentages reporting they engage in each practice "a moderate amount" or a "great deal" as a result of the state tests.

These questions were not presented to PA science teachers because of the lack of a statewide science test.

suggest greater effects in math than in science. Some prevalent responses are consistent with the presumed benefits of greater accountability—for example, searching for more effective teaching methods and spending more time teaching content. However, others suggest the risk of an undesirable narrowing of curriculum that could lead to score inflation; these include emphasizing specific problem styles and formats and teaching test-taking strategies. Whether or not these responses are problematic depends in large part on how much time is devoted to them and on the activities from which teachers are reallocating their time and effort. As with the shifts in instructional time across subjects described in the previous paragraph, these responses appear to be reinforced by the actions of principals and district administrators, who in many districts have engaged in efforts to promote instruction that is aligned with state tests. For example, large majorities of principals reported encouraging teachers to engage in test preparation, and nearly all of them reported taking steps to align curriculum and instruction with state standards and tests.

Reallocation can occur not just among topics but also among students. Between 30% and 41% of elementary mathematics teachers report focusing more on students who are close to proficient (sometimes called "bubble kids"; see, e.g., Booher-Jennings, 2005), though we do not know to what extent this occurs at the expense of other students. Case study teachers in several schools described schoolwide policies intended to focus on this group of students and acknowledged that raising the scores of these students was the most efficient way to reach AYP goals.

There is also evidence that the format of the state accountability tests shaped responses. For example, Pennsylvania's state mathematics test included open-ended items, and teachers in that state were more likely than those in the other states to say they were relying more on open-ended assessments in their classes. Teacher interviews confirmed that many teachers had adopted open-ended assessments as a means of preparing students for the state assessment.

It is worth noting that an exploratory factor analysis suggests a single dimension underlying these items (see Hamilton et al., 2008)—in other words, teachers who reported engaging in the practices generally considered to be more desirable also reported engaging in the less desirable activities. There seems to be a general tendency for teachers to respond to high-stakes tests, and when they do respond, they do it in a variety of ways.

These responses are consistent with a large body of research examining not only NCLB but also the state accountability systems that preceded it (Hamilton, 2003; Stecher, 2002). Beginning in the 1990s, when many states were experimenting with new forms of assessment that were intended to measure higher-order thinking and other complex processes and skills (Resnick & Resnick, 1992), teachers tended to report engaging in many of the activities that the tests were designed to promote, such as having students solve open-ended problems in mathematics (Koretz, Stecher, Klein, & McCaffrey, 1994; Lane, Parke, & Stone, 2002; Taylor, Shepard, Kinner, & Rosenthal, 2003). Although these responses in some cases were considered beneficial by those who advocated for performance-based assessment, there is also evidence that even these types of assessments have led to narrowing that has resulted in score inflation (Koretz & Barron, 1998). These lessons from the performance assessment movement should be kept in mind as new, presumably better and more complex assessments are developed over the next few years in response to the common standards initiatives and new federal funding opportunities (Sawchuk, 2009). We currently do not know how to develop assessments that will be resistant to the negative effects of high-stakes tests, though the final section of this chapter provides some suggestions that could mitigate some of the most problematic responses.

One additional set of responses from ISBA illustrates teachers' opinions regarding the appropriateness of test-focused accountability policies. Table 3.3 summarizes the responses of elementary and middle school mathematics teachers to a set of questions regarding attitudes toward their states' NCLB-mandated accountability systems. It shows that large majorities of teachers in each state agree that the system has increased their focus on improving student learning, but similarly large majorities say it leaves little time to cover untested content. Minorities of teachers in Pennsylvania and California, and about half in Georgia, agree that the system has been beneficial for students, and at the same time roughly half express concern that high-achieving students may be shortchanged. These views, both the positive ones and the ones expressing concern, should be considered as new evaluation systems are developed, as teachers may be in the best position of anyone in the school system to understand how test-based accountability policies affect the teaching and learning environment.

The research described in this section examined school-level accountability systems such as those mandated under NCLB, and there is currently insufficient research evidence to determine the extent to which they will generalize to teacher-focused accountability policies. On the one hand, some teachers' responses were influenced by actions taken at the school and district levels, and it is possible that school and district administrators would be less likely to engage in these responses under a system that places most of the incentives directly on teachers. However, many of the relevant teacher-focused policies are accompanied by new compensation or evaluation systems for principals and other administrators, so they may

Table 3.3. Percentages of Elementary and Middle School Mathematics Teachers Agreeing with Statements about State Accountability System, 2006

Statements About State Accountability System	California		Georgia		Pennsylvania	
	Elementary	*Middle*	*Elementary*	*Middle*	*Elementary*	*Middle*
The state's accountability system supports my personal approach to teaching and learning	33 (5)	33 (4)	53 (3)	47 (3)	27 (3)	28 (5)
The state's accountability system leaves little time to teach content not on the state tests	89 (2)	88 (3)	82 (2)	83 (2)	87 (2)	95 (2)
Because of pressure to meet the AYP target, I am focusing more on improving student achievement at my school	78 (3)	72 (4)	84 (2)	81 (2)	80 (4)	78 (4)
The possibility of my school receiving rewards or sanctions is a very strong motivator for me	35 (5)	31 (4)	57 (3)	50 (3)	36 (3)	38 (4)
Overall, the state's accountability system has been beneficial for students at my school	37 (5)	34 (5)	54 (3)	50 (2)	31 (4)	28 (3)
As a result of the state accountability system, high-achieving students are not receiving appropriately challenging curriculum or instruction	52 (4)	54 (3)	46 (3)	51 (2)	46 (3)	56 (5)

Standard errors are provided in parentheses.

Response options were "strongly disagree," "disagree," "agree," and "strongly agree." Percentages in table are those responding "agree" or "strongly agree."

face similar or even greater incentives to try to shape teachers' responses. In any case, these findings illustrate the potential danger of relying heavily on standardized assessments as measures of institutions' or individuals' effectiveness, especially given all the other responsibilities teachers have and the outcomes they are expected to promote, such as improved social skills and citizenship.

The findings reported in this section addressed broad effects stemming from use of tests in high-stakes accountability or evaluation systems. There are two specific implementation issues that should also be examined: the development of data systems to support this type of evaluation and the construction of measures that are attached to individual teachers and used for making personnel decisions. These topics are addressed in the next two sections.

DEVELOPMENT OF NEW DATA SYSTEMS: HOW WILL THEY INFORM PRACTICE?

Until fairly recently, one of the factors hindering efforts to use test scores to measure teacher effectiveness was a technical one—most districts and states lacked data systems that would allow them to link students with their teachers and to follow individual students over time. This situation has been changing rapidly, in no small part as a result of federal funding initiatives that have encouraged states to develop better data systems, as well as through the work conducted by organizations such as the Data Quality Campaign, which offers guidance and assistance to help states tackle the challenges associated with assembling data systems.

The development of new statewide longitudinal data systems is likely to influence the nature of new teacher evaluation policies and practices. If all goes as planned, most states will have systems that can be used to calculate teacher-level growth-based measures for accountability purposes. These measures could provide more accurate information about the performance of a teacher's students than is currently available, particularly if they focus on growth and on measuring change at all points in the score distribution rather than relying on the percent above a cut score as is done under NCLB.

Although the development of these new data systems may be driven in large part by the need to accommodate new teacher evaluation reforms, they are also intended to provide better data for instructional decision making (Halverson, Grigg, Prichett, & Thomas, 2005; Hamilton et al., 2009; Ikemoto & Marsh, 2007). Making standardized test score data more readily accessible to teachers and other educators could promote some of the desired outcomes of accountability by providing information to help teachers identify and respond to students' instructional needs, but it is important to recognize the limitations and potential drawbacks of encouraging greater use of this type of data, such as the potential to reinforce the curriculum-narrowing effects of high-stakes tests.

Findings from ISBA suggest that teachers and administrators do use state test-score data extensively for instructional decision making but that they also rely heavily on other sources of information about student learning. Table 3.4 shows the percentages of mathematics teachers who reported using student achievement data of all types for various instructional purposes either "sometimes" or "often." It shows widespread adoption of data-based practices, somewhat more so among elementary than middle school teachers. Table 3.5 provides an additional set of responses that focused exclusively on opinions about the utility of scores on the statewide accountability tests. Majorities in all three states reported using them to identify their own strengths and weaknesses, which suggests that the content and nature of these tests could influence teachers' decisions about their own professional learning. Smaller but still sizable percentages reported using state test results to identify gaps in the curriculum and to determine individual students' needs. In interviews, teachers acknowledged the utility of state tests but expressed concerns about possible narrowing effects of practices that fall within the domain of "data-driven decision making." These kinds of uses of test-score data could reinforce the tendency, discussed earlier, for teachers to reshape their instruction to align it with tests in ways that lead to both desirable and undesirable changes.

As with other responses to accountability reported by teachers, their use of data appears to be supported by actions taken by school and district administrators. In 2006, almost all principals reported data use as an improvement strategy in their schools, and more than half of elementary principals in each state listed this as one of their three most important school improvement strategies (percentages were somewhat lower among middle school principals). District superintendents who participated in ISBA also reported extensive reliance on data use as an improvement strategy, taking steps such as offering professional development focused on data use and requiring teachers to administer interim assessments aligned with the state standards and tests.

It is likely that reliance on data will increase as new state data systems provide more detailed and accessible information. Of course, as was pointed out by many of the teachers we interviewed, end-of-year tests have limited value for informing day-to-day instructional decisions, especially when considered in light of the massive amount of information that teachers gather through their instruction. State tests do not lend themselves to the kind of useful instructional guidance that is provided through systems that are truly formative (Perie, Marion, &

Table 3.4. Percentage of Elementary School Mathematics Teachers Reporting Use of Data for Instructional Decision Making, 2006

	California		Georgia		Pennsylvania	
Approach to Using Data	*Elementary*	*Middle*	*Elementary*	*Middle*	*Elementary*	*Middle*
Plan different assignments based on performance	80 (3)	67 (5)	87 (2)	83 (2)	79 (3)	73 (5)
Reteach topics because performance on assignments or assessments did not meet expectations	97 (1)	97 (1)	98 (1)	95 (1)	95 (1)	90 (3)
Review assessment results to identify individual students who need supplemental instruction	94 (2)	91 (3)	96 (1)	91 (1)	93 (1)	80 (5)
Review assessment results to identify topics requiring more or less emphasis in instruction	93 (2)	86 (2)	96 (1)	95 (1)	91 (1)	81 (5)
Conduct a pre-assessment to find out what students know about a topic	67 (3)	51 (5)	76 (3)	68 (1)	58 (3)	56 (10)

Standard errors are provided in parentheses.
Response options were "never," "rarely," "sometimes," and "often."
Cell entries are percentages reporting they engage in each practice "sometimes" or "often."

Table 3.5. Percentage of Mathematics Teachers Agreeing with Statements About the State Tests, 2006

State Test Results	California		Georgia		Pennsylvania	
	Elementary	*Middle*	*Elementary*	*Middle*	*Elementary*	*Middle*
Allowed me to identify areas where I need to strengthen my content knowledge or teaching skills	73 (3)	62 (5)	89 (2)	79 (2)	62 (4)	57 (5)
Helped me identify and correct gaps in curriculum and instruction	67 (3)	60 (6)	88 (2)	80 (3)	56 (4)	61 (4)
Helped me tailor instruction to individual student needs	59 (3)	42 (7)	85 (2)	79 (3)	36 (3)	42 (6)

Teachers who said they did not receive test results are excluded.
Response options were "strongly disagree," "disagree," "agree," and "strongly agree."
Standard errors are provided in parentheses.

Gong, 2007), and they inevitably exclude at least some content that is important for understanding students' strengths and weaknesses, such as extended essays or responses to complex mathematics problems. Still, there is likely to be continued pressure for teachers and administrators to engage in data-driven decision making, especially if it is viewed as a means of promoting improved performance on test-based accountability measures. Developers of test-based teacher evaluation policies should consider the ways in which these policies are likely to encourage teachers to use the available data in appropriate ways and should strive to mitigate any risks that these actions will detract from more appropriate data-driven instruction, such as that guided by formative assessment systems. It is particularly important to be alert for ways in which increased reliance on data from externally mandated tests reduces teachers' exposure to other valuable sources of information that could help them address students' needs.

CONSTRUCTION OF MEASURES OF TEACHER EFFECTIVENESS

One topic of debate that has characterized recent developments in teacher evaluation is illustrated by the phrases *effective teachers* and *effective teaching*, both of which are used in discussions of teacher accountability but which have different meanings. The former reflects an assumption that effectiveness is an attribute that characterizes an individual teacher and, by extension, that teachers carry this "effectiveness" with them as they move from one classroom or school to another. The phrase "effective teaching," by contrast, can be interpreted to suggest that effectiveness is an attribute of a particular teaching situation rather than a person. Many of the policies that have been discussed recently, such as proposals to transfer effective teachers into high-need schools, have implicitly adopted the former characterization. However, the notion that the attributes that promote high-quality instruction exist primarily within an individual and are not influenced greatly by the context in which that individual works conflicts to some degree with the idea that schools that promote effective instruction tend to be characterized by a highly collaborative environment and extensive support from principals and other instructional leaders (Leithwood, Louis, Anderson, & Wahlstrom, 2004; McLaughlin & Talbert, 2006). Moreover, although the literature on what constitutes effective professional development is limited, today's reformers emphasize professional development that is school based and collaborative (Garet et al., 2010; Rice, 2010). Emphasizing individual measures of teacher effectiveness not only has the potential to exert a negative effect on the collaborative culture of schools, particularly if teachers are competing against one another for limited rewards (Podgursky & Springer, 2007), but also fails to recognize the extent to which measures of teachers' effectiveness may be shaped by the broader context in which they work, including the effectiveness of other teachers in their schools (Jackson & Bruegmann, 2009). And it does not account for the fact that multiple teachers may contribute to a student's achievement in any given subject (Valli, Croninger, & Kirk, 2007).

Data from ISBA provide some evidence of the extent to which responses to test-based accountability are driven by schoolwide, collaborative activity rather than by the actions of individual teachers working independently. Of course, a shift to teacher-level accountability could result in a different set of responses that emphasize individual teacher actions to a greater degree, but it is important to understand the ways in which school improvement efforts have in the past involved collective action. The findings present a mixed picture. School-level action is common and appears to shape what happens in classrooms. As discussed earlier, school and district administrators have engaged in a number of responses to NCLB that are directly linked with the work teachers do in the classroom. They include promoting use of data for instructional decision making, requiring teachers to administer interim assessments that are aligned with the state standards and assessments, providing resources to assist teachers in aligning their instruction with standards and tests (e.g., pacing guides), distributing test-preparation materials, and providing professional development to promote standards-based instruction. Table 3.6 provides an illustration; it shows that nearly all principals report engaging in numerous activities to promote standards-aligned instruction. Although our study design does not support strong causal conclusions, our interviews with teachers and administrators suggest that many of the actions teachers have taken have occurred in response to school- or district-level initiatives. These findings are consistent with other research that indicates an important role for school leaders in shaping teachers' responses to reforms (Firestone et al., 2004; Kirby, Berends, & Naftel, 2001; Knapp, Copland, & Talbert, 2003). Teachers in the ISBA study also described high levels of collaboration with colleagues that contributed to their instructional responses to the accountability policies. Together these findings indicate that teachers' actions are influenced by a variety of factors that are not necessarily under their control, which raises questions about the utility of teacher-level accountability measures as a means to promote instructional change.

Analysis of relationships among district, school, and teacher practices provides additional evidence that teachers' responses to accountability pressures are related to school or district conditions. For example, a set of multilevel models discussed in Hamilton et al. (2008) showed that teachers' use of the test-focused instructional practices listed in Table 3.2 was higher in schools where principals reported pressure to achieve AYP than in schools whose principals reported less pressure. Similarly, teachers reported less test-focused instruction in schools that had met their previous AYP targets than in those that hadn't.

At the same time, we observed a high degree of variation among the practices, beliefs, and attitudes of teachers within the same schools, which suggests that teachers retain considerable autonomy and may not respond to district or school mandates with as much fidelity as administrators might hope. The ISBA survey data were subjected to an intraclass correlation analysis, which partitions the total variance in teacher responses into separate components representing variance between teachers in the same schools (as well as measurement error), variance between

Table 3.6. Percentage of Principals Employing School Improvement Strategies, 2006

School Improvement Strategies	California		Georgia		Pennsylvania	
	Elementary	*Middle*	*Elementary*	*Middle*	*Elementary*	*Middle*
Matching curriculum and instruction with standards, assessments, or both	95 (5)	98 (2)	100 (0)	100 (0)	100 (0)	100 (0)
Using existing research to inform decisions about improvement strategies	95 (3)	85 (8)	100 (0)	99 (1)	88 (7)	90 (6)
Providing additional instruction to low-performing students	100 (0)	98 (2)	99 (1)	98 (2)	85 (7)	90 (6)
Increasing the use of student achievement data to inform instruction	90 (6)	98 (2)	100 (0)	98 (2)	100 (0)	92 (7)
Increasing the quantity of teacher professional development	93 (4)	80 (10)	95 (3)	96 (4)	71 (9)	72 (10)
Improving the school-planning process	94 (5)	83 (8)	100 (0)	94 (3)	73 (9)	72 (15)
Providing before- or after-school, weekend, or summer programs	97 (2)	62 (14)	93 (5)	95 (3)	69 (10)	63 (14)
Promoting programs to make the school a more attractive choice for parents	80 (9)	78 (9)	87 (6)	56 (11)	47 (10)	42 (12)
Restructuring the day to teach content in greater depth (e.g., a literacy block)	75 (10)	43 (13)	79 (5)	59 (11)	73 (9)	38 (12)
Increasing instructional time (lengthening school day or year or shortening recess)	31 (7)	12 (7)	42 (8)	23 (7)	20 (5)	24 (9)

Cell entries are percentages of principals reporting that they employed the strategy in the past year. Standard errors are provided in parentheses.

schools in the same district, and variance between districts. We observed extensive within-school variation, particularly on measures related to instructional practices or to teachers' opinions about the reforms. So even though school and district leaders' actions can exert significant influence on the curriculum materials, scheduling, and other resources that are available to teachers to support instruction, teachers maintain considerable autonomy over how they teach. This finding is not unexpected, given the large body of research that demonstrates the difficulty of implementing reforms that affect the classroom (Firestone, 2003; Ingersoll, 2003; Rowan & Miskel, 1999).

The numerous efforts by district and school personnel to shape instruction suggest that teachers' effectiveness at raising test scores could vary depending on the context in which they are working and that a teacher who demonstrates a high level of "effectiveness" in one school may not achieve the same results in a different school with different policies and leadership. Of course, it is an empirical question whether value-added-based effectiveness estimates are consistent for the same teacher across different contexts. The research examining this issue is limited. Sanders, Wright, and Langevin (2008) observed only small changes in teacher effectiveness estimates based on value-added modeling when Tennessee mathematics teachers moved from low-poverty to higher-poverty schools and vice versa (while remaining in the same grade), and they found that these estimates looked more like the pre-move estimates after a teacher had spent 2 years in the new school. Lockwood and McCaffrey (2009) found significant interactions between value-added-based teacher effects and predicted student achievement, but these tended to be modest in size except when classes are heterogeneously grouped (e.g., in the presence of tracking or ability grouping). In addition, these estimates were generated using within-class differences in achievement and do not provide information on how teachers would function across classrooms with very different student populations.

A somewhat contrasting set of findings was provided by Jackson (2010), who found substantial improvements in measured teacher effectiveness when teachers voluntarily moved to new schools, suggesting that teachers had strategically moved to achieve a better match between their skills and the school's context. In general, however, there is a lack of evidence regarding the effects of moving teachers to contexts that differ from their own. Hess (2010) points out, for example, that in charter schools that use models such as the Knowledge Is Power Program (KIPP; a national network of public schools that emphasizes specific approaches, including partnerships between schools and families, a strong culture of achievement, and extended learning time) or in schools that rely heavily on technology for delivery of instruction, the kinds of skills and background experience that contribute to effecting teaching may be different from those that are relevant in more traditional classroom settings. Efforts to predict a teacher's future effects on test scores based on evidence gathered in a different school context should therefore be carried out with caution.

PROPOSED IMPROVEMENTS IN TEST-BASED TEACHER EVALUATION

This chapter drew on prior research, with a focus on a recent study of educators' responses to NCLB, to identify some of the likely effects and challenges stemming from proposed efforts to use student achievement tests as measures of teacher effectiveness. As noted earlier, the goal was not to identify every potential drawback to these policies but to examine what we know about how teachers and administrators have responded to test-based accountability policies in the past and to explore the implications of these findings for future test-based evaluation systems. Our evidence suggests that all three of the mechanisms identified earlier were operating to some degree: Teachers and other school staff, experiencing pressure to meet AYP targets and raise proficiency rates, responded to incentives to engage in actions to improve tests scores. They also made use of information regarding students' performance to design new programs or policies to meet students' needs, and educators at each level received assistance and support from higher levels through resources such as curriculum and pacing guides, test-preparation materials, and test-focused professional development. In many ways, these responses are consistent with the goals of test-based accountability policies, but they also raise concerns about efforts to use student achievement data to evaluate teachers. In particular, findings suggest that instruction can be narrowed in undesirable ways, existing data systems are of limited utility for informing instruction, and efforts to measure individual teachers' performance are hampered by factors not under the teacher's control. Again, we need to be cautious in making inferences about the extent to which these responses will generalize to other contexts such as test-based teacher evaluation systems. At a minimum, however, the findings suggest some reasons to be concerned about unintended negative effects and suggest a few approaches for diminishing the likelihood of these effects as new teacher evaluation policies are designed and enacted.

Create a Balanced System of Accountability Using Multiple Measures of Performance

Test-based accountability systems, whether at the school or teacher level, are typically intended in part to promote specific types of instructional change, but the findings from ISBA and other studies suggest that many of the resulting changes are not consistent with developers' original intentions. The risk of curriculum narrowing and score inflation stemming from reliance on specific tests suggests a need to adopt systems that provide incentives, information, and assistance in other, nontested areas that are viewed as important and that could mitigate a tendency to place undue emphasis on tested content. One approach is to broaden the range of subjects tested, as well as the content of the tests. However, increased testing imposes significant costs and may backfire by increasing the likelihood of curriculum narrowing in subjects that have not traditionally been tested. In addition, certain skills and processes are not easy to measure through the kinds of large-scale tests that are used in accountability systems, though increasing use of technology has the potential to expand the range of material that can be feasibly included (Quellmalz & Pellegrino, 2009; Tucker, 2009).

Efforts to reduce narrowing do not need to rely exclusively on additional achievement tests. In particular, systems could incorporate direct measures of teachers' work, including measures of instruction, where possible. Most systems already devote some attention to teachers' work; the Denver Pro-Comp program, for example, is a performance-based compensation system that involves a partnership between the Denver Public Schools and the Denver Classroom Teachers' Association. The system links teachers' annual pay to a broad range of outcomes, practices, and job characteristics. It includes bonuses for teachers who work in high-need schools, as well as a rubric-based evaluation of instruction (Denver Public Schools, 2011). Moreover, work is under way in several sites across the United States to develop higher-quality measures of teaching effectiveness (see, e.g., Bill and Melinda Gates Foundation, 2010). If these measures are designed carefully, they may create incentives for teachers to engage in activities that are valued but that are not captured by test-score-based measures. For example, the inclusion of measures of teachers' assignment quality, with a focus on capturing high levels of cognitive demand, might reduce teachers' tendencies to emphasize low-level instruction in response to standardized tests. These additional measures may also provide more useful information to teachers to help them improve their own practices than the information teachers receive based on test scores and can serve an important assistance function by supporting improved professional development (Stein & Matsumura, 2008). Similarly, measures that focus on whether teachers take on new and challenging roles might offset incentives for teachers to choose situations (e.g., classrooms or schools with high-performing students) that they believe will maximize their performance on test-based measures. Of course, there is still a risk that these alternative measures could lead to undesirable narrowing or be subject to the same kinds of corruption that has occurred with student tests, so careful monitoring of effects is critical, as discussed at the end of this chapter.

Design Tests in Ways That Mitigate Narrowing

Regardless of the amount of weight given to test-score-based measures in an evaluation system, it is likely that tests will continue to influence curriculum and instruction. Evidence suggests that the content and format of tests shapes what teachers do, but that even high-quality assessments do not necessarily lead to high-quality instruction. One feature of tests that may reduce the likelihood of narrowing and score inflation is the extent to which their content is predictable from one administration to the next. Teachers' reallocation in response to tested material leads to score inflation because of the consistency in what is measured and how it is measured over time. Varying the content and format of test items could make it more difficult for teachers to engage in test-focused instruction that is effective at raising scores without generalizing to the broader achievement domain, so that over time it becomes clear that the most effective way to improve students' performance is to cover the full curriculum effectively. It may not be possible to eliminate narrowing and score inflation, but careful test design could reduce the magnitude of these outcomes. Of course, designing new and better items is likely to increase testing costs, but these may be mitigated to some degree by the cross-state collaborative testing efforts that are being explored and, possibly, by strategic use of information technology.

Explore Opportunities to Balance Individual- and Group-Level Accountability Measures

An important design consideration is the extent to which teacher evaluation systems should rely on test score–based measures for individual teachers, given the challenges inherent in making inferences about the extent to which students' achievement growth can be attributed to a single teacher. Decisions about individual versus group-based measures require careful consideration of both the validity of inferences these measures support and the nature of the incentives they are likely to create. School-level measures, for example, may do a better job of recognizing the collaborative nature of teachers' work with students, but could lead to teachers' avoiding working in schools that have performed poorly on these measures.

The ideal approach might be a flexible system that involves a hybrid of school-level and individual-level measures, customized to a teacher's particular situation. For some teachers it may be nearly impossible to make reasonably valid inferences about effectiveness based on student growth; these include teachers for whom there is no existing high-quality measure of student outcomes as well as those who provide instructional services that supplement other teachers' instruction and who therefore do not have any students for whom they are exclusively responsible. Given the wide variety of roles and contexts in which teachers work, a one-size-fits-all evaluation system may not be feasible or effective. As Hess (2010) points out, an effective compensation system is likely to involve flexibility to accommodate various career paths, skills, and degrees of specialization.

Develop Comprehensive Data Systems with a Focus on Instructional Improvement

An additional strategy for reducing the likelihood that externally mandated assessments will play an outsize role in shaping teachers' practices is to create a data system that not only provides the information and links necessary for external evaluation purposes but also includes elements designed to support more effective instructional use of data. These might include high-quality formative assessments linked to specific instructional strategies, as well as reporting tools that provide detailed information on individual students' performance rather than emphasizing coarse categorizations such as whether students are performing above or below proficiency. And these revamped data systems should be accompanied by professional development and by opportunities for teachers to collaborate and learn from one another.

Conduct Validity Investigations Targeted to Accountability Uses of Tests

Those who develop, mandate, and implement test-based teacher evaluation systems should gather and document evidence of validity for their intended uses of tests, to ensure, to the extent possible, that tests are used appropriately and in ways that will promote desired outcomes. Validity refers to "the extent to which an assessment measures what it is supposed to measure and the extent to which inferences and actions made on the basis of test scores are appropriate and accurate" (Center for Research on Evaluation, Standards, and Student Testing, 2008). A validity investigation should be designed to gather a variety of evidence to support proposed interpretations of test scores and should begin with a clear statement regarding the interpretations the test is intended to support and with a rationale for how these interpretations are related to proposed uses. Even when a test is supported by validity evidence for one purpose (such as providing information about the extent to which a student has mastered the grade-level content in a particular subject), if the test is used for a very different purpose (such as determining which teachers should be granted tenure), additional validity evidence should be gathered to support the inferences and decisions relevant to that purpose and to identify the likely consequences.

Validity investigations should incorporate multiple sources of evidence relevant to each desired inference and should examine the consequences of specific uses on educators' practices and student outcomes, including outcomes other than the high-stakes test itself. Because tests are often used for multiple purposes, it is also important to assess the extent to which practices that promote effective use for one purpose may diminish the utility of those tests for other purposes. For example, designing a testing system that provides useful information might require a higher level of disclosure of items than would be ideal for a high-stakes testing program. These types of trade-offs should be examined, and program designers should take the steps necessary to promote appropriate use, recognizing that it may require difficult decisions regarding time and budgets (e.g., the use of different tests for different purposes). Of course, a full understanding of consequences can probably be attained only once a new system is implemented on a large scale, but some likely outcomes can be predicted based on other research and evaluation. Developers should build into the new programs a careful evaluation that monitors consequences and that can provide guidance to inform modifications to the system if undesirable effects are observed. The large number of current and planned efforts to develop test-based teacher evaluation systems across the United States provides an opportunity to figure out what works and what doesn't, as long as these programs are carefully designed and monitored.

CONCLUSION

Efforts to expand and refine test-based teacher evaluation systems are widespread and are likely to continue to grow as a result of federal, state, and local policy trends. These efforts should be informed by careful analysis of the likely consequences of adopting test-based teacher evaluation and by consideration of ways to design systems to maximize the likelihood of beneficial effects. As this chapter suggests, the use of student achievement tests for high-stakes purposes has been accompanied by both desirable and undesirable responses on the part of teachers and other educators. Lessons from these experiences provide guidance for creating tests, accountability measures, and data systems that have the potential to improve outcomes associated with the use of tests for teacher evaluation, while simultaneously mitigating some of the negative effects. Research on the effects of test-based teacher evaluation systems is limited, however, and it is impossible to determine how any policy or design feature will work in the context of a specific system. It is crucial that the consequences associated with the adoption of these new systems be monitored so that midcourse corrections can be made in the interest of improving the quality of teaching and learning in all classrooms.

NOTE

This work was supported in part by the National Science Foundation under Grant No. REC-0228295. Any opinions, findings and conclusions, or recommendations expressed in this paper are those of the author(s) and do not necessarily reflect the views of the National Science Foundation.

REFERENCES

American Educational Research Association, American Psychological Association, and National Council on Measurement in Education. (1999). *Standards for educational and psychological testing*. Washington, DC: Author.

Bill and Melinda Gates Foundation. (2010). *Learning about teaching: Initial findings from the Measures of Effective Teaching project*. Seattle: Author. Retrieved from http://www.gatesfoundation.org/college-ready-education/Documents/preliminary-finding-policy-brief.pdf

Booher-Jennings, J. (2005). Below the bubble: "Educational triage" and the Texas accountability system. *American Educational Research Journal, 42*, 231–268.

Braun, H. (2005). Value-added modeling: What does due diligence require? In R. Lissitz (Ed.), *Value added models in* education*: Theory and practice* (pp. 19–38). Maple Grove, MN: JAM Press.

Center on Education Policy. (2006). *From the capital to the classroom: Year 4 of the No Child Left Behind Act*. Washington, DC: Author.

Center for Research on Evaluation, Standards, and Student Testing. (2008). *Glossary*. Los Angeles: Author. Retrieved from http://www.cse.ucla.edu/products/glossary_2.html

Denver Public Schools. (2011). *Welcome to Teacher ProComp*. Denver: Denver Public Schools. Retrieved from http://denverprocomp.dpsk12.org/

Firestone, W. A. (2003). The governance of teaching and standards-based reform from the 1970s to the new millennium. In M. T. Hallinan, A. Gamoran, W. Kubitschek, & T. Loveless (Eds.), *Stability and change in American education: Structure, process, and outcomes* (pp. 153–170). Clinton Corners, NY: Eliot Werner.

Firestone, W. A., Monfils, L. F., Hayes, M., Polovsky, T., Martinez, M. C., & Hicks, J. E. (2004). The principal, test preparation, and educational reform. In W. A. Firestone, L. F. Monfils, & R. Y. Schorr (Eds.), *The ambiguity of teaching to the test: Standards, assessment, and educational reform* (pp. 91–112). Mahwah, NJ: Lawrence Erlbaum.

Garet, M., Ludwig, M., Yoon, K., Wayne, A., Birman, B., & Milanowski, A. (2010). *Making professional development more strategic: A conceptual model for district decisionmakers* (Report prepared for the U.S. Department of Education, Policy and Program Studies Service). Washington, DC: American Institutes for Research.

Goldhaber, D., & Hannaway, J. (Eds.). (2010). *Creating a new teaching profession.* Washington, DC: Urban Institute Press.

Halverson, R. R., Grigg, J., Prichett, R., & Thomas, C. (2005, July). *The new instructional leadership: Creating data-driven instructional systems in schools.* Paper presented at the National Council of Professors of Educational Administration, Washington, DC.

Hamilton, L .S. (2003). Assessment as a policy tool. *Review of Research in Education, 27,* 25–68.

Hamilton, L. S., Halverson, R., Jackson, S., Mandinach, E., Supovitz, J., & Wayman, J. (2009). *Using student achievement data to support instructional decision making* (NCEE 2009-4067). Washington, DC: National Center for Education Evaluation and Regional Assistance, Institute of Education Sciences, U.S. Department of Education.

Hamilton, L. S., Stecher, B. M., Marsh, J., McCombs, J. S., Robyn, A., Russell, J., Naftel, S., & Barney, H. (2007). *Implementing standards-based accountability under No Child Left Behind: Responses of superintendents, principals, and teachers in three states.* Santa Monica, CA: RAND.

Hamilton, L. S., Stecher, B. M., Russell, J. L., Marsh, J. A., & Miles, J. (2008). Accountability and teaching practices: School-level actions and teacher responses. In B. Fuller, M. K. Henne, & E. Hannum (Eds.), *Strong state, weak schools: The benefits and dilemmas of centralized accountability (Research in the Sociology of Education, Vol. 16)* (pp. 31–66). St. Louis, MO: Emerald Group.

Hess, F. M. (2010). The human capital challenge: Toward a 21st-century teaching profession. In D. Goldhaber & J. Hannaway (Eds.), *Creating a new teaching profession* (pp. 115–136). Washington, DC: Urban Institute Press.

Ikemoto, G. S., & Marsh, J. A. (2007). Cutting through the "data-driven" mantra: Different conceptions of data-driven decision making. In P. A. Moss (Ed.), *Evidence and decision making, Vol. 106* (pp. 105–131). Malden, MA: Blackwell.

Ingersoll, R. M. (2003). *Who controls teachers' work? Power and accountability in America's schools.* Cambridge, MA: Harvard University Press.

Jackson, C. K. (2010). *Match quality, worker productivity, and worker mobility: Direct evidence from teachers (NBER Working Paper 15990).* Cambridge, MA: National Bureau of Economic Research. Retrieved from http://www.nber.org/papers/w15990.pdf

Jackson, C. K., & Bruegmann, E. (2009). Teaching students and teaching each other: The importance of peer learning for teachers. *American Economic Journal: Applied Economics, 1,* 85–108.

Kane, M. (2006). Validation. In R. Brennan (Ed.), *Educational measurement* (4th ed.) (pp. 18–64). Westport, CT: American Council on Education/Praeger.

Kirby, S. N., Berends, M., & Naftel, S. (2001). *Implementation in New American Schools: Four years into scale-up*. Santa Monica, CA: RAND.

Knapp, M. S., Copland, M. A., & Talbert, J. E. (2003). *Leading for learning; Reflective tools for school and district leaders.* Seattle: Center for the Study of Teaching and Policy.

Koretz, D. (1992). State and national assessment. In M. C. Alkin (Ed.), *Encyclopedia of educational research* (6th ed.) (pp. 1262–1267). Washington, DC: American Educational Research Association.

Koretz, D. (2008). *Measuring up: What educational testing really tells us.* Cambridge, MA: Harvard University Press.

Koretz, D. M., & Barron, S. I. (1998). *The validity of gains on the Kentucky Instructional Results Information System (KIRIS).* Santa Monica, CA: RAND.

Koretz, D., & Hamilton, L. S. (2006). Testing for accountability in K–12. In R. L. Brennan (Ed.), *Educational measurement* (4th ed.) (pp. 531–578). Westport, CT: American Council on Education/Praeger.

Koretz, D., Stecher, B., Klein, S., & McCaffrey, D. (1994). The Vermont portfolio assessment program: Findings and implications. *Educational Measurement: Issues and Practice, 13*, 5–16.

Lane, S., Parke, C. S., & Stone, C. A. (2002). The impact of a state performance-based assessment and accountability program on mathematics instruction and student learning: Evidence from survey data and school performance. *Educational Assessment*, *8*, 279–315.

Leithwood, K., Louis, K. S., Anderson, S., & Wahlstrom, K. (2004). *Review of research: How leadership influences student learning.* Minneapolis: Center for Applied Research and Educational Improvement, University of Minnesota.

Linn, R. L. (2000). Assessments and accountability. *Educational Researcher, 29*, 4–16.

Lockwood, J. R., & McCaffrey, D. F. (2009). Exploring student-teacher interactions in longitudinal achievement data. *Education Finance and Policy, 4*, 439–467.

McCaffrey, D., Han, B., & Lockwood, J. R. (2008). *From data to bonuses: A case study of the issues related to awarding teachers pay on the basis of their students' progress* (Working Paper No. 2008–4). Nashville, TN: National Center on Performance Incentives, Vanderbilt University.

McLaughlin, M. W., & Talbert, J. E. (2006). *Building school-based teacher learning communities: Professional strategies to improve student achievement.* New York: Teachers College Press.

Perie, M., Marion, S., & Gong, B. (2007). *A framework for considering interim assessments.* Dover, NH: National Center for the Improvement of Educational Assessment.

Podgursky, M. J., & Springer, M. G. (2007). Teacher performance pay: A review. *Journal of Policy Analysis and Management*, *26*, 909–949.

Quellmalz, E. S., & Pellegrino, J. W. (2009). Technology and testing. *Science, 323*(5910), 75–79.

Resnick, L. B., & Resnick, D. P. (1992). Assessing the thinking curriculum: New tools for educational reform. In B. R. Gifford & M. C. O'Connor (Eds.), *Changing assessment: Alternative views of aptitude, achievement, and instruction* (pp. 37–75). Boston: Kluwer.

Rice, J. K. (2010). Investing in human capital through teacher professional development. In D. Goldhaber & J. Hannaway (Eds.), *Creating a new teaching profession* (pp. 227–247). Washington, DC: Urban Institute Press.

Rivkin, S. G. (2010). The estimation of teacher value added as a determinant of performance pay. In D. Goldhaber & J. Hannaway (Eds.), *Creating a new teaching profession* (pp. 181–193). Washington, DC: Urban Institute Press.

Rowan, B., & Miskel, C. (1999). Institutional theory and the study of educational organizations. In J. Murphy and K. S. Louis (Eds.), *Handbook of research on educational administration* (2nd ed.) (pp. 359–383). San Francisco: Jossey-Bass.

Sanders, W. L., Wright, S. P., & Langevin, W. E. (2008). Do teacher effect estimates persist when teachers move to schools with different socioeconomic environments? (Working Paper No. 2008–20). Paper prepared for *Performance Incentives: Their Growing Impact on American K–12 Education* (National Center on Performance Incentives). Nashville, TN: NCPI, Vanderbilt University. Retrieved from http://www.performanceincentives.org/data/files/directory/ConferencePapersNews/Sanders_et_al_2008b1.pdf

Sawchuk, S. (2009, November 18). Funding for common assessments poses challenge. *Education Week, 29:12, 16.*

Stecher, B. M. (2002). Consequences of large-scale, high-stakes testing on school and classroom practices. In L. S. Hamilton, B. M. Stecher, & S. P. Klein (Eds.), *Making sense of test-based accountability in education* (pp. 79–100). Santa Monica, CA: RAND.

Stecher, B. M., Epstein, S., Hamilton, L. S., Marsh, J. A., Robyn, A., McCombs, et al. (2008). *Pain and gain: Implementing No Child Left Behind in California, Georgia, and Pennsylvania, 2004 to 2006.* Santa Monica, CA: RAND.

Stein, M. K., & Matsumura, L. C. (2008). Measuring instruction for teacher learning. In D. Gitomer (Ed.), *Measurement issues and assessment for teaching quality* (pp. 179–205). Thousand Oaks, CA: Sage.

Taylor, G., Shepard, L., Kinner, F., & Rosenthal, J. (2003). *A survey of teachers' perspectives on high-stakes testing in Colorado: What gets taught, what gets lost* (CSE Tech. Rep. 588). Los Angeles: Center for Research on Evaluation, Standards, and Student Testing.

Tucker, B. (2009). Beyond the bubble: *Technology and the future of student assessment.* Washington, DC: Education Sector.

U.S. Department of Education. (2009). *Race to the Top program executive summary.* Washington, DC: Author. Retrieved from http://www2.ed.gov/programs/racetothetop/executive-summary.pdf

Valli, L., Croninger, R. G., & Kirk, W. (2007). Who (else) is the teacher? Cautionary notes on teacher accountability systems. *American Journal of Education, 113,* 635–662.

CHAPTER 4

Beyond High-Stakes Tests

Teacher Effects on Other Educational Outcomes

Jennifer L. Jennings
Sean P. Corcoran

In August 2010, the *Los Angeles Times* published a series of articles titled "Who's Teaching L.A.'s Kids?" Alongside these articles, the newspaper made available a database linking individual teachers' names to measures of teachers' "value-added" on state standardized tests. Teachers were divided into five categories ranging from "least effective" to "most effective." Explaining their decision to publish these ratings, the paper editorialized:

> Research has repeatedly found that teachers are the single most important school-related factor in a child's education, yet until now, parents have had no objective information about their effectiveness. The Los Angeles Unified School District has had the underlying data in hand for years but has not used them to inform parents—or teachers themselves—about how instructors are doing. The *Times* made the decision to release the information because it bears on the performance of public employees who provide an important service, and in the belief that parents and the public have a right to judge it for themselves (*Los Angeles Times*, 2010).

With this paragraph, the *Times* encapsulated much of supporters' rationale for using value-added measures to evaluate teachers. On the evidence of a recent body of literature finding that teacher effects on test scores are substantial in size (Clotfelter, Ladd, & Vigdor, 2006; Rivkin, Hanushek, & Kain, 2005; Rowan, Correnti, & Miller, 2002) but poorly predicted by observable characteristics such as certification, educational credentials, and experience (Hanushek, Kain, O'Brien, & Rivkin, 2005; Kane, Rockoff, & Staiger, 2008; Rockoff, 2004), many policy makers believe that using these measures to evaluate, retain, and reward teachers will improve the quality of American education, particularly for the most disadvantaged students.

The *LA Times'* statement also nicely captures the popular sentiment that these measures represent "objective information" about teacher effectiveness, in contrast with subjective evaluations by supervisors that are less trusted. This view extends all the way to the White House, as President Barack Obama, speaking about teacher evaluation this year, remarked, "Success should be judged by results, and data is a powerful tool to determine results. We can't ignore facts. We can't ignore data" (Obama, 2010). Teacher value-added measurement has been further bolstered by the movement for more accountability in public education, and its core idea that the public has the right to hold employees of public institutions responsible for the quality of the services they provide. The Obama administration's "Race to the Top" initiative, a competitive grants program that places substantial weight on states' and districts' willingness to evaluate teachers based on student achievement, has increased the number of states and districts seeking to require that teachers' evaluation, pay, and tenure be tied to measures of their value-added on standardized tests. For example, in 2010, legislators in Tennessee and Colorado committed to tying 50% of teachers' evaluations to value-added, and many other states have similar bills pending in their legislatures.

In this chapter, we explore two largely untested assumptions on which these proposals are based. First, policy makers supporting these systems believe that the high-stakes tests from which value-added measures are derived provide sufficient and accurate information—information that is not contaminated by well-documented behavioral responses to accountability systems—to determine which teachers are "good." Second, these policy makers assume that value-added measures are predictive of other outcomes, such as long-term educational attainment, earnings, and participation in civic life, that we care about, and thus the use of test scores to make evaluation and compensation decisions is not problematic. In other words, the belief is that a "good teacher," as measured by value-added to test scores, is good at all components of the job. In what follows, we explore both propositions by examining elementary school teachers' effects on outcomes beyond high-stakes tests.

HOW TEACHER ACCOUNTABILITY SYSTEMS MIGHT AFFECT CLASSROOM PRACTICE

To assess whether and how teacher-value added systems may affect teachers' attention to the full range of educational goals, it is useful to consider the existing literature on the effects of school-level accountability systems on classroom practice. A consistent finding of this literature is that test-based accountability systems have large impacts on behavior in ways that both promote and undermine policy makers' intentions. This is unsurprising in light of a large body of literature that finds that the introduction of social indicators fundamentally alters social processes. As Campbell (1979) most famously described, "The more any quantitative social indicator is used for social decision making, the more subject it will be to corruption pressures and the more apt it will be to distort and corrupt the social processes it is intended to monitor" (p. 85).

Stecher (2002) describes a number of ways that school accountability could positively influence classroom practices. They include supporting diagnosis of student needs, identifying strengths and weaknesses in the curriculum, identifying content not mastered by students that can be used to inform instruction, motivating teachers to "work harder and smarter," changing instruction to better align instruction with standards, and encouraging teachers to obtain professional development that will improve their instruction. Recent evidence suggests that accountability policies have resulted in some of these intended outcomes (Hamilton et al., 2007). Other researchers have identified instructional practices that potentially invalidate the inferences that we can draw from test scores, the most relevant of which are *reallocation of instructional time and attention* and *teaching to the test format*. Reallocation spans a continuum of activities, which may be more or less desirable depending on the extent to which the state standards fully capture the knowledge and skills desired for students, and the inferences that policy makers hope to make based on state test results. At one end of the continuum is aligning instruction with state standards; for example, it may be the case that teachers previously did not adequately cover a desired skill, but then are incentivized to do so because of its presence in the state standards. In this case, it is possible to make inferences about students' knowledge of the state standards based on the test, but depending on the capaciousness of the state standards, these inferences may not generalize to a broader set of skills not included in the standards. "Teaching to the format" captures the idea that teachers are responsive to the structure and representation of tasks on state tests. For example, if tests require a five-paragraph writing prompt, teachers are likely to assign similar tasks in their classrooms. In some respects, this is policy makers' goal in presenting tasks in certain ways. However, if students are taught formulaic approaches to approaching tasks, their scores may improve without improving their underlying skills.

Instructional Reallocation

A common form of reallocation involves the shifting of a teacher's attention between subject areas (Diamond, 2007; Marsh, Pane, & Hamilton, 2006). Simply testing a subject appears to affect classroom time use, and more so in high-stakes settings (Pedulla et al., 2003). For example, Hannaway (2007) found that in a national sample, the amount of time spent on instruction in mathematics in elementary school increased 40% from 2000 to 2004, which roughly captures pre- and post-NCLB (No Child Left Behind) periods. A study of NCLB implementation in three states by the RAND Corporation found increases in time spent on reading and mathematics (Hamilton et al., 2007), echoing the findings of other RAND studies during the 1990s in Kentucky, Maryland, Vermont, and Washington (Koretz, Barron, Mitchell, & Stecher, 1996; Stecher & Barron, 1999; Stecher & Chun, 2002). Another recent study by the Center on Education Policy (2008) concluded that nontested subjects such as science, social studies, and art were taught less in schools struggling to meet NCLB's targets. Depending on one's goals for public education, this shift can be viewed as having a salutary or detrimental effect on educational accountability.

Another form of reallocation involves the reallocation of time within a tested subject. The high predictability of tested content may lead teachers to narrow their instruction to focus only on the parts of the state curriculum represented on state tests, and to teach these skills in the specific format that appears on the test. These behaviors can produce what is known as "score inflation." *Score inflation* refers to the phenomenon by which test results overstate students' skills in the tested area and thus do not provide a valid measure of students' knowledge and skills in the larger knowledge domain that the test intends to measure. Because tests are based on a sampling principle, whereby only a fraction of the full knowledge domain of mathematics or reading is tested, state test results can become inflated when only a small fraction of state curriculum standards are tested and the content and form of test items is similar across years. As a result of this process, it is difficult to make inferences about students' proficiency in the larger domain that the test is intended to capture—the state standards—as students will appear to have made more academic progress than they truly have.

Gaming activities extending beyond reallocation can also have the effect of inflating state scores, including classifying students as special education so they can be exempted from state tests (Cullen & Reback, 2006; Figlio & Getzler, 2002; Jacob, 2005; Jennings & Beveridge, 2009), focusing on students close to passing (Booher-Jennings, 2005; Neal & Schanzenbach, 2010; Reback, 2008), and suspending low-scoring students close to the test date (Figlio, 2005). However, it is likely that instructional reallocation and teaching to the format are most consequential for understanding teachers' likely responses to value-added systems, so we focus on these activities in the balance of this section.

Some states have created opportunities for targeting material most likely to appear on future tests by providing teachers with guidance about which standards will appear on the tests. For example, from 2006 to 2009 New York published "pre-March" standards (those that were eligible to appear on the state test in March), while Pennsylvania has provided teachers with "Assessment Anchors" that identify standards eligible for testing (Hamilton et al., 2007). Even when such standards are not formally designated, the sampling of standards—what is actually covered on the tests—may also affect instructional responses. A number of studies have demonstrated that teachers use this approach. In the aforementioned RAND survey of teachers in California, Pennsylvania, and Georgia, teachers reported that because there were many standards to be tested, they identified "highly assessed standards" on which to focus their attention (Hamilton & Stecher, 2006). Studies of standard coverage on the New York, Massachusetts, and Texas tests over the period 2006–2009 have found that state tests do not cover the full curriculum and are predictable across years in ways that facilitate test-specific instruction, though there is substantial variation across subjects and across states within subjects (Holcombe, Jennings, & Koretz, 2010; Jennings & Bearak, 2010). At one end of the continuum is New York; in both subjects, the tests assess only a small fraction of the state curriculum. In mathematics, in no grade was more than 55% of the state math curriculum tested in 2009. By contrast, the Texas math tests covered almost every standard in 2009, while the Massachusetts exams covered roughly four-fifths of the standards in that year. Uneven weighting of standards that are tested creates the optimal opportunity for score inflation. For example, in New York, just eight of New York's 48 8th-grade math standards made up 40% of test points over the years 2006–2009. Using item-level data, Jennings and Bearak (2010) analyzed teachers' responses to these features and found that in three states, students perform better on items testing these frequently assessed standards.

Teaching to the Format

Features of the assessment also affect instructional responses to accountability, and a group of studies on "teaching to the format" address this issue. Studies by Borko and Elliott (1999), Darling-Hammond and Wise (1985), Smith and Rottenberg (1991), McNeil (2000), Pedulla et al. (2003), and Wolf and McIver (1999) all demonstrate how teachers focus their instruction not only on the content of the test, but also on its format by presenting material in formats as they will appear on the test and designing tasks to mirror the representation of content of the tests. To the extent that students learn how to correctly answer questions when they are presented in a specific format, but struggle with the same skills when they are presented in a different format, teaching to the format inflates test scores. A useful example reported in Shepard's (1988) study was a set of questions involving decimals. When addition was presented in a vertical format on the state test, 86% of students answered these questions correctly, but in horizontal format, only 46% of students did.

Broad test-preparation activities may also fall into the category of "teaching to the format," with many studies finding increases in instructional time spent specifically on test preparation in high-stakes contexts (Bulkley, Fairman, Martinez, & Hicks, 2004; Diamond, 2007; Jones et al., 1999; Koretz, Barron, Mitchell, & Stecher et al., 1996; Koretz, Mitchell, Barron, & Keith, 1996; Pedulla et al., 2003; Smith, 1994; Tepper, 2002). Koretz, Barron, Mitchell, and Stecher (1996) and Koretz, Mitchell, Barron, and Keith (1996) surveyed teachers in Kentucky and Maryland and found that teachers attributed test score gains in their schools to increased familiarity with the test and the use of practice tests and preparation materials, rather than to general improvements in skills. While many argue that there is nothing wrong with "teaching to the test" so long as the tests are worth teaching to, the issue is whether we can make inferences from the test results to the knowledge domain of interest, or whether higher scores merely reflect students' growing familiarity with specific question formats. To the extent that student learning is tied to the specific format of an isolated test, we may not be able to make inferences from students' scores to the knowledge domain of interest.

It is worth briefly commenting on the current research on the implications of these responses for the validity of inferences we can make based on test scores. Much of the evidence that we have on this question is at the level of states rather than at the level of schools or classrooms. For example, it is well documented that state test gains under accountability systems typically outpace national test gains (Center on

Education Policy, 2008; Fuller, Wright, Gesicki, & Kang, 2007; Klein, Hamilton, McCaffrey, & Stecher, 2000; Koretz & Barron, 1998; Linn, 2000). While we would not expect state and national gains to perfectly track each other, the magnitude of these differences is striking. For example, Koretz and Barron (1998), studying gains on the Kentucky state assessment, found that 4th- and 8th-grade math scores increased 3 to 4 times as much on the state test as on the National Assessment of Educational Progress (NAEP) between 1992 and 1996. Klein et al.'s (2000) study of Texas's state test and NAEP trends also uncovered a similar pattern and found that inflation for Black students appeared to be greater than inflation for White students, potentially because Black students are more likely to be educated in low-performing schools facing pressure to quickly increase scores. More recently, Jacob (2007) found that state scores grew twice as much as NAEP scores in Texas, North Carolina, Arkansas, and Connecticut.

Other studies of score inflation have examined performance on other high- and low-stakes exams and found similar patterns. For example, Koretz, Linn, Dunbar, and Shepard's (1991) study administered two separate mathematics, reading, and vocabulary tests—one from a commercial publisher and one that paralleled the state test—to students in elementary grades and found evidence of substantial score inflation that was greatest in mathematics. Another recent study by Jacob (2005) used item-level data to better understand the mechanisms underlying score inflation. Jacob analyzed data on high- and low-stakes tests from the Chicago Public Schools and found large gains on the high-stakes test following the introduction of accountability, but no similar effects of the accountability system on the low-stakes. He determined that students improved more on the basic math skills emphasized in the high-stakes test, but exhibited little improvement on questions testing skills like estimation, data interpretation, and multiple-step problem solving. However, he did not find unequal gains across skill types on the reading exam and suggested that the skill-specific nature of mathematics may make test preparation more effective than for reading.

What are the implications of these findings for measuring teacher effectiveness? To the extent that instructional reallocation and teaching to the format behaviors differ across teachers, true value-added comparisons will be compromised. What's more, teachers may amplify these actions as pressure increases to improve high-stakes scores. In the next section, we explore this possibility by asking whether the teachers who appear effective on high-stakes tests are similarly effective on low-stakes tests of the same subject areas.

THE RELATIONSHIP BETWEEN TEACHERS' EFFECTIVENESS ON HIGH-STAKES TESTS AND THEIR EFFECTIVENESS ON OTHER MEASURES OF ACHIEVEMENT

Evidence that the choice of test can make a difference to value-added comes from recent research comparing value-added measures on multiple tests of the same content area. Since 1998, Houston has administered two standardized tests every year—the state TAKS and the nationally normed Stanford Achievement Test. Using data from the Houston Independent School District (HISD), we calculated separate value-added measures for 4th- and 5th-grade teachers for the two tests (Corcoran, Jennings, & Beveridge, 2011). These measures were based on the same students, tested in the same subject, at approximately the same time of year. The key difference between the two tests is their stakes: One is used for accountability purposes, while the other is not. While there are other reasons why value-added measures may vary across tests, our interest is primarily in the role high stakes play in their divergence.

High- and Low-Stakes Tests in Houston

Like all school districts in Texas, HISD has administered annual state assessments since the 1980s. The Texas Assessment of Academic Skills (TAAS) was a minimum-competency test given annually from 1991 until 2003, when it was replaced by the Texas Assessment of Knowledge and Skills (TAKS), a criterion-referenced test. In 1996, HISD added the Stanford Achievement Test under pressure from a business task force that sought a nationally normed benchmark test (McAdams, 2000). Since that time, all students receiving instruction in English, except those with serious disabilities, have been required to take the Stanford. Limited English proficient students who receive reading and language arts instruction in Spanish are given the Spanish-language Aprenda. Both the TAKS and the Stanford are untimed. During this period, all these tests were given in the spring, from early March (Stanford/Aprenda) to mid- to late April (TAAS/TAKS). (For a more detailed description of the features of the tests, see Corcoran et al., 2011).

The TAAS/TAKS is HISD's "high-stakes" test, for several reasons. First, passing rates on these tests have been an integral part of Texas's accountability system since 1994 (Reback, 2008). Under this system, which served as the model for No Child Left Behind, schools and districts are labeled "exemplary," "recognized," "acceptable," or "low-performing" based on their pass rates in each subject area. In most years, monetary rewards were available for high-performing or improving schools, while low performers were subject to sanctions, up to and including school closure or reconstitution. Second, HISD has operated a performance pay plan since 2000 that provides monetary rewards to schools and teachers for TAAS/TAKS results. Historically the district based these rewards on campus accountability ratings, but in recent years it has rewarded individual teachers and schools based on their value-added on these tests. Third, Texas has required 3rd-grade students to pass the TAKS reading test for grade promotion since 2003. Since 2005, 5th-grade students have been required to pass both the math and reading TAKS to be promoted.

The Stanford can be considered HISD's "low-stakes" test, in that it is not tied to the state accountability system. However, the test plays several important roles in the district. For example, it is used as one criterion for grade promotion in grades 1–8. HISD students are expected to perform above a minimum standard on both the Stanford (e.g., at least one grade level below average) and the TAKS. In addition, the Stanford is used to aid in the placement of students in special programs, including gifted and special education. School-level results on the Stanford are publicly reported in the local media, and in recent years value-added measures on the Stanford were integrated into HISD's performance pay plan.

Reading and math skills covered on the TAKS and Stanford are broadly similar. TAKS tests in all grades are mapped to specific state standards. For example, the 4th- and 5th-grade TAKS math test includes items pertaining to number operations and quantitative reasoning; patterns, relationships, and algebraic thinking; geometry and spatial reasoning; measurement; probability and statistics; and underlying processes and tools. The TAKS English/Language Arts and reading tests cover such areas as reading comprehension (literary and informational); vocabulary development; writing; oral and written conventions; research; and listening. On the Stanford, the 4th- and 5th-grade math tests are composed of two subtests: problem solving (such as number sense and operations, statistics, and geometry) and procedures (including computation with fractions and decimals). The reading subtests include word study skills (structural and phonetic analysis), reading vocabulary (e.g., synonyms and context clues), and reading comprehension (including literary, informational, and critical analysis). Thus, while there are content differences across the two tests, they overlap considerably. An analysis by Hoey, Campbell, and Perlman (2001) mapped the standards on Texas's 4th-grade TAAS math test to those covered on the analogous Stanford test and found that 83% of the Texas state standards were represented on the Stanford.

Two Different Stories About Teacher Effectiveness

In line with previous research on teacher effects, we found that teachers had a large impact on achievement as measured on both tests. However, our results indicated that the magnitude of these effects—as evidenced by the variation in teacher value-added—depended on the nature of the test. Overall, teacher effects on the high-stakes TAKS were 17 to 35% larger than those on the low-stakes Stanford Achievement Test. In other words, teachers appeared to be more different from one another on the high-stakes test than on the low-stakes test. Although the difference between, say, a teacher at the 75th percentile of effectiveness and a teacher at the 25th percentile is still quite large, the difference is not nearly as large as the high-stakes test would suggest.

Perhaps more important, the *correlation* between teachers' value-added on the two tests is modest at best. Measures of correlation between the two sets of value-added estimates offer some indication of whether teachers deemed effective on the high-stakes tests are similarly effective on the low-stakes tests of the same subject. Any meaningful difference in teacher rankings that exists across the two tests are potentially important in light of recent proposals to reward the highest-performing teachers (e.g., the top 20%) or deny tenure to the lowest-performing teachers (e.g., the bottom 20%; see Gordon, Kane, & Staiger, 2006; Hanushek, 2009). We found correlations on these two tests to be 0.52 in reading and 0.60 in math. While measurement error plays some role in these modest correlations, these estimates were based on all years of available data for each teacher—in some cases up to 8 years—and are thus less affected by year-to-year noise. As expected, we found weaker correlations between single-year teacher effect estimates (0.47 in reading and 0.53 in math). While multiyear estimates are always preferred to measures based on a single year, in practice an important fraction of teachers will always have no more than a single year that can be used in a value-added calculation.

Not surprisingly, this modest correlation yields many inconsistent rankings of effective teachers. This is illustrated in Figure 4.1 where we group teachers into five performance categories on each test (1–5), with the five TAKS categories on the horizontal axis. We see that teachers who had high value-added on one test tended to have high value-added on the other, but there were many inconsistencies. For example, 13% of exceptional (top quintile) teachers in reading—as measured by the state test—were deemed well below average (bottom two quintiles) on the low-stakes reading test, and another 14% were deemed no better than average (middle quintile). The opposite pattern emerges for low-performing (bottom quintile) teachers on the state test. Here, 49% of bottom-quintile

Figure 4.1. Teacher Value-Added on High and Low-Stakes Reading Tests: Houston 4th- and 5th-Grade Teachers

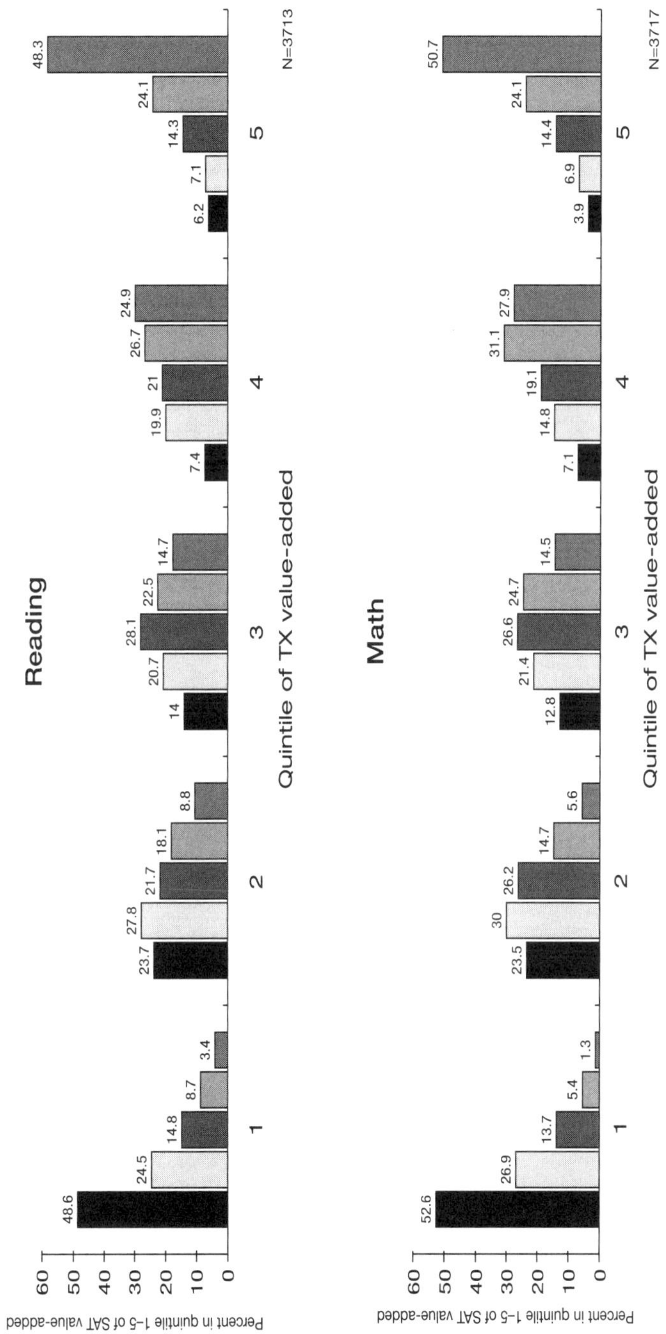

reading teachers appeared in the bottom quintile of the Stanford. One in eight (12%) ranked in the top two quintiles. A similar pattern is observed in math, though the quintile rankings are a bit more consistent than in reading.

These findings are consistent with those from other districts, including several large districts in Florida (Sass, 2008) and a large anonymous district in the Northeast (Papay, 2010). To show what kind of impact these inconsistencies can have in practice, Papay (2010) simulated teacher bonuses using his two differing sets of value-added estimates and the current Houston incentive plan. He found that "simply switching the outcome measure would affect the performance bonus for nearly half of all teachers, and the average teacher's salary would change by approximately $2,200" (p. 5). Like our study, he concludes that the two value-added estimates "are not sufficiently comparable to rank the same individual teachers as high or low performing" (p. 5).

THE RELATIONSHIP BETWEEN EFFECTIVE TEACHING OF ACADEMIC SKILLS AND OF SOCIAL AND BEHAVIORAL SKILLS

In the previous section, we showed that teachers who are effective at improving performance on high-stakes tests are not necessarily effective at improving performance on low-stakes tests. A second set of issues with measuring teacher effectiveness stems from the fact that public education has multiple goals, including promotion of social and behavioral skills. Analysts and policy makers measure test scores because they assume they are correlated with these outcomes and current policy assumes that a "good" teacher is effective across domains, but in fact we know little about whether teachers who are good at supporting one set of competencies are similarly capable at supporting others.

The only evidence that we do have on this issue comes from studies estimating the effects of schools on test scores and other outcomes. In these studies, scholars have examined school effects on incarceration and college enrollment rates and found that students who won the lottery to attend their school of choice committed fewer crimes and were also more likely to attend a 4-year college, but there was no evidence that their test scores rose more than the scores of students who lost the same lottery (Booker, Gill, Zimmer, & Sass, 2009; Deming, forthcoming; Deming, Hastings, Kane, & Staiger, 2009). Cullen, Jacob, and Levitt (2006) also found that winning high school choice lotteries in Chicago did not improve winners' test scores, but lottery winners were less likely to be arrested or have disciplinary infractions than were lottery losers. Taken together, these results suggest that teacher and school quality may be multidimensional;

the things schools do to increase test scores may not also increase performance in these other domains, and vice versa.

We build on this literature by reviewing the results of a recent study by Jennings and DiPrete (2010), which analyzed data from the Early Childhood Longitudinal Study—Kindergarten Cohort and asked whether kindergarten teachers who are good at promoting academic growth are also good at promoting social growth. Their measures of academic growth focused on progress made between the beginning and end of kindergarten, while their measures of social growth included three different sets of skills. They included "approaches to learning," which rate the child's attentiveness, task persistence, eagerness to learn, learning independence, flexibility, and organization; self-control skills, which indicate the child's ability to control behavior by respecting the property rights of others, controlling temper, accepting peer ideas for group activities, and responding appropriately to pressure from peers; and interpersonal skills, which include the child's skill in forming and maintaining friendships, getting along with people who are different, comforting or helping other children, expressing feelings, ideas, and opinions in positive ways, and showing sensitivity to the feelings of others.

Jennings and DiPrete (2010) found that the correlation between math and reading teaching was higher than were the correlations between social teaching and either math or reading teaching. The math-reading correlation ranged from .42–.48, while the social-academic correlation ranged from .13–.17. Because of the relatively low number of students per teacher in the Early Childhood Longitudinal Study-Kindergarten Class of 1998-99 sample, these correlations are almost certainly underestimated. Nonetheless, these results suggest that social and behavioral teaching is a distinct competency from the teaching of math or reading.

Based on these results, it is worth considering why teachers may differ in their promotion of social and behavioral skills and what the implications of this are for value-added estimates of teacher effectiveness. At the most basic level, we know that teachers bring a diverse toolkit of skills to the classroom. Just as teachers vary in their ability to promote academic skills, teachers, we expect, vary in their capacity to increase student stocks of social and behavioral skills. Teachers' professional beliefs have a potentially important role to play along with teacher competencies. Teachers vary in their valuation of academic and social competencies, particularly in kindergarten (Dombkowski, 2001), which would generate differences in how much they emphasize the teaching of each type of skill. Even if teachers agreed on the relative importance of academic achievement versus the enhancement of social and behavioral skills, they may disagree about the extent to which these skills are of instrumental importance in promoting academic achievement, which would produce heterogeneous teaching styles even among those teachers who were primarily focused on academic goals. They may also disagree about their ability to affect the stocks of these skills, with some teachers believing that student behavioral deficits are impervious to change and others seeing social and behavioral skills to be potentially as teachable as reading and mathematics.

Nonschool factors, such as parents and state regulatory systems, may matter for producing these differences as well. There is some evidence that high–socioeconomic status (SES) parents value academic and social competencies differently than do low-SES parents and parents may demand different approaches for their children as a result (Jacob & Lefgren, 2007). Parents of different backgrounds may see different types of social skills as appropriate for their children; as Lareau (2003) has discovered, high-SES parents privilege the use of language to negotiate with authority, while low-SES parents prefer that their children do not question authority. Finally, and most relevant to this chapter, states, schools, and districts differ in the incentives they offer teachers to focus on academic versus social and behavioral skills (Russell, 2007). For example, teachers in states with more stringent accountability systems may face stronger incentives to emphasize academic skills. In sum, both the socioeconomic and the regulatory context of the school would be expected to produce variation in the extent to which teachers focus on enhancing social and behavioral skills in early elementary school.

CONCLUSION: POLICY IMPLICATIONS

In this chapter, we demonstrated that a teacher who appears effective on one outcome of schooling is not necessarily effective on others. Even when the outcome measured taps a general body of academic skills, for example, 4th-grade mathematics, teachers who are effective as measured by a test used for state accountability purposes are not necessarily effective on a second low-stakes test of academic performance. We also provided evidence that teachers who are effective at promoting academic skills are not necessarily effective at improving students' social and behavioral skills. In this section, we consider the implications of these findings in light of current education policy and the public conversation about what it means for a teacher to be "good."

Our review of the educational accountability literature suggests that placing a heavy weight on performance on high-stakes tests is likely to distort the educational process, particularly in light of the current weaknesses of state standardized tests. The accountability literature clearly demonstrates that unwanted responses to accountability are most likely when performance pressures are heightened, and holding teachers individually accountable for student test scores is likely to ramp up such pressure. Policy makers can attempt to minimize these unintended consequences by designing tests that create fewer opportunities for test-specific instruction that does not generalize to other assessments. Current tests are extremely predictable both in their content (which standards are likely to make up a high fraction of the test year after year) and in their format (the way that this content is represented). While short tests like those used for accountability will be able to test only a sample of the domain about which we wish to make inferences, varying this sample from year to year will create fewer incentives for teachers to engage in the narrowing that undermines the validity of state test results. Some states like Massachusetts have attempted to address this issue for school accountability by including a block of "matrix-sampled" items in addition to the common items that all students answer. In other words, as with the National Assessment of Educational Progress, each student is given a subset of the domain of interest, since the goal is to make inferences about a school's effectiveness in teaching the full domain rather than to make inferences about individual students. While such adjustments will not eliminate unwanted responses to test-based accountability, they may reduce some of their most problematic consequences.

A common response to concerns about distortion described above is to recommend that value-added estimates be used only for diagnostic purposes or that they function in a system of multiple measures that puts lower weights on the value-added component. Certainly such systems would give teachers reason to invest in cultivating a broader range of skills among their students, including the social and behavioral outcomes addressed in this chapter, and are an improvement on using only high-stakes tests for these purposes. At the same time, the discussion of multiple-measures systems has ignored that value-added measures may inform and color subjective evaluations of teachers. There is much evidence of this phenomenon in social science. For example, in an experiment in which subjects were given false information about the popularity of a song—that is, subjects were told that the highest-ranked song was ranked last, and so on—this information influenced their ratings of song quality, even as they could listen to the entire song (Salganik, Dodds, & Watts, 2006). Other studies of *US News and World Report* rankings suggest that subjective evaluations of universities are shaped by their relative ranking in prior years (Espeland & Sauder, 2007). Taken together, these findings suggest that arguments that value-added measures "will only be one small part of the evaluation" need to be evaluated in light of how real users of these data integrate both qualitative and quantitative data.

REFERENCES

Booher-Jennings, J. (2005). Below the bubble: "Educational triage" and the Texas accountability system. *American Educational Research Journal, 42*, 231–268.

Booker, K., Gill, B., Zimmer, R., & Sass, T. R. (2009). *Achievement and attainment in Chicago charter schools*. Santa Monica, CA: RAND.

Borko, H., & Elliott, R. (1999). Hands-on pedagogy versus hands-off accountability: Tensions between competing commitments for exemplary math teachers in Kentucky. *Phi Delta Kappan, 80*, 394–400.

Bulkley, K., Fairman, J., Martinez, M. C., & Hicks, J. E. (2004). The district and test preparation. In W. A. Firestone & R. Y. Schorr (Eds.), *The ambiguity of test preparation* (pp. 113–141). Mahwah, NJ: Lawrence Erlbaum and Associates.

Campbell, D. T. (1979). Assessing the impact of planned social change. *Evaluation and Program Planning*, 2(1), 67-90.

Center on Education Policy. (2008). *Has student achievement increased since 2002? State test score trends through 2006–07*. Washington, DC: Center on Education Policy.

Clotfelter, C. T., Ladd, H. F., & Vigdor, J. L. (2006). Teacher-student matching and the assessment of teacher effectiveness. *Journal of Human Resources, 41*, 778–820.

Corcoran, S. P., Jennings, J. L., & Beveridge, A. A. (2011, March 4). *Teacher effects on high- and low-stakes tests.* Paper presented at the Society for Research on Educational Effectiveness, Washington, DC.

Cullen, J. B., Jacob, B. A., & Levitt, S. (2006). The effect of school choice on student outcomes: Evidence from randomized lotteries. *Econometrica, 74*, 1191–1230.

Cullen, J. B., & Reback, R. (2006). *Tinkering towards accolades: School gaming under a performance accountability system* (Working Paper No. 12286). Cambridge, MA: National Bureau of Economic Research.

Darling-Hammond, L., & Wise, A. E. (1985). Beyond standardization: State standards and school improvement. *The Elementary School Journal, 85*, 315–36.

Deming, D. (Forthcoming). Better schools, less crime? *Quarterly Journal of Economics*.

Deming, D., Hastings, J., Kane, T. J., & Staiger, D. O. (2009). *School choice and college attendance: Evidence from randomized lotteries* (Working Paper). Cambridge, MA: Harvard University.

Diamond, J. B. (2007). Where rubber meets the road: Rethinking the connection between high-stakes testing policy and classroom instruction. *Sociology of Education, 80*, 285–313.

Dombkowski, K. (2001). Will the real kindergarten please stand up? Defining and redefining the 20th century US kindergarten. *History of Education, 30*, 527–545.

Espeland, W., & Sauder, M. (2007). Rankings and reactivity: How public measures recreate social worlds. *American Journal of Sociology, 113*, 1–40.

Figlio, D. N. (2005). *Testing, crime, and punishment* (Working Paper No. 11194). Cambridge, MA: National Bureau of Economic Research.

Figlio, D. N., & Getzler, L. (2002). *Accountability, ability, and disability: Gaming the system* (Working Paper No. 9307). Cambridge, MA: National Bureau of Economic Research.

Fuller, B., Wright, J., Gesicki, K., & Kang, E. (2007). Gauging growth: How to judge No Child Left Behind? *Educational Researcher, 36*, 268–78.

Gordon, R., Kane, T. J., & Staiger, D. O. (2006). *Identifying effective teachers using performance on the job*. Washington, DC: Brookings Institution.

Hamilton, L. S., & Stecher, B. M. (2006). *Measuring instructional responses to standards-based accountability*. Santa Monica, CA: RAND.

Hamilton, L. S., Stecher, B. M., Marsh, J. A., McCombs, J. S., Robyn, A., Russell, J. L., Naftel, S., & Barney, H. (2007). *Implementing standards-based accountability under No Child Left Behind: Responses of superintendents, principals, and teachers in three states*. Santa Monica, CA: RAND.

Hannaway, J. (2007, November). Unbounding rationality: Politics and policy in a data rich system. In *Mistisfer Lecture, University Council of Education Administration*, Alexandria, VA.

Hanushek, E. A. (2009). Teacher deselection. In D. Goldhaber & J. Hannaway (Eds.), *Creating a new teaching profession* (pp. 165–180). Washington, DC: The Urban Institute Press.

Hanushek, E. A., Kain, J. F., O'Brien, D. M., & Rivkin, S. G. (2005). *The market for teacher quality* (Working Paper No. 11154). Cambridge, MA: National Bureau of Economic Research.

Hoey, L., Campbell, P. B., & Perlman, L. (2001). *Where's the overlap? Mapping the SAT9 and TAAS 4th grade test objectives*. Groton, MA: Campbell-Kibler Associates.

Holcombe, R. W., Jennings, J. L., & Koretz, D. M. (2010). Opportunities for score inflation: an examination of tests from two states [Working Paper]. Cambridge, MA: Harvard University.

Jacob, B. A. (2005). Accountability, incentives, and behavior: Evidence from school reform in Chicago. *Journal of Public Economics, 89*, 761–796.

Jacob, B. A. (2007). *Test-based accountability and student achievement: An investigation of differential performance on NAEP and state assessments* (Working Paper No. 12817). Cambridge, MA: National Bureau of Economic Research.

Jacob, B. A., & Lefgren, L. (2007). "What Do Parents Value in Education? An Empirical Investigation of Parents' Revealed Preferences for Teachers." *The Quarterly Journal of Economics, 122*(4), 1603-1637.

Jennings, J. L., & Bearak, J. M. (2010, August). *State test predictability and teaching to the test: Evidence from three states.* Paper presented at the annual meeting of the American Sociological Association, Atlanta, GA.

Jennings, J. L., & Beveridge, A. A. (2009). How does test exemption affect schools' and students' academic performance? *Educational Evaluation and Policy Analysis, 31*, 153–175.

Jennings, J. L., & DiPrete, T. A. (2010). Teacher effects on social and behavioral skills in elementary school. *Sociology of Education, 83*, 135–159.

Jones, G., Jones, B. D., Hardin, B., Chapman, L., Yarbrough, T., & Davis, M. (1999). The impact of high-stakes testing on teachers and students in North Carolina. *Phi Delta Kappan, 81*, 199–203.

Kane, T. J., Rockoff, J. E., & Staiger, D. O. (2008). What does certification tell us about teacher effectiveness? Evidence from New York City. *Economics of Education Review, 27*, 615–631.

Klein, S., Hamilton, L., McCaffrey, D., & Stecher, B. (2000). *What do test scores in Texas tell us?* Santa Monica, CA: RAND.

Koretz, D. M., & Barron, S. I. (1998). *The validity of gains on the Kentucky instructional results information system (KIRIS)*. Santa Monica, CA: RAND.

Koretz, D., Barron, S., Mitchell, K., & Stecher, B. (1996). *The perceived effects of the Kentucky instructional results information system*. Santa Monica, CA: RAND.

Koretz, D., Linn, R. L., Dunbar, S. B., & Shepard, L. A. (1991, April). *The effects of high-stakes testing: Preliminary evidence about generalization across tests*. Paper presented at the annual meeting of the American Educational Research Association, Chicago.

Koretz, D., Mitchell, K., Barron, S., & Keith, S. (1996). *The perceived effects of the Maryland school performance assessment program (CSE Tech. Rep. No. 409)*. Los Angeles: University of California, National Center for Research on Evaluation, Standards, and Student Testing (CRESST).

Lareau, A. (2003). *Unequal childhoods: Class, race, and family life*. Berkeley: University of California Press.

Linn, R. L. (2000). Assessments and accountability. *Educational Researcher, 29*, 4–16.

Los Angeles Times. (2010). *Los Angeles teacher ratings: FAQ and about*. Retrieved from http://projects.latimes.com/value-added/faq/

Marsh, J. A., Pane, J. F., & Hamilton, L. S. (2006). *Making sense of data-driven decision making in education: Evidence from recent RAND research (OP-170)*. Santa Monica, CA: RAND.

McAdams, D. R. (2000). *Fighting to save our urban schools . . . and winning!* New York: Teachers College Press.

McNeil, L. M. (2000). *Contradictions of school reform: The educational costs of standardized testing*. London: Routledge.

Neal, D., & Schanzenbach, D. W. (2010). Left behind by design: Proficiency counts and test-based accountability. *The Review of Economics and Statistics, 92, 263-283.*

Obama, B. (2010, July 24). *Remarks by the president at the Department of Education*. Retrieved from http://www.whitehouse.gov/the_press_office/Remarks-by-the-President-at-the-Department-of-Education/

Papay, J. P. (2010). Different tests, different answers: The stability of teacher value-added estimates across outcome measures. *American Education Research Journal, 48*, 1–30.

Pedulla, J. J., Abrams, L. M., Madaus, G. F., Russell, M. K., Ramos, M. A., & Miao, J. (2003). *Perceived effects of state-mandated testing programs on teaching and learning: Findings from a national survey of teachers*. Boston: National Board on Educational Testing and Public Policy.

Reback, R. (2008). Teaching to the rating: School accountability and the distribution of student achievement. *Journal of Public Economics, 92*, 1394–1415.

Rivkin, S. G., Hanushek, E. A., & Kain, J. F. (2005). Teachers, schools, and academic achievement. *Econometrica, 73*, 417–458.

Rockoff, J. E. (2004). The impact of individual teachers on student achievement: Evidence from panel data. *American Economic Review, Papers and Proceedings, 94*, 247–252.

Rowan, B., Correnti, R., & Miller, R. J. (2002). What large-scale, survey research tells us about teacher effects on student achievement: Insights from the Prospects Study of elementary schools. *Teachers College Record, 104*, 1525–1567.

Russell, J. (2007). *Not kid stuff anymore? An analysis of institutional change in kindergarten education.* Unpublished doctoral dissertation, University of California–Berkeley, School of Education, Berkeley.

Salganik, M. J., Dodds, P. S., & Watts, D. J. (2006). Experimental study of inequality and unpredictability in an artificial cultural market. *Science*, 311, 854–856.

Sass, T. R. (2008). *Policy brief: The stability of value-added measures of teacher quality and implications for teacher compensation policy.* Washington, DC: CALDER.

Shepard, L. A. (1988). *The harm of measurement-driven instruction.* Paper presented at the annual meeting of the American Educational Research Association, Washington, DC.

Smith, M. L. (1994). *Old and new beliefs about measurement-driven instruction: "The more things change, the more they stay the same."* Los Angeles: Center for Research on Evaluation, Standards, and Student Testing.

Smith, M. L., & Rottenberg, C. (1991). Unintended consequences of external testing in elementary schools. *Educational Measurement: Issues and Practice, 10,* 7–11.

Stecher, B. M. (2002). Consequences of large-scale, high-stakes testing on school and classroom practice. In L. S. Hamilton, B. M. Stecher, & S. P. Klein (Eds.), *Making sense of test-based accountability in education* (pp. 79–100). Santa Monica, CA: RAND.

Stecher, B. M., & Barron, S. I. (1999). *Quadrennial milepost accountability testing in Kentucky* (CSE Technical Report 505). Los Angeles: National Center for Research on Evaluation, Standards, and Student Testing, University of California.

Stecher, B. M., & Chun, T. J. (2002). *School and classroom practices during two years of education reform in Washington State.* CSE Technical Report 550. Los Angeles: National Center for Research on Evaluation, Standards and Student Testing.

Tepper, R. L. (2002). *The influence of high-stakes testing on instructional practice in Chicago.* Unpublished dissertation. Chicago: Harris Graduate School of Public Policy, University of Chicago.

Wolf, S. A., & McIver, M. C. (1999). When process becomes policy: The paradox of Kentucky state reform for exemplary teachers of writing. *Phi Delta Kappan, 80,* 401–406.

CHAPTER 5

Power, Accountability, and the Teacher Quality Problem

Richard M. Ingersoll

Few educational issues have received more attention in recent times than the problem of ensuring that our nation's elementary and secondary classrooms are all staffed with quality teachers. Concern with teacher quality is not surprising. Elementary and secondary schooling is mandatory in the United States and it is into the care of teachers that children are legally placed for a significant portion of their lives. The quality of teachers and teaching is undoubtedly among the most important factors shaping the learning and growth of students. Moreover, the largest single component of the cost of education is teacher compensation. Especially since the seminal *Nation at Risk* report in 1983, a seemingly endless stream of studies, commissions, and national reports have targeted teacher quality as one of the central problems facing schools. Critics have blamed the performance of teachers for myriad social ills: the erosion of American economic competitiveness and productivity, the decline in student academic achievement, teenage pregnancy, juvenile delinquency and crime, the coarsening of our everyday discourse and culture, a decline in morals, gender and racial stereotyping and discrimination, and on and on (see e.g., Bennett, 1993; Levin, 1998; Sadker & Sadker, 1994; Urban League, 1999). As a result, in recent decades a host of initiatives and programs seeking to upgrade teacher quality have been pushed by reformers at the federal, state, and local levels.

Although ensuring that our nation's classrooms are all staffed with quality teachers is a perennially important issue in our schools, it is also, however, among the least understood. This misunderstanding centers on the sources of the problem, the reasons behind the purportedly low quality of teachers and teaching in American schools, and it has undermined the success of reform efforts. Behind the criticism and reforms are a variety of differing perspectives as to the sources of the problems plaguing the teaching occupation.

One of the most popular perspectives has to do with the control and accountability of the teaching force. Schools, this view claims, are marked by low standards, a lack of coherence, poor management, and little effort to ensure adequate supervision and control, especially in regard to their primary activity—the work of teachers with students. Teachers are not held accountable and simply do what they want behind the closed doors of their classrooms. The predictable result, this view holds, is low-quality performance on the part of teachers and students.

In this chapter I offer a critique of this accountability perspective. My argument is that this view overlooks some of the most important sources and forms of organizational control and accountability that already exist in schools and, as a result, overlooks the ways schools themselves, and in particular the ways they are managed and organized, contribute to the teacher quality problem. In plain terms, poorly run schools can make otherwise excellent teachers not so excellent.

For those who subscribe to the accountability perspective, the obvious antidote to the ills of the education system is to increase the centralized control of schools and to seek to hold teachers more accountable, in short, to "tighten the ship." Typically, proponents of this view advocate methods and mechanisms, such as teacher entry examinations, the use of standardized curricula, and especially the implementation of explicit performance standards coupled with more rigorous teacher evaluation. A prominent focus in the accountability movement is to change the traditional ways that teachers have been assessed, evaluated, and rewarded, in regard to employment decisions about teacher hiring, assignment, transfer, layoffs, promotions, and salary. The traditional public school approach largely bases these kinds of decisions on measures of teachers' qualifications, usually the amount of teaching experience, postsecondary courses completed, and type of licensure or certification. The thrust of many accountability critics is to deny a strong link between these traditional measures of qualifications and the actual quality and performance of teachers and to therefore push to replace the former with new approaches that better capture quality and merit. A variety of new approaches have been developed and implemented, such as the controversial "value-added" model, which attempts to assess teachers by assessing gains in their students' test scores. Many of these accountability mechanisms have become widely used since the advent of the No Child Left Behind Act in 2002.

A lack of control and accountability is, of course, not the only explanation given for the problem of low-quality teachers and teaching. Nor is this perspective universally believed; indeed, it is the subject of much contention. But it is a prominent view, a growing part of the conventional wisdom about what ails teaching, and has had an increasing impact on reform and policy.

Over the past 2 decades, I have undertaken a series of research projects on the levels, distribution, and effects of control and accountability in schools (Ingersoll, 2003). This research has involved analyses of a wide array of data, both qualitative and quantitative. A major source of data was the nationally representative Schools and Staffing Survey (SASS) conducted by the National Center for Education Statistics, the statistical arm of the U.S. Department of Education. Conducted every few years since the late 1980s, this survey is the largest and most comprehensive source of information on teachers that is available (each cycle of SASS includes about 55,000 teachers in both the public and private sectors). From this survey I analyzed data on an unusually wide range of information on the characteristics, work, and attitudes of both teachers and administrators, and on the characteristics and conditions of schools and districts across the country.

Another quantitative data source I used is the International Survey of the Locus of Decision-Making in Educational Systems, conducted by the Center for Educational Research and Innovation, part of the Organization for Economic Co-Operation Development (OECD). OECD is a leading international research and development organization based in Paris and one of the best sources of international data on education; this particular survey collected information on the control of schooling across a range of nations. These data proved valuable because they allowed me to compare the system of school governance and control in the United States to that in other nations.

Finally, I also undertook a field study of four schools in the Philadelphia area, chosen to be as varied as possible. My fieldwork included observing life in school cafeterias, halls, meetings, and classrooms; conducting in-depth interviews with administrators and teachers; and examining school documents, faculty manuals, and policy handbooks. From this research I have come to the conclusion that the accountability movement often involves wrong diagnoses of, and wrong prescriptions for, problems of teacher quality.

Often underlying accountability initiatives is what might be called a "teacher deficit" viewpoint. The assumption underlying this view is that the primary source of low-quality teaching in schools lies in various deficits in teachers themselves—their ability, commitment, engagement, or effort. Hence, the attendant assumption is that the best way to fix schools is to fix these deficits in individual teachers through increased rules and regulations, incentives, and sanctions, "sticks and carrots."

Proponents of the accountability perspective identify important issues and problems. Accountability in schools is reasonable and necessary and the public has a right and, indeed, an obligation to be concerned with the performance of teachers. There is no question that some teachers are poorly performing and inadequate for the job, in one way or another.

However, my argument in this chapter is that the accountability perspective offers only a partial, one-sided explanation and as a result the reforms it has spawned often do not work and can even make things worse. In this chapter I offer an alternative theoretical perspective drawn from the sociology of organizations, occupations, and work. My operating premise, drawn from this perspective, is that fully understanding issues of teacher quality requires examining the character of the teaching occupation and of the organizations in which teachers work. In contrast to a teacher deficit viewpoint, this perspective seeks to illuminate the ways the organizational characteristics of schools and of the teaching occupation themselves contribute to the problem of teaching quality. In other words, the goal of this alternative perspective is to illuminate the ways in which individual teacher troubles are really public issues, indelibly shaped by the larger occupational and organizational context, a way of looking that the sociologist C. Wright Mills (1959/2000) referred to as the "sociological imagination."

WHO CONTROLS TEACHERS' WORK?

Historically, in the United States the control of elementary and secondary schooling developed in an unusual manner. In contrast with most European nations, public schooling in this country was originally begun on a highly democratized, localized basis. The resulting legacy is a current system of some 15,000 individual public school districts, governed by local school boards of citizens, each with legal responsibility for the administration and operation of publicly funded, universal, mandatory, elementary and secondary schooling. Of course, local school districts in the United States are clearly no longer the autonomous bodies they once were. Over the past half century, myriad other organizational actors have increasingly exerted or sought to influence control of schooling, including state governments, external pressure groups, and the judicial system. Most recently, we have seen an unprecedented expansion of the federal role in education through the No Child Left Behind Act. Nevertheless, comparative data from a number of nations indicate that, despite these changes, schooling in the United States still remains a far more nonfederal and local affair than in most other systems.

While the education system in the United States is relatively decentralized, schools themselves are not. Most public and private secondary schools are highly centralized internally. In other words, the data show that while school principals and school governing boards often have substantial control over many key decisions in schools, teachers usually do not. There are differences among different types of schools but overall and on average, teachers have had little power, influence, or control over many key decisions concerned with the day-to-day management of their work and their workplaces. For instance, teachers often have little influence over larger schoolwide decisions that shape the instructional program, such as establishing the overall curriculum for the school, conceiving changes and innovations to the curriculum, and even choosing their own course textbooks. Teachers often have little input over decisions concerned with their course schedule, their class sizes, the office and classroom space they will use, and the use of school discretionary funds for classroom materials. On average, teachers have very limited control over which courses they are assigned to teach.

Teachers usually have little input into hiring, firing, and budgetary decisions. They further have little input into the means and criteria by which they, or school administrators, are evaluated. Teachers frequently have little say in the determination over the content of their own on-the-job development and in-service training programs.

A similar account holds for teachers' influence over the clients they serve—students. For example, teachers often have little say over what kind of student ability grouping the school has and which students are placed into which tracks or ability levels. Teachers typically have little say over decisions surrounding whether to promote particular students or to hold them back to repeat a grade. Teachers, overall, have little input into schoolwide behavioral and disciplinary rules and standards for students. Likewise, teachers have little influence over the assignment of students and who is enrolled in their courses. In addition, rarely do teachers have the authority to have disruptive students removed from their classroom, even temporarily. Teachers also usually have almost no influence over the rules and standards of student expulsion from schools. In other words, teachers rarely have the right to not teach particular students, even if they are disruptive and regardless of whether the student wishes to be in school or not. As described by Lortie (1975), the relationship between teacher and student continues to be one of "dual captivity"; teachers are public servants who cannot chose not to serve their clients and their clients are recipients of a public service who cannot chose not to be served. This stands in sharp distinction to members of the traditional professions, such as lawyers, academics, accountants, physicians, or psychotherapists, who often can have a substantial degree of choice over whom they serve. For instance, unlike teachers, within the constraints of the market, and depending on the type of institutions and organizations in which they are employed, lawyers, accountants, and psychotherapists may have the option not to work with particular clients.

The degree of power and control practitioners hold over workplace decisions is one of the most important criteria distinguishing the degree of professionalization and the status of a particular occupation or line of work (Freidson, 1986). Professionalized employees usually have control and autonomy approaching that of senior management when it comes to organizational decisions surrounding their work. University professors and other academics, for example, often have equal or greater control than that of university administrators over the content of their teaching and research, over the hiring of new colleagues and, through the institution of peer review, over the evaluation and promotion of members and, hence, over the ongoing content and character of their profession. Members of lower-status occupations usually have little say over their work. The data show that in comparison with traditional professions, teachers have only limited power and control over key workplace decisions that affect their work.

This hierarchy in schools is both understandable and consequential, given the nature of the work of teachers. Schools are not simply formal organizational entities engineered to deliver academic instruction and schools do not simply teach children reading, writing, and arithmetic. Schools are a major mechanism for the socialization of children and youth, a process captured in the contemporary concept of social capital (see chapter 9). The task of deciding which behavior and values are proper and best for the young is not trivial, neutral, or value free. Hence, it is no surprise that those who do this work—teachers—and how they go about it are matters of intense concern. Indeed, underlying the accountability movement is the understandable assumption that education is far too important to be left up solely to educators.

As a result, teaching is an occupation beset by tension and imbalance between expectations and resources, responsibilities, and powers. On the one hand, the work of teaching, helping prepare, instruct, and rear the next generation of children is both important and complex. But on the other hand, those who are entrusted with the training of this next generation are not entrusted with much control over many of the key decisions concerned with this crucial work. Moreover, the data suggest this imbalance is increasing. After little change from the late 1980s to 2000, levels of individual teacher classroom autonomy in schools across the nation, especially in regard to the selection of texts, content, topics, and evaluation of students in their courses, have decreased in the past decade.

THE TEACHER IN THE MIDDLE

Control and accountability can be exerted in a wide range of different ways in schools, as in other workplaces. These are not necessarily a matter of direct and obvious mechanisms, such as rules and regulations, incentives and sanctions, "sticks and carrots." Indeed, organizational analysts have long held that the most effective mechanisms by which employees are controlled and held accountable are often embedded in the day-to-day culture of the workplace and, hence, are often taken for granted and invisible to both insiders and outsiders alike (Perrow, 1986). This is reflected in the role of teachers in schools. Teachers are akin to men or women in the middle. A useful analogy is that of supervisors caught between the contradictory demands and needs of their superiors, school administrators, and their subordinates, students. In this analogy teachers are not typically part of the management of schools, nor are teachers the workers. Teachers are in charge of, and responsible for, the workers—their students. While teachers are allowed limited input into crucial decisions concerned with the management of schools and into crucial decisions concerned with their work, teachers are delegated a great deal of responsibility for the implementation of these decisions. Like middlemen and -women in other occupations, teachers usually work alone and may have much latitude in seeing that their students carry out the tasks assigned to them. This responsibility and latitude can easily be mistaken for a kind of professional-like autonomy, especially in regard to tasks within classrooms. A close look at the organization of the teaching job shows, however, that while it involves the delegation of much responsibility, it involves little real power.

The motives, values, and aspirations of those entering teaching dramatically differ from those entering many other occupations. An unusually large proportion of teachers are motivated by what is called an "altruistic" or "public service" ethic. Such individuals place less importance on extrinsic rewards (such as income and prestige) and less emphasis on intrinsic rewards (such as intellectual challenge or self-expression) and more importance on the opportunity to contribute to the betterment of society, to work with people, to serve their community, to help others, in short, to do "good." Numerous studies over the past several decades have concluded that those entering teaching are more likely to value service and less likely to value pecuniary rewards than are those entering most other occupations, including law, engineering, natural or social science, sales, advertising, business, architecture, journalism, or art (Farkas, Johnson, & Foleno, 2000; Lortie, 1975; Miech & Elder, 1996; Rosenberg, 1957/1980).

This altruistic ethic, combined with teachers' mixed role of great responsibility along with little power is reflected in the widespread practice among teachers of spending their own money on classroom materials. Teachers often find, for various reasons, that their school does not, or will not, provide the curriculum materials, stationery, and supplies they deem necessary to do an adequate job with their students. The national data show that teachers have little access to, or control over, school discretionary funds. They must request these monies through administrative channels, a sometimes frustrating and unsuccessful experience. As a result, teachers commonly pay for such materials out of pocket.

Since 1989 there have been a half dozen different national surveys documenting this phenomenon. For example, in analyses of SASS data from the 2007–8 school year, I found that teachers had spent, on average, about $395 of their own money the prior year for classroom supplies, without reimbursement. Only 9% of teachers reported spending none of their own money that year for such materials. Notably, this commitment and public service was not merely a matter of youthful idealism; the data show that older and veteran teachers spent more of their own money, on average, than did younger and beginning teachers. Moreover, public school teachers spent more than did private school teachers and teachers employed in high-poverty schools spent more than those in low-poverty schools.

These data on out-of-pocket expenditures illustrate a remarkable responsibility, commitment, and accountability on the part of individuals, in the face of a remarkable lack of responsibility, commitment, or accountability on the part of the organizations and publics that employ these individuals. The data suggest that in that year alone, a workforce of teachers, mostly female, numbering almost 4 million, donated over $1.5 billion of educational materials to schools! This kind of teacher public service and subsidization of the school system received unprecedented recognition in federal legislation, proposed by the George W. Bush administration in 2001, to provide tax deductions to teachers for their out-of-pocket expenditures for classroom materials.

Teacher financial subsidization of public schools is all the more notable because teaching is a relatively low-paying occupation. The SASS data indicate that in 2007–8 the average starting salary in public schools for a teacher with a bachelor's degree and no teaching experience was about $32,000 and the average maximum salary possible at the end of one's career was $61,000. The salaries of new college graduates who become teachers have long been consistently and considerably below those of new college graduates who choose many other occupations. For example, the average salary (one year after graduation) for college graduates who become teachers is typically almost 50% less than the average starting salary of their classmates who take computer science jobs (Ingersoll & Merrill, 2011). Moreover, this disparity remains throughout the career span. Teachers' salaries are less than those in many other lines of work and far less than those of most traditional professionals. For instance, data from the Bureau of Labor Statistics show that in 2007 the average annual salaries of teachers were less than one-third of the average annual salaries of physicians, less than one-half those of lawyers, and about two-thirds those of college and university professors in the arts and sciences. Using these salary data, it is possible to make a crude calculation of an equivalent level of personal out-of-pocket accountability and public service for these professions. The $395 estimate for teachers represented almost 1% of the average school teacher salary that year. Thus, a rough equivalent of average out-of-pocket expenditures for the purchase of materials necessary to serve their clients would come to (in 2007 dollars) about $630 a year on the part of professors; about $1,100 a year for lawyers; and about $1,500 a year for doctors.

THE DIFFERENCE THAT TEACHER CONTROL CAN MAKE

What difference does the amount of teacher control over their work make for how well schools function? Does increasing the amount of influence exercised by teachers in schools have a positive or negative impact on life inside schools?

From the public's viewpoint, a safe and harmonious environment in schools is as important as academic achievement. From much of the public's viewpoint the "good" school is characterized by well-behaved students; a collegial, committed staff; and a general sense of cooperation, communication, and community. Likewise, the "bad" school is characterized by conflict, distrust, and turmoil between students, teachers, and administrators. Problems of student discipline; lack of respect for teachers; improper behavior in classrooms; and conflict, distrust, and turmoil between teachers and administrators have long been considered of great importance to parents; however, in recent years increased concern over school violence has made these even more prominent. To evaluate some of the consequences of teacher control and influence, I undertook a series of advanced multilevel regression analyses of the SASS data focusing on the relationship between the amount of control and power held by teachers and these kinds of school climate outcomes. In these analyses I controlled for the effects of other school characteristics, such as school size; student poverty levels; whether a school is in an urban, rural, or suburban setting; and whether it is private or public and also for other teacher characteristics, such as experience, fields, gender, and race.

I found in my analyses that, after the characteristics of schools and teachers are held constant, school problems are directly connected to the distribution of power and control in a wide range of schools. The data show that, while most schools are centralized, there is substantial variation in the degree of teacher control among different kinds of schools and the latter is strongly linked to how well schools function. Schools where teachers have more control over key schoolwide and classroom decisions have fewer problems with student misbehavior, have more collegiality and cooperation among teachers and administrators, have a more committed teaching staff, and do a better job of retaining their teachers.

However, I also found that the effects of teacher control and influence on these outcomes varies by the type of decision or issue involved. Interestingly, the data show that one of the most consequential sets of decisions has to do with a particular group of nonacademic issues—school and classroom student behavior and discipline policies. For instance, I examined the relationship between the average amount of teacher influence over decisions concerned with school and classroom discipline issues and the likelihood that teachers stay in or depart from their schools. In order to focus on those kinds of departures that were more likely to be related to the character of schools, I excluded from the analysis teachers who departed their jobs because of retirement, layoffs, or school closings or because of being fired or terminated. I found that teacher control over such issues in a school is very strongly related to the percentage of turnover. Almost 1 in 5 teachers in schools with a low level of teacher control over student discipline issues was likely to depart, while far fewer, less than 1 in 20, was likely to do so from schools with a high level of teacher control over such issues.

Why is teacher control over this particular set of issues so consequential? The data also indicate that teachers have substantial responsibility for the enforcement of student behavioral and discipline rules and for maintaining an orderly school and classroom. But the data tell us that teachers often have little input into schoolwide behavioral and disciplinary rules, norms, and standards for students; they are largely conceived by others. And teachers often have little say over the types of sanctions used to enforce these rules. For example, teachers are often not allowed to remove students who are disrupting their classrooms, teachers often must first obtain permission to sanction a student infraction, and teachers are often not allowed to punish students who are caught cheating on tests. These limitations on teacher control can also undermine their ability to be in charge of their classrooms and to meet their responsibilities. The data suggest that this lack of control also leads to high turnover rates.

At the crux of the role and of the success of teachers, as the man or woman in the middle, is their level of control and power over the tasks and issues for which they are responsible. On the one hand, if teachers have sufficient say over the decisions surrounding those activities for which they are responsible, they will be more able to exert sufficient influence to see that the job is done properly and, in turn, derive respect from administrators, colleagues, and students. On the other hand, if teachers' power and control over school and classroom policies is not sufficient to accomplish the tasks for which they are responsible, they will meet neither group's needs and will sour their relationships. The teacher who has little control and power is the teacher who is less able to get things done, is the teacher with less credibility. Students can more easily ignore such a teacher; indeed, timidity seems to invite challenge. Principals can more easily neglect backing them. Peers may be more likely to shun them. This, in turn, could lead such teachers to feel less commitment to their teaching job or the teaching career.

BALANCING POWER AND ACCOUNTABILITY

The accountability perspective, and many of the reforms to come out of it, commonly suffers from several problems. The first involves the accuracy of their diagnosis. The data show that the high degree of centralization in schools and a lack of teacher control of their work, rather than the opposite, is often the source of problems in how well schools function. As a result, these kinds of top-down accountability reforms may divert attention from the organizational sources of school problems.

Second, accountability reforms are sometimes unfair. For instance, proponents of top-down accountability reforms often overlook the unusual character of the teaching workforce. It is common among these analysts and reformers to subscribe to a teacher deficit viewpoint assuming that the blame lies with the caliber of individual teachers. A litany of such critics has told us again and again that teachers lack sufficient engagement, commitment, and accountability. But the earlier data suggest that teachers have an unusual degree of public service orientation and commitment and a relatively high "giving-to-getting" ratio, compared with many other occupations. Unrecognized and unappreciated by these critics is the extent to which the teaching workforce is a source of human, social, and even financial capital in schools.

Third, for the preceding reasons accountability reforms often don't work. Top-down reforms draw attention to an important set of needs—accountability on the part of those doing the work. But these kinds of reforms sometimes overlook another equally important set of needs, the autonomy and goodwill of those doing the work. Too much organizational control may deny teachers the very control and flexibility they need to do the job effectively and undermine the motivation of those doing the job. A high degree of centralized control may squander a valuable human resource—the unusual degree of commitment of those who enter the teaching occupation. Having little say in the terms, processes, and outcomes of their work may undermine the ability of teachers to feel they are doing worthwhile work, the very reason many of them came into the occupation in the first place, and end up contributing to the high rates of turnover among teachers. As a result, such reforms may not only fail to solve the problems they seek to address but also end up making things worse.

There is no question that there are problems with the quality of teachers and teaching. Moreover, it is neither convincing nor valid to simply pass most of the blame for low-quality teaching and educational failure elsewhere, for instance, onto families. Proponents of accountability in schools are right; schools, like all organizations designed to serve the collective needs of the public, need to be accountable to that public. However, the accountability perspective typically offers only a partial, one-sided explanation and as a result often overlooks the ways schools themselves, and in particular how they are managed and organized, contribute to the teacher quality problem. In plain terms, simply recruiting quality candidates and holding them more accountable will not solve the problem of quality if the manner in which the job itself is organized and managed undermines those same candidates.

Experts on organizational management and leadership (e.g., Whyte & Blasi, 1982) have long advocated a balanced approach. Accountability and power must go hand in hand in workplaces, and increases in one must be accompanied by increases in the other. Imbalances between the two can result in problems for both the employee and for the organization. Delegating power to employees or management without commensurate responsibility is irresponsible and can even be dangerous and harmful. That is, giving teachers more power alone is not the answer. Likewise, accountability without commensurate power is unfair and can also be harmful. In other words, it does not make sense to hold employees accountable for something they do not control, nor does it make sense to give someone control over something for which they are not held accountable. Both these changes are necessary, but neither alone is sufficient. Promising examples of this more balanced model or school organization have sprung up in recent years. For example, there is a growing network of charter schools in the Midwest that are operated and run by teachers (Kolderie, 2008). These schools are often referred to as "partnership schools" because they are modeled after law partnerships, where lawyers, as professionals, both manage and ultimately are accountable for the organization and its success (Hawkins, 2009). From this alternative perspective, solving the problem of teacher quality will require addressing the underlying roots of the problem. The focus of reform would need to shift from solely getting (or producing) "better people for the job" to also getting "a better job for the people" (Kolderie, 2008). Rather than solely focusing on trying to force the existing arrangement to work better, this alternative view suggests the importance of viewing teacher quality issues as organizational and occupational design issues, suggesting the necessity of a different arrangement, better built for those who do the work of teaching.

REFERENCES

Bennett, W. (1993). *The book of virtues*. New York: Simon & Schuster.

Farkas, S., Johnson, J., & Foleno, T. (2000). *A sense of calling: Who teaches and why*. New York: Public Agenda.

Freidson, E. (1986). *Professional powers: A study in the institutionalization of formal knowledge*. Chicago: University of Chicago Press.

Hawkins, B. (2009). Teacher cooperatives: What happens when teachers run the school? *Education Next, 9*, 37–41.

Ingersoll, R. (2003). *Who controls teachers' work? Power and accountability in America's schools*. Cambridge, MA: Harvard University Press.

Ingersoll, R., & Merrill, E. (2011). The status of teaching as a profession. In J. Ballantine & J. Spade (Eds.), pp. 185-198 in *Schools and society: A sociological perspective* (4th ed.). Belmont, CA: Wadsworth Press.

Kolderie, T. (2008). *The other half of the strategy: Following up on systemic reform by innovating with school and schooling*. St. Paul, MN: Education Evolving.

Levin, H. (1998). Education performance standards and the economy. *Educational Researcher, 27*, 4–10.

Lortie, D. (1975). *School teacher*. Chicago: University of Chicago Press.

Miech, R., & Elder, G. (1996). The service ethic and teaching. *Sociology of Education, 69*, 237–253.

Mills, C. W. (2000). The sociological imagination. New York: Oxford University Press. Original work published 1959.

National Center for Education Statistics. (2005). *Schools and staffing survey (SASS) and teacher followup survey (TFS)*. Washington, DC: U.S. Department of Education.

Perrow, C. (1986). *Complex organizations: A critical essay*. New York: Random House.

Rosenberg, M. (1980). *Occupations and values*. New York: Arno Press. Original work published 1957.

Sadker, M., & Sadker, D. (1994). *Failing at fairness*. New York: Scribner.

Urban League. (1999). *The state of Black America*. New York: Urban League.

Whyte, W. F., & Blasi, J. (1982). Worker ownership, participation, and control: Toward a theoretical model. *Policy Sciences, 14*, 137–163.

CHAPTER 6

In Search of Equity

Teacher Tracking in Math

Colette Cann

Education production function research is concerned with identifying and quantifying the effect of various school resources (such as small student-to-teacher ratios, teachers with many years of experience and high-quality facilities) on student performance and well-being. Such research informs educational policy, evaluation, and budgeting. Applied estimates of teacher effects generated by districts and states certainly have great practical relevance in the work lives of teachers. The greatest line item expense in any school budget is teacher salaries, and teacher evaluations and merit pay are based increasingly on value-added estimates. Value-added estimates of teacher effectiveness may mean, quite literally, the difference between tenure and a pink slip. Most recently, value-added estimates have become the difference between public humiliation and glorification, as the media prepares to print the rankings of teachers who add value (or not) to student test scores (Felch, Song, & Smith, 2010).

Although value-added teacher estimates continue to be used in high-stakes ways, I argue in this chapter that they tell us more about a teacher's ability to politick for preferred high-level courses than about his or her teaching ability. In particular, this research looks at the teacher assignment process in high schools to understand why and how teachers are assigned to particular classrooms. Prior research indicates that teachers have not been historically, nor are they presently, distributed equitably across districts, schools, or classrooms. Yet while existing research shows that inequitable distribution is the norm, it offers few clues about why and how this occurs. In this chapter, I review the research on teacher tracking looking at both the quantitative research that explores the distribution of teachers across schools and the qualitative research that examines the tracking of teachers within schools.

In addition, I offer new findings from a qualitative study to deepen our understanding of the district- and school-level dynamics at play in teacher tracking. Specifically, I look at the contexts of districtwide equity reform, math as a subject area, and departmental politics in teacher tracking. Finally, this chapter considers the implications of these new findings for research and practice.

WHAT 50 YEARS OF RESEARCH TELLS US ABOUT TEACHER TRACKING

The Inequitable Distribution of Teachers Across Schools

Despite their importance to student achievement, there is substantial literature that finds that "high-quality" teachers are not equitably distributed across schools. A review of this literature reveals that indeed the least qualified of the teaching force are disproportionately assigned to regions, districts, schools, and classrooms populated by low-income or low-performing students or students of color or a combination. In a report conducted by the Public Policy Institute of California, Betts, Rueben, and Danenberg (2000) analyzed data from the California Department of Education to describe the distribution of teachers across schools. With regard to teacher resources, measured as years of experience, highest level of education attained, and possession of a full teaching credential, Betts et al. found that some schools employed a disproportionate share of teachers with less experience, less education, and less than a full credential. These same schools with less qualified teachers also had less of their share of other resources. Betts et al. also found that these resources were predictably distributed across rural, urban, and suburban areas and according to the socioeconomic status of the student body (as measured by percentage of students who participate in the free and reduced-price lunch program). For example, urban schools had fewer experienced, credentialed teachers than did both rural and suburban areas (suburban areas had the highest percentage of teachers who were most qualified). This discomforting pattern of staffing continued in looking across schools with varying levels of socioeconomic status. Schools enrolling low-income students had a higher percentage of teachers who were not fully certified, had only a bachelor's degree (or less), and had less than two years of experience.

Also using years of experience as a proxy for teacher quality, Clotfelter, Ladd, and Vigdor (2005) examined the skewed distribution of new, inexperienced teachers. They hypothesized that if less experienced, and therefore less qualified, teachers were inequitably distributed across classrooms and districts according to student body composition, then opportunities to make substantial gains in a year's time were accordingly distributed. This had serious implications for equity concerns in schools. Clotfelter et al. found that across districts, teachers were indeed unevenly distributed according to years of experience. Schools with higher percentages of students of color had higher percentages of teachers with no prior teaching experience. This finding held and was statistically significant even when controlling for income level, geographical location (rural, urban, or suburban), and the size of the district. However, this finding alone did not draw an accurate picture of teacher staffing inequalities, since there are many aspects of teacher work conditions that vary across districts. When looking across districts, researchers also look across labor markets. Different salary scales, for example, might influence the distribution of teachers as much as student populations. Thus, Clotfelter et al. also looked within districts to observe the distribution of teachers across schools. In doing so, they found that across schools, African American students had a higher probability of being exposed to inexperienced teachers than White students in both math and English. This probability increased for African American students when they limited their analysis to schools within urban school districts.[1]

Using a large, descriptive database, Lankford, Loeb, and Wyckoff (2002) tracked the careers of 180,000 teachers across schools within the state of New York to study how teachers were distributed across schools by their qualifications (educational background and teaching experience). They created school-level averages of the following teacher characteristics to use as variables for teacher quality: teaching experience, certification status, certification test scores, the selectivity of the teacher's undergraduate institution, highest level of education achieved, and whether or not the teacher passed the certification exam on the first attempt. They examined how these teacher characteristics were related to student body characteristics and how teachers were distributed across schools, districts, and labor markets. They found that teachers were inequitably distributed across schools according to the geographical location of the school, ethnic background and income level of the students, and the average achievement level of the students. Specifically, they found that the least qualified teachers (i.e., teachers with the fewest years of teaching experience and who attended the least selective undergraduate institutions) were disproportionately employed at urban schools with low-income students of color. They also concluded that most of the variation in teacher qualifications occurred across school districts within the same region and across schools within the same school districts.

Wayne (2002) used measures of teacher academic skill as a proxy for teacher quality. Assuming that teachers with less academic skill were less effective in the classroom, Wayne argued that results from his study had implications for how the opportunity of students to learn may be disproportionately distributed across groups of students. Using two separate national data sets, Wayne found that teachers with lower scores on entrance exams and who attended less selective colleges were disproportionately concentrated in schools with higher percentages of low-income students.

Sunderman and Kim (2005) found in California that although 48% of all core classes were taught by qualified teachers, only 35% of classes in schools educating low-income students were taught by qualified teachers as compared with 53% of classes at their wealthier counterparts. Disparities in teacher qualifications such as levels of education, years of experience, and credential levels were also found between schools educating low-income populations of color and those serving student populations that were primarily White and wealthy.

In an observational study, Bruno (2002) compared rates of absenteeism at different schools, illuminating how substitute teachers (considered less qualified than full-time teachers) were distributed across schools and how school budgets were affected at schools with higher rates of absenteeism. Bruno used status as a substitute teacher as a proxy for being underqualified because there were fewer training, education, or experience requirements for substitute teachers. Further, substitute teachers often did not have access to lesson plans and materials needed to conduct class sessions. Bruno found that the location of a school in "negative geographic space," neighborhoods with more crime, poverty, students of color, and lower test scores, was related to higher rates of teacher absenteeism,[2] as well as more unfilled substitute teacher positions. He also found that full-time teachers with less experience and less than a full credential were disproportionately represented at these same schools. Importantly, students at schools with lower-quality teachers indeed had lower test scores than students at other schools.

Teacher Tracking within Schools

Thus far, I have described how teachers are distributed across schools. I now turn to research that examines the allocation of teachers to classrooms within schools. It is appropriate to begin this discussion with a review of Finley's seminal 1984 case study of a tracked high school, since subsequent studies of teacher tracking build on her work. Finley conducted a case study of an English department in a school she called Suburban High School.

Within the context of a community struggling to desegregate its schools while maintaining its structure of privilege, Finley introduced Suburban High School. In the late 1960s, this high school was described as a "good" high school, one that enrolled a student population that teachers desired to work with. Subsequently, a desegregation mandate increased the population of minority students at Suburban. The English department responded by tracking students within the school along race and class lines. As the student population became more racially and economically diverse, the school curriculum, particularly in the English department, became more differentiated. At the time of her case study, Finley found that most students of color and low-income students were found in low-level English courses. The teachers at Suburban considered the new low-track classrooms undesirable. The tracking of students created the opportunity for an informal career ladder at Suburban as teachers sought to secure the desirable high track classrooms. That is, teachers could now increase their intrinsic rewards by teaching the "good" classes—those with White, wealthy students left over from the days when Suburban was considered a good school.

Teachers described students in the "good" classes as highly motivated, hardworking, and likely to attend high-ranking colleges and universities. They had few absences and rarely missed assignments. Further, these students were described in terms of the type of skills they demanded of teachers, namely, the ability to academically challenge students with stimulating discussion questions that required higher-order thinking. Alternatively, students in remedial classes were perceived as difficult to motivate, lacking in long-term college plans, often absent, failing to complete assignments, and unenthusiastic about learning. School staff believed that the low-track classrooms required teachers who were more like police officers—teachers who could control students' behavior while attempting to teach them a little along the way. Low-track teachers were challenged by disciplinary problems, rather than by the intellectual demands of their students. Teachers at Suburban believed the rewards of teaching a classroom of remedial students were few and far between.

Through political maneuvering, teachers with more seniority and who had garnered a reputation for themselves managed to secure the highly desirable classes. These teachers created their own advanced classes or inherited other advanced classes outside the official allocation process. Even within the official allocation process, these more powerful teachers encouraged students and parents to pressure the administrators to give them more desirable classes. When less desirable students found their ways into these teachers' classrooms, these students were removed through subtle means such as constant behavioral referrals or discouragement. Teachers with the least amount of power, part-time teachers in the department, new teachers, and the least educated teachers were given what was left over, despite an official policy of distributing the desirable and undesirable classes equitably to all teachers. Instead of such an arrangement, Finley found "student resources" (here defined as classes with easy-to-work-with students and the accompanying intrinsic rewards) were inequitably distributed across teachers.

This tracking of teachers had adverse effects on both the teachers and students in low-track classes. Teachers of these classes came to feel that they deserved those classes, since they did not have enough intellectual knowledge of the subject or enough experience to teach advanced courses. The students in these courses were exposed to an inferior and substandard curriculum as well as the least experienced and least knowledgeable teachers. Importantly, Finley argued that reforms such as merit pay and career ladders (designed to differentiate teachers by status) were "unlikely to touch these teachers because their very association with these students makes it unlikely that they will be singled out as good teachers worthy of either merit pay or status as master teachers" (p. 242). Finley's (1984) model of teacher tracking finds support in Kelly's (2004) quantitative study of teaching assignments.

In a later study of the micro contexts of school and math department cultures, Yu and Talbert (1994) considered how and why lesser-qualified teachers found their ways into classrooms with the weakest math students and how their assignment to these courses guaranteed that they would remain unqualified teachers. Yu and Talbert found that in some departments, official administrative and department policies conspired to create an assignment policy that tracked teachers by background characteristics among highly differentiated math courses. These departments were described as ones with "rigid assignment patterns" (low rotation of teachers among high level courses) (p. 18). Teachers blamed this on the fact that there were only a few teachers in their department who were capable of teaching the higher-level courses. Yet the rigidity belied the fact that the department was doing little to train low-ability teachers to be able to teach higher-level courses.

Other math departments did a better job of evenly distributing high-track courses among teachers and of training teachers to be able to teach the most academically demanding classes. These departments had highly desirable work conditions, as well as qualified math teachers and low levels of attrition. The fact that a greater percentage of the teaching staff had a background in math allowed the departments to rotate levels of courses among teachers from year to year. Yu and Talbert described these departments as "organized to advance" students and teachers (p. 19). These departments invested in moving teachers and students through increasingly difficult levels of math.

FACTORS INFLUENCING TEACHER COURSE ASSIGNMENTS: THE CASE OF THREE SCHOOLS IN A NORTHERN CALIFORNIA SCHOOL DISTRICT

The Three High Schools

The study that I conducted, reported here, builds on the work of Finley and Yu and Talbert to give more depth to the inner workings of schools and teaching assignments. Such research informs the modeling of teacher effects; for researchers to control for the nonrandom assignment of teachers to students, they need to understand more about how they are presently assigned. While Finley discussed teacher tracking in English and language arts, researchers need to understand how teachers' preferences and assignment policies work in math departments. Math is a high-status subject area, standardized tests are concerned with this subject area, and it factors heavily into most value-added models. Making use of administrative, historical, observational, and interview data, this chapter looks at three high schools within a district experiencing equity reform; thus, this study can speak to how differently tracked schools respond to equity mandates. I consider the implications of teacher tracking for increasing student access to opportunities to learn; issues of equity and social justice arise in the distribution of valuable resources such as highly qualified teachers.

In this study, I worked with over 20 math teachers at three high schools in a northern California school district, Eastland Unified School District (EUSD)[3] from May 2002 through May 2004. Eastland City, in which the district is located, has a rich racial and sociopolitical history characterized first by waves of Chinese American and African American immigration prior to and during World War II, a wave of White flight in the postwar era, and social upheaval during the civil rights era of the 1960s and 1970s. At the time of this study, EUSD had six large comprehensive high schools in the district, of which I selected three for this study: Madera, Pinewood, and Ingleside high schools.

Madera High School. Madera served an underperforming (only 7% of the student body was proficient in math), low-income (63.7%), and primarily African American and Latino population (over 99% of the student body was composed of students of color) in Eastland. Considering this district's tumultuous relationship with its communities of color, it was important to include a school context that reflected this historically difficult relationship. This school also employed the least experienced math teachers in the district. Madera High School's student population reflected the characteristics of schools that prior research has shown receive the least qualified teachers, namely, a school with a high percentage of African American students and a low percentage of students performing above the 50th percentile on standardized tests. Though Madera has the smallest student population at 1,723 students, it has the highest dropout rate (16.3%).

Pinewood High School. Pinewood enrolled one of the highest percentages of White students in the district and served the wealthiest neighborhood of Eastland City. Math teachers at this school were relatively experienced—none were substitute teachers and all but one had been at the school more than a year. Reputed as a safe campus located in the wealthy Hills area of the city, Pinewood opened in the 1960s amid controversy over how the attendance boundaries were drawn to include mostly students from the Hills area. Test scores and grade point averages of students, particularly in math, were above those of students at Madera (36.8% of the student body was proficient in math and the Academic Performance Index Base Score of Pinewood was 610, as compared with 422 for Madera). Academic performance on standardized tests in this school is among the highest in the district. This school also included more sections of math honors classes than the other two schools combined.

Ingleside High School. Ingleside served a racial and socioeconomically diverse student population—diversity that extended to academic performance. Ingleside High School represented a school where the extremes existed *within* its walls. In addition, the teachers at this school were also fairly experienced and had worked within the district for many years (with a couple who had transferred to Ingleside from Madera). Ingleside was also a top-tier secondary school in EUSD with a reputation for sending students to 4-year institutions. Yet, as this school is located halfway between the lower-income neighborhood of the Corridor and the upper-income neighborhood of the Hills, it struggled at times with issues similar to those at Madera.

ORGANIZING FOR EQUITY: THE SOCIOPOLITICAL CONTEXT OF TEACHER TRACKING IN MATH

Within the context of California's math state standards and admissions requirements for its competitive state universities, EUSD created equity policies designed to increase the access of African American and Latino students to upper-level math courses. A long history of de facto residential and school segregation had limited educational opportunities for African American, Asian American, and Latino students. Although Eastland's school board formally voted to end de jure segregation in its public schools in the late 1800s, over a century later, EUSD still struggled with de facto segregation that concentrated lower-income youth of color in Corridor schools. A history of residential isolation, wartime migration, and fights over the boundaries of neighborhood schools triggered seemingly intractable school segregation and accompanying inequities in resources.

Eastland similarly has a history of political activism; residents concerned about how this segregation affected the academic opportunities of lower-income students of color worked steadily to combat inequities in the school system. In the 1990s, the efforts of these residents to increase the academic opportunities and achievement of all students resulted in a call for equity policies that brought the district math curriculum *at all schools for all students* in line with the state curriculum and universities' admissions requirements.

By September 1998, all high schools were required to offer math courses that fulfilled state universities' entrance requirements as well as upper-level math courses such as calculus (which only a few high schools had previously offered). In response, high schools cut all math courses that did not meet eligibility requirement for admissions into a state university; thus, all math courses below Algebra 1 were cut from the math program. All freshmen were required to take Algebra 1 (unless they had taken it in middle school), regardless of whether they had the necessary background math skills. I refer to this program as the "Algebra for All" program.

The result of the Algebra for All program was that the student characteristics of the courses changed dramatically after its implementation. An influx of students previously assigned to Math A and pre-algebra courses (primarily students of color) were suddenly placed in Algebra 1. Further, Algebra for All was rejected almost across the board by math teachers in the district. Students failed Algebra 1 at high rates (as high as 70% in the first year) and few teachers wanted to teach these courses. A few years after implementation, the district retreated from its reform efforts and split the one-year Algebra 1 course into an Algebra A/B 2-year sequence. Again, African American and Latino students were concentrated in these lower-level math courses.

Math Teachers' Preferences for Courses and Students

Math teachers' preferences for higher-level courses are, in part, informed by district-level equity reforms, particularly, those reforms designed to increase access to college preparatory coursework. Math teachers' preferences are also, though, affected by the cultural norms of their subject matter. Such norms structure how they view teaching, their students, and educational issues (Siskin, 1994). Contributing to the formation of this cultural norm is that math teachers, unlike teachers of other subjects such as foreign language, science, and social studies, have the same disciplinary training; they undergo a socialization process that informs their ways of thinking about the organization of their subject, their students, and even themselves. Thus, they are more likely to be consistent in how they think about their subject area.

Further, math as a high school subject has clear and well-defined curricula and courses of study. Despite debates over how topics should be taught, the high school math curriculum has been relatively stable since the turn of the 20th century. History courses, by contrast, vary substantially across schools. For example, some schools offer African American history, while others do not. Unlike in the social sciences, what "counts" as math is not contested at the high school level (Stodolsky, 1993).

Moreover, math is a high-status subject. Math courses are required for graduation, higher-level courses serve as a gatekeeper to academic opportunity beyond high school, and it is a subject tested on state standardized exams. As a high school subject, it is also sequential and hierarchically organized. Each course in the curriculum, with few exceptions, is a prerequisite to the next course in the sequence. And math teachers are more likely than science teachers, for example, to believe that mastery of one course is required for success in subsequent coursework.

And finally, as a subject area with a host of required coursework, the math department serves *every* student in the high school at one point. They see students at all ability levels and with varying levels of interest for their subject. Students are more highly differentiated in math than in other subject areas (Kelly, 2007).

In my interviews with math teachers, they elaborate on aspects of math students that influence their interests in teaching particular courses. In addition, they discuss how the district's math equity mandate affects the composition of math courses in ways that create spaces that are less desirable to teach. Finally, although most teachers prefer to teach high-track math classes, I also explore exceptions in my sample—those teachers who prefer and request to work with students in lower-track math courses.

Classroom Demographics and Ways of Being a Student. The math teachers in this study are consistent in regard to what they express as accepted student ways of being in the classroom. Whereas movement, unsolicited interjections, and creative input might be accepted in other disciplines, math teachers describe "proper" student behavior in very specific and detailed ways—from what students put on their homework papers to how students should talk to teachers. In all, there is a common culture of math seen across all three schools in this study. Students who are well versed in the culture of math and fluent in the academic discourse of the subject have access to opportunities in the tracking system. Beyond knowing the math content, academically successful students also know the rules of engagement, communication, and discourse in the classroom. And overwhelmingly, math teachers want to work with these students.

Javier Agostino, a 1st-year fully credentialed teacher, describes this classroom expectation. What distinguishes the Algebra 1 students from the students in the higher-track courses are behavioral responses to what he describes as the primary mode of instruction in upper-track math courses (a didactic, lecture-based teaching style):

> I feel like I need more experience to be good at [teaching Algebra 1] because what you find in the general algebra is all the students that other teachers have given up on. And it's not that they can't do it. It's not like they're stupid or whatever. It's that they don't have certain skills or they don't *understand the behavioral expectation*. No one has ever done that with them and they don't have a supportive home.
>
> It's harder to teach those students. It's easy to teach calculus. That's why the calculus classes are bigger. You can have like 40-something in calculus because *they all sit there quietly. They have their books, the materials, calculator, everything they need.* And *they're paying attention.* [They say], "[I'm] ready. Give it to me. I want to go to college." So the teacher just stands in front, does a few examples, you know.

Sunil Chandra, a veteran teacher at Ingleside, more pointedly argues that the ways of being a math student are associated more with behavior than with math competency. He links this behavior with experience and age, as Algebra 1 students are more likely to be 9th-grade students and students in the 9th grade have other social realities associated with becoming teenagers to contend with:

> I think the algebra is basically a structural issue. . . . I think the students don't have the structure to really, the habits to really study right in a course of algebra. In other words, they can't sit still for a very long time. They have to move around. They have to talk around and they have all kinds of other things happen and it's not that the course is difficult. It's that they're not really structured to sit down and say, "Okay. I'm going to sit down and do it." Their listening capabilities need to be improved so that when a teacher is talking,

> they are listening. Because they don't listen as good because their mind is wandering in all kinds of other places and they're different kinds of issues in the first course of algebra. . . . So in algebra class we really have a different issue altogether. It's a structural issue. It's a behavioral issue. Your mind is not focused. You're not listening very carefully to what's being said.

Chris Patchett, a Teach for America teacher in the 2nd year of his commitment and 1st year at Pinewood, describes the ways of being of students in his advanced core course in the following way:

> The students in that class are really motivated. If they see something they don't know, they're *listening*. So I don't have to ask, "[Does everyone understand?]" And *especially* when they see something they don't know.

Students who know how to be students know to listen when they don't understand. They know to pay particular attention when they see something new that they don't know how to do. These visible manifestations of being a good math student indicate to this teacher that he is working with a group of motivated students who are in class to learn.

Response to Equity Mandate. Already hesitant to teach students in lower-level courses because those students don't exhibit traditional ways of being math students, teachers were further discouraged from teaching lower-track courses by the equity mandate (Algebra for All). Teachers argue that reform policies, such as Algebra for All, introduce a range of student ability in the class that is challenging for teachers to create lesson plans for. Further, students who are not prepared, skillwise, for the content of a more challenging course are unable to access the material in a meaningful way. Sunil Chandra even mentions that he feels that he compromises the material and himself to teach watered-down content to students who are not truly prepared for algebra. Policy decisions at the district level to push students into algebra regardless of skill level and prerequisite knowledge have forced teachers to confront the reality of students who struggle with the course content.

> *Colette*: Which of the three courses did you find the most challenging to teach . . . ?
>
> *Daniel Schorr:* I think I'd . . . say the 9th-grade algebra—doing the Algebra for All—because trying to keep students engaged in the class and moving forward with the material was what I found

> most challenging in both those years. I mean, there are some students who probably actually did finish their algebra course the year before and should've been in geometry, but were advised to repeat algebra. And they were always at the top of the class. So, for them, they would do whatever the assignment for the day was with no problems. *But for those students who probably should never have been in the algebra class, I'm trying to get them engaged with the material and so forth and making that jump to symbolic logic and so forth was the challenging part.*

The equity mandate had repercussions for the way that teachers experience courses that sequentially follow Algebra 1. Steeped in the culture of his academic discipline, Nick Sanders, a new teacher to EUSD (although an experienced high school math teacher), feels that the boundaries between levels of math were breached:

> There are problems with Advanced Algebra, too, but more with Intermediate Algebra. My understanding is that more than half the students in Intermediate Algebra failed Algebra 1 and were passed on. The overwhelming majority of the students in my Intermediate Algebra class have, I don't think it's an exaggeration to say, no algebraic skills. They seemed to have learned zero in Algebra 1, zero in geometry and are on some maybe 3rd- or 4th-year level in terms of arithmetic. Many can't do simple arithmetic. I'm afraid to use 2-digit numbers. . . . They are not ready for Algebra 2. . . . You can have the state saying that algebra is a requirement. You can have the district saying that 2 years of algebra and a year of geometry are a requirement. And you will be able to, you know, to flash statistics which show that you have it. But, it doesn't matter. It doesn't mean a thing.

Social Justice Teachers: The Exception to the Rule. While the overwhelming majority of teachers in my sample preferred to avoid lower-level math courses, particularly Algebra 1, there were two teachers who came into the teaching profession specifically to work with students in lower-track math courses. Both teachers were relatively new to teaching and came from preparation programs with a focus on education as social justice work. The first teacher, Michelle Schumer, was a 2nd-year Teach for America teacher. Michelle stated that she truly enjoys teaching Algebra 1, despite the fact that she struggles with classroom management. She entered the teaching profession because she enjoys teaching, not because she enjoys math. In her interview, she made this point emphatically: It is the mentoring aspect of working with youth that engages her intellectually and provides the challenge that she desires. Mentoring and teaching, she believed, happen more at the lower levels of math than at the upper levels.

Javier Agostino, a 1st-year teacher from a progressive local university credential program, entered the teaching profession to make a change in the life outcomes of students in need, particularly African American and Latino youth in Eastland. Earlier we heard from Javier that the upper-track courses, in his opinion, were easier to teach. Despite this, he enjoys teaching the lower-track courses and, in fact, came into teaching to work with youth in lower-track math courses. As a teacher with a social justice agenda, he believes that, *politically*, the work that he needs to do is with students in lower-track classes.

As seen in EUSD, teachers for the most part resisted the math equity mandate because it challenged their notions of how math should be organized and taught. More likely than other subject area teachers to believe that students must master lower levels of math before being promoted, math teachers in this study resisted the Algebra for All mandate that placed all students (regardless of background) into Algebra 1. Not only were students unprepared to take this course (from their perspective), but students in this lower-level course were not fluent in the cultural norms of math. Thus, the equity policy to implement a more rigorous curriculum for all students regardless of race and socioeconomic status did not succeed in changing how teachers thought about math or about students. This reform left intact traditional, math-specific ways of relating to students and to bodies of knowledge. Where the equity reform at the district level failed to inspire teachers to request lower-level courses, the social justice framework of preparation programs succeeded. Although inexperienced and struggling in their classes, teachers with a social justice perspective requested and remained committed to students in Algebra 1.

High School Math Departments as Context: Three Departments, Three Identities

While teachers in general prefer higher-level courses, they cannot always garner a schedule filled with their preferred courses, as these more advanced math courses are in demand within the department. In this section, I turn to the allocation of higher-level math courses to consider, at the department level, how preferences of teachers are mediated.

Subject-matter departments affect the everyday work lives of teachers (Siskin, 1994). Relevant to the present analysis, teaching assignments often originate in the academic department and are mediated by an *intra*departmental, micropolitical process. While seniority and background characteristics of teachers (credentialing and training) certainly play a role in the assignment process (Kelly, 2004), across all three departments, I find that the policies of *attention to fairness, politicking,* and *multiple credential status* are also important aspects of the assignment process. However, across the three schools, local context affected assignment processes such that no two processes were exactly alike.

At Madera, math teachers, because of the overall organization of the school, are spread out across three buildings. Students are grouped in the various buildings by grade level. Freshmen and teachers of courses that enroll freshmen are located in one building. Characterized by chaos and increased volume, this building eventually placed a guard in the building to police student movement and behavior in the hallways.

Efforts to separate the math teachers by grade level into different buildings, a focus on looping (a policy of teachers' staying with the same group of students for 2 years), and increased centralization efforts have decreased the strength of the department chair and the ability of the department to organize for its own political purposes. Instead, the Madera administrative team makes all decisions about the assignment of math teachers to courses. While they do allow input from teachers, the department chair does not have a say in the assignment of teachers to courses. Rather, in the assignment of teachers to classes, the administrative team is guided by the school policy of looping and "credential eligibility" of the teacher (site administrator, Madera High School).

Thus, administrative and organizational concerns drive the process of assigning teachers to courses. Yet teachers do have some input in the process; they are asked about their preferences for teaching particular courses. Also, there is politicking. To the contrary, Madera is a site of micropoliticking that takes place behind closed doors and through individual teacher maneuvering. Aria Chateau, the department chair, gives an example of this "behind closed door" politicking. Even after officially placing her request for courses on the request form, she lobbied her case with the administrator in charge of teacher assignment:

> Well, I wrote it on there *and then I went and bugged the principal and the administrators*. And I said, "Please, I want to move up." And then they're like, "Okay."

Jeffrey Berg moved from Madera to Ingleside High School because, at Madera, he had been confined to lower-level courses. First, as a strong disciplinarian, he did not have classroom management issues. The administration assigned strong disciplinarians to lower-track math classes. Second, Madera did not offer many upper-level courses while he was there. The opportunity to grow into more advanced classes simply was not there.

> I'm here at Ingleside having an opportunity to more rapidly be able to teach some of the higher-end courses than I did at Madera. I understood what was going on at Madera. And that was fine but it is good to be able to teach a variety of courses because if you don't use it, you lose it even as someone who has that background.

Madera participated in whole-school reform during the following (2005–06) school year. They transitioned into contiguous small schools organized around a theme and grade levels. Teachers applied to particular small schools for the 2005–06 school year. This provided a unique opportunity for strategizing. Kelly Vesela, a teacher at Madera, provides an example:

> Well, to make sure that I don't get moved down to a 9th-grade (class), I would apply to an upper-division (school) so that at least my lowest-level class would be geometry. I would have no problem taking a geometry class because I love it. I'd have to just secure that for myself. I don't know if it was because it was my 1st year or I don't know if it was because of the book that I had, [but] I just hated teaching Algebra 1. I just struggled with it. Not in the sense that I didn't know how to teach it. Well, in the sense that I didn't know how to teach it so that people would understand it.

Ingleside's academic campus is composed of one large building, a smaller building near a garden, and several small trailers on either side of the track behind the main building. The large building has two stories, with long hallways, students moved between classes in a flow of enthusiastic teenage chatter, ringing cell phones, and bantering with security guards and administrators. Hallways during classes retained some students who lagged behind to talk to friends or, avoiding security guards, to skip class.

Generally, math teachers were grouped together (two to three teachers were in proximity to each other). Most were located in the main building. There was a level of assumed collegiality among teachers in this department. Teachers were generally aware of the work of others in their department and there was an overall sense of friendliness among the teachers. Yet there were no overt efforts to collaborate or in-depth involvement in each other's work. Department meetings, few and far between, were used to handle business affairs.

As department chair, Martin Henry exhibited quiet control over his department. He handled administrative work efficiently and tried not to unnecessarily impose on his peers. His involvement in recruitment and hiring depended on the administration. Ingleside had a high turnover rate of principals; some principals called him in for the interview process and others did not.

Martin had been a member of the faculty at Ingleside for over 10 years. During his tenure, he served as department chair twice, once early in his career with the school and, most recently, this past year. He currently advocates a policy of fairness to all members of his department in the assignment process, a stance influenced by his experience under the leadership of another department chair. He recalls well the history of the assignment process in his department when "good courses" were handed out to friends of the department chair, an ethos he now actively rejects. Recently the department as a whole set the goal of becoming a teaching force that could teach "up and down the ladder," meaning all teachers could teach all courses offered. Specifically, teachers were not forced to teach beyond their comfort level in the upward direction, but all teachers were required to teach at the low end.

While he did not have the final say about the scheduling of his teachers to math courses, Martin Henry exerted much influence. He first solicited course requests from teachers before making a preliminary assignment schedule. Then, taking these requests into account, he moved courses around so that each teacher had some "up-rank" (higher-track courses). He hoped to avoid having any teacher "stuck" in all required core courses. As department chair, he noted that he could probably get away with giving himself only up-rank courses. Yet, to be fair, he also took a spread of courses. In fact, he taught six different preps in the 2nd year of the study.

> Nobody's going to get the perfect schedule. They try to provide people with a schedule that they're going to be sort of happy with, comfortable with, and I think enthusiastic about as opposed to I don't want anybody to feel like dread. Right? So, very often, say, if you have a teacher who really doesn't like necessarily teaching lower-level classes very often, they have a couple of top-end classes. They don't mind because they feel like, "I have energy to do that."

The downside to "spreading courses around" to make sure that teachers have both higher-level and lower-level classes was that, in order to make that happen, teachers had more than two preps. Their union contract required that teachers had no more than two preps. Yet teachers at Ingleside were willing to take on additional preps in return for having advanced courses in their schedule. A third priority in the assignment process (behind teacher preference and spreading courses around) was to make sure that teachers had the opportunity to teach courses 2 years in a row so that they could master teaching those courses. In all, the chair hoped that his policies would create a department that could teach up and down the ladder.

Jeffrey Berg, who previously taught at Madera, describes his experience of the assignment process at Ingleside:

> At Ingleside I've been comfortable with the process. The intention of the department is to . . . I guess in a way live up to teachers having fundamental-through-more-advanced courses in their teaching in some kind of balance, in some kind of mix. So I think the intention of this math department is that teachers can do exactly that—teach at multiple levels. . . . And I think that's good. It's refreshingly good.

Generally, teachers in the Ingleside math department believe that the assignment process is fair to themselves and to their peers. They have faith in their leadership to create a schedule that balances the desires and capabilities of all teachers. Teachers in this department have bought into the fairness ethic exhibited by their department chair. His institutional memory of an assignment process based on personal connections encouraged him to create a fair process of sharing rewards (advanced courses). All teachers now shared in the burdens of more challenging-to-teach courses (lower-level classes), while also getting at least one or two courses that are more desirable to teach.

Yet there was a subset of teachers at Ingleside who were disadvantaged in course assignments—teachers with bilingual credentials (BCLAD) and science teachers teaching math classes out of field. BCLAD certification locked teachers into teaching structured English immersion courses (which were mostly lower-track math classes), as they were the only teachers in the department who could teach those courses. The other teachers whose preferences were disregarded outright were the "honorary members" of the math department. Teachers certified in science could take "singleton math classes"—classes that were left over after assignments had been made to math teachers. Although one of these two teachers requested high-track math courses year after year, he rarely got any. Although luck of the draw often determined what would be left over, high-track classes were never singletons.

Pinewood is located on a sprawling campus in the Hills area of Eastland. Overlooking the city and surrounded by towering conifers, the campus is composed of several single-story buildings with portables concentrated at the rear of the campus. Over 70% of the math teachers are congregated in the southeastern portion of the campus; seven occupy portables. Of the remaining four teachers, two are located next door to each other in a building on the north side of campus. Pinewood would turn out to be as different from Madera and Ingleside in its course assignment process as it is in physical layout, location, and reputation.

At Pinewood, the department, *as a group*, worked to design a schedule that they could agree upon. The teachers took myriad things into account when creating the teacher course schedule. For example, they looked at what the school needed, how many sections of each course were needed, and how many students would be taking which math courses the following year. Teachers were then asked to write down their "dream schedule" and the department co-chairs took those schedules to look them over. The department co-chairs then called another meeting during which teachers, *as individuals*, negotiated for course schedules.

The co-department chair, Gregory Quinley, noted that the department meeting, when they discussed the assignment of mathematic teachers, was well attended. Attendance at this meeting was not mandatory; however, for a teacher to ensure that he or she got a desirable course schedule the following year, attendance was unofficially required. Teachers were responsible for representing their own interests in the negotiation process at this meeting. According to Quinley:

> It's very interesting because we have department meetings throughout the year. When we do the one to select your courses for next year, that's the height of interest for any meeting. I mean people come to the other meetings but this one they really want to be there and sometimes people aren't and *they don't always get the best schedule if they're not there kind of lobbying for themselves. For a lot of people they are very motivated to get certain classes because it can make a big difference. If you get a certain class, it can make your day really tough.*

Teachers considered different factors in the negotiation process. Not all teachers requested high-track classes, particularly if they were novice teachers, because it was unlikely they would have had enough political power in the department to successfully lobby for advanced core courses. In these instances, teachers negotiated for other desirable aspects of a course schedule such as having only one prep or *not* teaching Algebra 1 or the Algebra A/B sequence. One teacher, for example, requested courses other teachers *did not want*, but that were not the least desired of offered courses. Another teacher requested all Algebra 1 courses so that he would have only one prep for the school year.

A veteran teacher credentialed in both science and math, Lionel Malone is a particularly savvy politician in the math department. Experience has taught him how to maneuver the system such that he can protect his own interests without alienating his peers:

> *Lionel Malone:* But what made me choose math . . . [was that] the principal asked me if I would consider teaching physics instead of math. And I said I would. But I said, "What else do you have in that assignment?" And this goes to your research because when she said, "Ninth-grade physical science," I lost interest unfortunately.
>
> *Colette:* When she said, "Are you interested in teaching physics," it was a package deal? It came with something else?
>
> *Lionel Malone:* Yes.
>
> *Colette:* I'm just intrigued. What made you ask that question? What made you think that it might come with something else?
>
> *Lionel Malone:* Because it generally does. It's pretty rare to teach five physics classes.

After many years as a teacher in various schools, he has come to understand how rare a full schedule of upper-level classes is and how unlikely it is that a teacher can avoid teaching lower-level classes. He has navigated these waters successfully (defined as avoiding as many low-level classes as possible) primarily by moving into the math field rather than working in both math and science or just science, where there were fewer opportunities for a schedule with high-track classes.

As at Ingleside, credential and training limitations affect course schedules. However, the focus at Pinewood is on the training necessary to teach advanced placement (AP) courses. This requirement influenced assignment policy mostly at Pinewood, as Madera, for example, did not offer any AP math courses. Scott Tanzi at Pinewood explained how this limitation affects the process:

> There are several classes, like calculus that are the calculus series. Not everybody can really get them even though you're qualified because [there is] this training that people go through [to be able to teach] the AP classes. . . . So unless you've gone through that, those things you don't even ask because they'll say, "Do you have the training," [and you'll have to reply], "Not yet." So you have to wait until you go through those things.

Ultimately though, departmental autonomy, and thus teachers' individual control over their course schedules, was constrained by administrative oversight. Teachers invested considerable time in deciding their ideal schedule. And the principal took the schedule they created under advisement. The administration, though, was not obligated to use this suggested schedule. Final authority over course schedules rested solely with the front office, and they exercised that authority as needed.

The math departments at Madera, Pinewood, and Ingleside can be contrasted on four dimensions: physical proximity of teachers, role in hiring process, participation in assignment process, and level of competition among department members for desired courses (see Table 6.1). At Madera, the math department was fragmented, was spread across the campus, and lacked a political power to select classes for its members. The department chair at Madera played a limited role in the recruitment and hiring of teachers for her department. Thus, creating a department of like-minded teachers could not occur through the recruitment process. Further, the department chair and teachers at Madera did not play a direct role in the creation of the assignment schedule; while they did give the administrator their preferences and lobbied for courses they wanted to teach, they did not participate in shaping the overall schedule. There were no negotiations that took place among department members. There were no opportunities for direct competition for courses, although politicking through the administrator did occur. This differs dramatically from the assignment processes at Ingleside and Pinewood.

At Ingleside, though teachers were located close to at least one other math teacher, they did not have the type of community that nurtured professional development. Despite this, the department culture encouraged a policy of fairness directed by the department chair. Teachers considered what was fair to students, to other math teachers and to themselves. Members of the department echoed the ethos of the department chair that teachers should not be stuck with less desired classes. The teacher buy-in to these philosophies of fairness and teaching "up and down the ladder" was so strong that they agreed to teach more than two preps even if it violated their contractual rights.

Teachers at Pinewood, though congregated for the most part together, exhibited the most competitive assignment process. In the Pinewood math department, the politicking took on the most extreme form, as they had a physical arena in which negotiating took place. Teachers could "make grabs" or "take possession of" desired courses. The co-department chairs organized the assignment process and worked as mediators in the negotiations for classes. Yet they did not have the power to truly assign teachers to courses. The administration at Pinewood exerted a powerful influence over the assignment processes (as well as the initial hiring of math faculty).

In the assignment process for each department, preferences of teachers played a critical role. Further, the individual character and context of each

Table 6.1. Characterization of Assignment Processes for the Three High Schools

<table>
<tr><th>Factors Affecting Assignment Processes</th><th>Madera</th><th>Ingleside</th><th>Pinewood</th></tr>
<tr><td>Physical separation of teachers' classrooms on campus:</td><td>High</td><td>Medium</td><td>Medium</td></tr>
<tr><td colspan="4">High: Teachers rarely inhabit the same building. Official policy on campus promotes segregation of teachers from the same department.

Medium: Teachers are occasionally in the same building. There is no official policy dictating teacher location on campus.

Low: Every effort is made to congregate math teachers in the same area of campus to encourage cooperation.</td></tr>
<tr><td>Role of department chair in hiring</td><td>Minimal</td><td>Minimal/ Advisory</td><td>Advisory</td></tr>
<tr><td colspan="4">Minimal: Department chair and other members of the department are rarely invited (or rarely are able) to participate in the recruitment, interviewing, and observation of candidates.

Advisory: Department chair and members of the department are solicited for referrals and occasionally invited to interview and observe candidates.

Critical: Department chair takes on full responsibility for recruitment and hiring responsibilities.</td></tr>
<tr><td>Level of autonomy of the department in creation of the assignment schedule</td><td>Low</td><td>High</td><td>Medium</td></tr>
<tr><td colspan="4">High: Department chair works with teachers to create a schedule that is submitted and accepted by the outside administrator.

Medium: Department chair works with teachers to create a schedule that is submitted as a suggestion to outside administrator (who makes minor changes).

Low: Administrator outside of the department creates the schedule based on teacher preferences.</td></tr>
<tr><td>Level of competition among teachers in the assignment process</td><td>Medium</td><td>Low</td><td>High</td></tr>
<tr><td colspan="4">High: Teachers are in physical proximity to each other as the schedule is made. Individuals are given a chance to give their preferences, but the final process is done in a politicized arena.

Medium: Teachers are not in physical proximity to each other in the assignment process. Teachers are unaware of the preferences of others and do not express a desire for fairness in the process. Decisions for requests are based on individual preferences and negotiations with the administrator only.

Low: Teachers are not in physical proximity to each other in the assignment process. However, they express an awareness of the preferences of others and a desire for a process that is fair to all teachers.</td></tr>
</table>

department also played a role. Yet there were also similarities across all departments. In each, soliciting teacher preferences was the first step in the assignment process. Further, policies of fairness and certification limitations influenced the assignment process. Politicking also played a role in the assignment process. Whether negotiations were mediated by department chairs or done face-to-face in a department meeting, department assignment policies could be manipulated by savvy teachers to ensure more favorable assignment schedules.

CONCLUSION

Math coursework is stacked in a hierarchical fashion that sheds students at each successive level. The students who remain exhibit ways of being math students whom teachers value and reward through higher grades and teacher recommendations to advanced coursework. This includes "good" classroom behavior, knowing how and when to take notes, independent learning styles, and having necessary materials ready and at hand at the start of class. Teachers overwhelmingly desire working with such students and believe that a schedule filled with advanced courses is an easier and more rewarding schedule.

And just as teachers in Finley's study fought against working with students of color bussed into their school following desegregation mandates, teachers in this study fought equity mandates. Math teachers in this study desire to teach high-track courses because they believe that students in these classes have earned their way into those classes and have a grasp of the knowledge necessary to succeed in those courses. Unlike high-track courses, Algebra 1 enrolls students who have been placed there as a mandate of the district's new equity policy. Math teachers in this study argue that these students are inappropriately placed in a course for which the latter do not have the requisite knowledge base. Thus, the equity mandate comes into conflict with these teachers' deep beliefs about how math is learned and what knowledge is necessary for students to succeed.

In contrast to Finley's findings, while English teachers could create new high-track seminars that could exclude these new students, math teachers have less leeway in this area. Their courses are more stringently defined, pushing them to find other ways to politick and maneuver within the department. Moreover, I found that for a small group of teachers, the equity mandate matched their vision for their own teaching. Teachers who come to teaching with a desire to teach students rather than teach a subject and who, most important, come to teaching with a desire to teach the students most in need, are the teachers who value a schedule that has a high concentration of lower-track courses. These teachers take on the work of teaching as a manifestation of how they can form positive and caring relationships with youth and as a way to transform the world.

These findings have implications for research on school effects. The debate about whether resources such as teachers "matter" began in the 1960s with the Coleman Report (Coleman et al., 1966) and took on an elevated presence in the 1980s with Hanushek's seminal meta-analysis (1989) and Hedges, Laine, and Greenwald's rejoinder in their 1994 article aptly titled "Does Money Matter?" While the production function has become more sophisticated in its modeling, it is still largely a discussion about resources and their importance to student achievement as measured by test scores. But production function research (as well as the teacher effects measures used frequently in school finance, teacher evaluation systems, and resource adequacy and equity court cases) often assumes a random assignment of teachers to classrooms. Unlike other resources typically considered in school effects studies, teachers play an integral role in their own allocation to student characteristics. This nonrandom assignment of teachers to students makes it difficult to ferret out the relationship between teacher characteristics and student achievement. Researchers cannot with certainty claim that any covariation between teacher characteristics and student achievement travels in the direction of teachers to students; it is possible that teachers with more experience and higher degrees *choose* to teach students with higher academic achievement. Researchers conducting teacher effects studies often hypothesize about the possible nonrandom assignment of teachers to classrooms; this present study not only confirms these assumptions, but also highlights the particular sociopolitical, subject-matter, and department contexts in which this nonrandom assignment is mired.

So too are there implications for teachers and administrators in this era of increased accountability. As evidenced by the teacher evaluation bill passed recently in Colorado (Banchero, 2010), the effects of teachers on student learning have taken on a new relevance in the lives of teachers. In Colorado, for example, teachers' tenure now rests on their ability to continually have a positive effect on student learning as measured by gains on test scores. The present study of school-level labor markets informs the use of value-added measures in two ways: First, the findings cast doubt on the accuracy of value-added measures, both because of nonrandom assignment of teachers to students and because of how low-track teaching assignments affect teachers; second, teacher tracking undermines teachers' faith in the ability of value-added models to identify "effective" teachers. There is still too much subject matter and local, site-based context responsible for the pairing of teachers with classrooms to reliably assume the nonrandom assignment of teachers to classrooms upon which much value-added modeling continues to rely. I found that for reasons related to subject matter, math teachers prefer to work with high-track students and politick fiercely to teach those courses. Thus, a teacher's value-added may be more a reflection of his or her ability to secure high-track classes than his or her talents and efforts in the classroom. Moreover, when left to teach lower-track math courses, courses that enroll students who stand to make the most gains (and thus, ironically, present the greatest potential for being identified as highly effective), they may not take full responsibility for the learning of their students. Steeped in subject-matter context, they see little hope that any action on their part can increase the outcomes for students who have not "mastered" earlier math concepts.

Teacher tracking also has implications for teacher buy-in to reforms based on value-added models. More likely to believe that learning is hierarchical than other subject teachers, math teachers may be less likely to believe that value-added measures tell them anything about their ability to teach; rather, they may surmise, the measures are more likely to reveal a student's lack of readiness to enroll in a math course.

This research, too, has implications for efforts to create greater opportunities for students to learn. We see time and again that organizational attempts to create greater opportunities to learn for all students hits a wall, falling short of its goal to make real, sustainable change for students. As seen in Eastland Unified, equity policy to implement a more rigorous curriculum for all students regardless of race and socioeconomic status did not succeed in changing how teachers thought about math nor about students. This reform left intact traditional ways of relating to students and to bodies of knowledge. However, hope exists in teachers with a social justice orientation; as they gain teaching experience, they may offer to lower-track math students both their experience and their desire to teach these classes. This research suggests that we consider engaging teacher belief systems and practices in addition to implementing equity mandates to create the change we desire.

NOTES

1. Clotfelter et al. (2005) made another interesting, if not unsurprising, finding. Districts with the least amount of segregation between African American and White students had the most even distribution of inexperienced teachers across schools.

2. Bruno hypothesized that teachers in schools in negative geographical space have more stressful, less desirable work conditions, causing them to use most of if not all their sick days. These schools responded by making heavier use of substitute teachers.

3. All names are pseudonyms.

REFERENCES

Banchero, S. (2010, May 14). Teacher-evaluation bill approved in Colorado. *The Wall Street Journal*. Retrieved from http://online.wsj.com/article/SB1000142405274870395080457524248316467 7818.html

Betts, J. R., Rueben, K. S., & Danenberg, A. (2000). Equal resources, equal outcomes? The distribution of school resources and student achievement in California. *Public Policy Institute of California*. San Francisco: PPIC.

Bruno, J. (2002). The geographical distribution of teacher absenteeism in large urban school district settings: Implications for school reform efforts aimed at promoting equity and excellence in education. *Education Policy Analysis Archives, 10*(32). Retrieved from http://epaa.asu.edu/epaa/v10n32

Clotfelter, C. T., Ladd, H. F., & Vigdor, J. L. (2005). Who teaches whom? Race and the distribution of novice teachers. *Economics of Education Review, 24*, 377–392.

Coleman, J. S., Campbell, E. Q., Hobson, C. J., McPartland, J., Mood, A. M., Weinfeld, F. D., et al. (1966). *Equality of educational opportunity*. Washington, DC: U.S. Government Printing Office.

Felch, J., Song, J., & Smith, D. (2010, August 14). Who's teaching L.A.'s kids? *Los Angeles Times*. Retrieved from http://articles.latimes.com/2010/aug/14/local/la-me-teachers-value-20100815

Finley, M. K. (1984). Teachers and tracking in a comprehensive high school. *Sociology of Education, 57*, 233–243.

Hanushek, E. A. (1989). The impact of differential expenditures on school performance. *Educational Researcher, 18*, 45–51, 62.

Hedges, L. V., Laine, R. D., & Greenwald, R. (1994). Does money matter? A meta-analysis of the effects of differential school inputs on student outcomes. *Educational Researcher, 23*, 5–14.

Kelly, S. (2004). Are teachers tracked? On what basis and with what consequences. *Social Psychology of Education, 7*, 55–72.

Kelly, S. (2007). The contours of tracking in North Carolina. *The High School Journal, 90*, 15–31.

Lankford, H., Loeb, S., & Wyckoff, J. (2002). Teacher sorting and the plight of urban schools: A descriptive analysis. *Educational Evaluation and Policy Analysis, 24*, 37–62.

Siskin, L. S. (1994). *Realms of knowledge: Academic departments in secondary schools*. Washington, DC: Falmer Press.

Stodolsky, S. S. (1993). A framework for subject matter comparisons in high schools. *Teaching and Teacher Education, 9*, 333–346.

Sunderman, G. L., & Kim, J. (2005). *Teacher quality: Equalizing educational opportunities and outcomes*. Cambridge, MA: The Civil Rights Project at Harvard University.

Wayne, A. J. (2002). Teacher inequality: New evidence on disparities in teachers' academic skills. *Education Policy Analysis Archives, 10*(30). Retrieved from http://epaa.asu.edu/epaa/v10n30

Yu, H. C., & Talbert, J. E. (1994). *Labor force conditions of high school math departments: Inequalities and the mediating effects of teacher community*. Stanford, CA: Center for the Research on the Context of Secondary Teaching.

CHAPTER 7

Teacher Education and Accountability

Adapting to Prospective Work Environments in Public Schools

Judson G. Everitt

Since the passage of the No Child Left Behind Act (NCLB) in 2002, ensuring there is a highly qualified teacher in every classroom has been a key component of accountability mandates in the United States. Teacher education is integral to this policy, as it provides the chief means by which states, districts, and schools meet this mandate of the law. In particular, university-based teacher education programs play a vital role, given that over 80% of incoming teachers acquire their certification in these programs, and thereby credential themselves as highly qualified under the law (U.S. Department of Education, 2006). Ample research on teacher education, however, finds that there is no guarantee of teacher quality among those who complete these programs. In fact, studies show that university-based teacher education does a poor job of equipping teacher candidates with the knowledge and skills necessary for their prospective work in public schools (Levine, 2006). As a result, teacher education programs are commonly blamed for failing to adequately train new teachers, and likewise, for failing to hold up their end of the bargain in improving our schools by improving teacher quality.

Rather than lay this blame entirely at the feet of teachers and teacher educators, however, we also have evidence that the problem of teacher quality may be as much in how the law defines it, as it is in how teachers are trained. I argue that our education policies should be more consistent with the ways that educators themselves—both teacher candidates and teacher educators—view the educational process. I show evidence in this chapter that what it means to be an "effective" teacher is much more locally defined than NCLB acknowledges. Effective teaching, according to teacher candidates, becomes defined through their training as the ability to adapt to the contingencies that students and schools throw at them on a daily basis. Teachers must make their own judgments on how to overcome challenges posed to them by forces beyond their control in order to accomplish their work goals with students. Such a perspective makes good professional sense among teachers, as it does among those in other lines of work.

To set the stage for the findings I present in this chapter, and highlight the disjuncture between NCLB mandates and teachers' work "on the ground," a brief comparison between teachers and physicians might be useful. Johnson (2011) and others have compared teachers to doctors in order to gain insight into school accountability and how this might affect teacher work conditions, and I outline a similar analogy here. Imagine if the U.S. federal government passed a very different type of health care reform from the bill recently signed into law. The alternative system (established by the "No Patient Left Behind Act") mandates that all licensed physicians now be responsible for ensuring that all their patients achieve an equal, minimum level of health within the next 10 years. Under this law, all practicing physicians must have completed a medical degree from an accredited institution to attain licensure and the "highly qualified" status the new law requires. Moreover, physicians and the organizations that employ them must meet mandates of reaching "adequate yearly progress" (AYP) toward their goal of achieving an equal, minimum level of health among all their patients. If physicians do not meet AYP 2 years in a row, they and the practices, hospitals, or health maintenance organizations (HMOs) for which they work are labeled as "failing" by the state, which can then sanction them. The guiding principle of the new law is that if the state simply holds physicians more accountable for their patients' health, the health-care industry will become far more effective in guaranteeing that we have a healthy, productive citizenry.

Now imagine how medical professionals might respond collectively to such a policy. Existing debates about health care aside, it is rather safe to say that the prospect of being held "accountable" for an equal, minimum level of health would draw vehement protest on the part of physicians. We can imagine the likely bases for their opposition to such a policy. First and foremost, doctors would likely cite myriad factors affecting their patients' health over which they as physicians have absolutely no control. Even if we set aside issues like diseases for which there is no known cure, there remain all manner of social factors affecting different people's health that are rooted in conditions outside doctors' offices. Just to name a few, people have different occupational hazards, differential access to resources for a healthy diet and exercise, and varying amounts of stress from work and social relationships, all of which decidedly affect individuals' physical and mental health. Physicians can recommend to their patients the proper lifestyle habits for good health, but they cannot control the structural conditions that create health disparities by social class, among other social differences. As such, physicians would likely make the strong case that it would simply be unrealistic, unreasonable, and unfair for the state to label them as failing in their profession when they do not overcome health disparities among their patients, the sources of which they themselves are powerless to change.

Yet this is precisely what the No Child Left Behind Act has done to teachers. We know from all manner of research that family socioeconomic background is the most important factor affecting educational success, which is not to say that schools and teachers don't sometimes interact with families in ways that serve to aggravate class inequalities (e.g., Lareau, 2003). While we certainly must be attentive to the role schools and teachers play in perpetuating schooling inequalities, it is quite another thing to expect teachers to eliminate these inequities when we know they reflect, and are linked to, a wider system of social stratification. Indeed, many teacher organizations have reacted to the No Child Left Behind Act in ways similar to the hypothetical example I have described. Of course, there are many differences between the teaching and medical professions. I use this comparison simply to highlight a key structural condition currently influencing teacher education and the ways teacher candidates make sense of their prospective work in schools, namely, structured inequality in public education, and to raise concerns about the accountability system intended to eliminate it.

In this chapter, I present a view of teacher training from inside a university-based teacher education program, and I emphasize what this training process means to the people going through it. I spent over a year following the same group of teacher candidates through the conclusion of their coursework, through their student teaching experiences, and into their job search. Based on extensive field notes and interview data, I show how teacher candidates develop the perspective that adaptation in their work is of central importance to performing their future work roles with students. Teaching, newcomers learn, is inherently unpredictable and dynamic work, constantly influenced by contingencies beyond teachers' control, to which they nonetheless must adapt. I also show that teacher candidates develop a widely shared service ethic to students that equips them to benefit students' educational success by increasing their attachment to school. However, as I discuss in the conclusion, these elements of teaching are largely excluded from current measures of teacher performance under accountability mandates. As such, there is a fundamental disconnect between what the law defines as a "highly qualified" teacher and what the teachers in this study define as "effective" teaching based on their training. I further discuss these policy implications in the concluding section of this chapter.

GENERAL CHARACTERISTICS OF TEACHER EDUCATION

Teacher training is most commonly controlled by university schools of education, despite the availability of alternative routes to teacher certification such as Teach for America (U.S. Department of Education, 2006). Teacher education programs have certainly received their share of criticism. According to much of the available research, education coursework largely focuses on theories of student development, learning, and cultural diversity, which many teacher candidates feel they cannot apply practically to their classrooms (Britzman, 1991; Labaree, 2004). Similarly, studies find that methods coursework does not consistently match the realities of classroom instruction with students (e.g., Hargreaves & Jacka, 1995); in other words, many teacher candidates find their coursework to be more theoretical than practical and thus do not internalize it to guide their teaching practice. Student teaching is more practical and gives preservice teachers firsthand experience in the classroom. Many preservice teachers value this experience. However, its benefit depends largely on the relationship teacher candidates have with their supervising teacher; such relationships are individual and the placement process is beyond preservice teachers' control. Consequently, student teaching is a training experience that varies widely from person to person (e.g., Calderhead & Shorrock, 1997).

Prior studies find that teacher candidates draw upon their personal relationships—especially with former teachers—to inform their early perspectives on teaching. Lortie (1975) refers to this phenomenon as the "apprenticeship of observation." Students identify with their favorite teachers and develop perspectives on the work of teaching based on imitation. Such relationships are personal and affective rather than analytical; in other words, students judge effective teaching by their positive relationships with teachers as opposed to assessments of effective teaching practice. Studies find that the predispositions teacher candidates develop as students are quite strong (Britzman, 1991; Liston & Zeichner, 1991). Scholars argue that this contributes to the relative lack of uniformity among teachers, since preservice teachers base perspectives on their individual relationships and experiences rather than on collective knowledge of practice. In this sense, these scholars claim that teacher candidates resist much of the content of their coursework in favor of preserving their beliefs based on their individual experience.

If we turn our attention to the other literatures on adult and professional socialization, however, we see alternative ways in which people develop perspectives on their future work. In their classic study on professional socialization in medicine, Becker, Geer, Hughes, and Strauss (1961) find that medical students develop perspectives largely through student cultures. Through collective interactions, medical students construct shared meanings regarding the level and direction of effort in medical school as well as their future roles as doctors. They also find that students' perspectives often differ substantially from the expectations of medical school faculty (Becker et al., 1961). While such findings expand upon functionalist theories of professional socialization (e.g., Merton, Reader, & Kendall, 1957), additional studies find that student cultures can foster both resistance and conformity depending on school and professional context (Garnier, 1973; Schleef, 2006). Teacher candidates appear to differ from students in other professional fields (i.e., medicine, law, business, military) in that they have relatively weak peer group ties during their formal training. As such, the influence of student cultures on preservice teachers' perspectives may be relatively low, a condition further contributing to their relative individualism as an occupational group.

Studies on professional socialization generally—and teacher training specifically—have focused on the perspectives entrants develop, but few studies have explicitly focused on professional socialization as a long-term process of social transition. Corsaro's work on early childhood, and theory of interpretive reproduction, highlight the importance of peer cultures as vehicles for how individuals make sense of the social world and actively reinvent the social conditions in which they are immersed (Corsaro & Molinari, 2000, 2005; Entwisle & Alexander, 1999). Building on Merton's (1968) concept of "anticipatory socialization," Corsaro and Molinari (2000, 2005) identify "priming events" in children's processes of transition from preschool to elementary school. Such events "involve activities in which children, by their very participation, attend prospectively to ongoing or anticipated changes in their lives" (2005, pp. 17–18). To be sure, individuals at all stages of the life course experience transition processes (Elder, 1994; Furstenberg, Cook, Eccles, & Elder, 2000), and the concept of priming events could be readily applied to analysis of adult transitions. In the case of teachers, their formal training constitutes a period of transition from the role(s) of student to that of teacher (Britzman, 1991) and largely coincides with the transition from the role(s) of adolescent to that of professional adult. Teacher candidates experience multiple priming events during coursework and student teaching that prepare them in some way for the work of teaching; moreover, such priming events emerge in social interaction that is necessarily enabled and constrained by social structures (Corsaro & Molinari,

2005). Empirical analysis of preservice teachers' transitions through formal training would contribute to a sociological understanding of the ways new teachers make sense of their prospective careers within the complex interplay of institutional and cultural conditions affecting teachers' work. Specifically, I focus on the concrete ways that accountability mandates and conditions of public schools shape the professional socialization process for prospective teachers.

THE EXPERIENCE OF TEACHER CANDIDATES IN UNIVERSITY-BASED TEACHER EDUCATION

In order to study teacher education from the perspective of the people going through it, I followed a sample of 49 teacher candidates over a 15-month period as they performed and completed their training. These teacher candidates include those training for both elementary education as well as secondary education. Among those in secondary education, the sample includes candidates in math, language arts, and social studies. I regularly observed their coursework and student teaching and interviewed them multiple times, as well as the faculty and teachers who supervised them. They include women and men in elementary and secondary education and across subject matters, and they performed their student teaching in a wide range of schools, including in both urban and rural areas.[1]

The Injunction to Adapt

Teacher candidates learn in their formal training a range of strategies for planning and executing their instruction. Many elements of these strategies are quite consistent among teacher candidates across different subject matters and grade levels. For instance, templates for lesson plans that all teacher candidates must use consistently require that they state learning objectives, connect to state standards, and include some form of both student-centered activities and guided practice from the teacher. Also, general strategies of pedagogy such as "scaffolding," the practice of building on what students already know to teach them new concepts or skills, were things that all teacher candidates were taught repeatedly in their training. As such, unlike prior studies of teacher education that claim the content of teacher education is chronically inconsistent (e.g., Levine, 2006), the candidates whose profiles are reviewed here show that there are basic principles of pedagogy that are consistently communicated to teacher candidates.

Within this general framework, however, teacher candidates are strongly encouraged to choose lesson plans from a variety of options and adapt them to fit their specific classroom needs. I refer to this central element of teacher candidates' training as the "injunction to adapt." Throughout their professional socialization, teacher candidates are primed to adapt their own practices to their individual classroom environments. A variety of concurrent routines and activities contribute to this perspective throughout their transitions though training, and it reflects specific structural conditions of public education. This adaptation perspective is consistent across teacher candidates in different grade levels and subject matter.

Course Work Routines and Prospective Work Environments

Teacher candidates are first exposed to the injunction to adapt in their coursework and interactions with education faculty through routines that are designed to help them think prospectively about their future work. However, we also see evidence of limited coordination in the different pedagogies and lesson plan models that are available to teacher candidates as they prepare for future work with students. In this excerpt, the faculty member (Bob) is explaining a major lesson-planning assignment to a class of teacher candidates in secondary mathematics.

> [Bob pulls up the template the website uses for lesson plans.] Here you can get a look at their template for lesson plans. . . . I actually don't like their objectives. These objectives are things that people do; they're not learning objectives. For example [pointing to example lesson plan on screen], analyze a report, they don't say what students will learn by doing this . . . make sure you actually write learning objectives. . . .
>
> Refer to your pink sheet; I want to go over the unit plan assignment. You're turning in your teaching philosophy assignments next Monday, and these are the next big assignments. . . . If your lesson plan for one of these assignments includes technology, it could double for your W401 assignment. . . . When writing these, make sure your objectives are truly learning objectives and you include a broad range of state standards . . . multiple content standards. I want you to include some NCTM standards with technology standards. . . . Check with [instructor of W401] about the template; they may not be using the same template [for lesson plans]. Last year we did, but I don't know if this year it's the same. . . .
>
> For the unit plan, you need three lesson plans that are linked together. . . . You want to think about how each lesson plan is linked to the others to meet your overall unit goal. . . . You have to have flexibility to adapt as you go. You have plans, and you anticipate how things will go, but you have to be responsive to how your students

> react to it and modify as you go. . . . For the last part of your grade, I will be looking for how insightful, creative, and cohesive the unit plan is and how does all this tie together.

Several aspects of this example evince the ways teacher candidates get primed to adaptation over coordination in practice. First, Bob expresses dissatisfaction with the very lesson plan template he models to them by criticizing the types of "objectives" it contains. For their unit plans, he wants them to articulate "learning objectives," and not adopt the objectives on the lesson plan template he offers. Moreover, he acknowledges that the lesson plans they will put together for this assignment in his class may not be the same as the templates they must use for similar assignments in another required course they all have in pedagogy and technology. Consequently, teacher candidates were forced to navigate competing pedagogical strategies during their training, while also becoming primed to cover a standardized curriculum and "adapt" and "modify" their instruction based on "how your students react to it."

Teacher candidates make sense of these types of planning routines in ways that shape how they think prospectively about their future work in their own classrooms. The following excerpt is taken from an online discussion forum among the teacher candidates taking Bob's methods course in secondary mathematics. Lindsay, a teacher candidate, is reacting to several of her classmates here regarding the assignments they have for the course, but discusses them in the context of their future work. Here, she emphasizes how they will have to balance the many conditions Bob warns them about while working within their own classrooms in the future:

> I also agree that until we are out in the classroom on our own, it's going to be hard to figure out just what our philosophies are. For now, I want my students to discover all there is about mathematics and be able to have a creative lesson (whether it involves technology or hands-on activities)—I don't want to just give them the information, but I think this is a lot harder said than done. Especially as a new teacher who has to figure out their classroom management techniques, writing up lesson plans, and with the weight on our shoulders to have our students succeed, while having administration keeping a close eye on us. I think in all of these aspects, we have to learn how to adapt, transition, and balance everything going on inside our classrooms.

Again, we see evidence of the adaptation perspective emerging in the context of their coursework routines and collective sense-making, but there are additional elements to this perspective here. Teacher candidates are keenly aware that they will be working in their own classrooms in the future, and they will be left largely on their own to "balance everything going on inside our classrooms." They will have curricula to cover, lesson plans to write, and students to manage, and as Lindsay articulates here, new teachers must figure out how to do these things simultaneously. These types of exchanges dominated teacher candidates' sense-making about their future work, and only rarely included widely shared strategies that consistently informed how teacher candidates would carry out instruction. Moreover, the goal of developing "creative" lessons to engage students was often important to both teacher candidates and the faculty teaching their courses. Such goals prioritize adapting to their work in innovative ways rather than relying on proven, coordinated methods for instruction.

The perspective among teacher candidates that they need to adapt to multiple and changing conditions in their future work was also shaped by school actors they encountered during their coursework in addition to education faculty. Beyond coursework in teaching methods, another required course for teacher candidates of all specialty areas was a class in "job search strategies." This class was taught by a current elementary school principal who was also an adjunct faculty member in the teacher education program. Several teacher candidates from my sample took this class, and the following is an excerpt from my field notes during a day in class when the principal is describing what she looks for in new teachers:

> When I'm looking through applications, I'm looking for teachers who are adaptable and flexible. There was one teacher who I had who was terrific like this. . . . Anytime I needed someone to do lunch duty, I could walk into the teachers' lounge and say, "I have a meeting I have to attend, I can't do lunch duty; can anyone fill in?" She would always volunteer to help, even if she were in the middle of her lunch. . . . That teacher, I would do anything for her. . . . That really means a lot. . . . Things always come up, and I'm looking for teachers who can adapt. . . . From one year to the next, I may need teachers to teach different grade levels; even if they've never done it before, those teachers who are willing to switch to another grade are the most helpful. . . . So adaptable and flexible are the most important.

Not only do faculty prime them to be adaptable in their planning and practices, an actual principal tells teacher candidates that adaptation and flexibility are the most important characteristics for getting and keeping a teaching job. We see here additional sources of the injunction to adapt that links closely with their coursework messages. Adapting instruction to different students is in part necessary because of management decisions by principals. Teacher candidates hear quite clearly that from year to year in their future work, they may be asked to teach different grades, "even if they've never done it before," and teachers who can adapt their instruction to such conditions are most attractive to potential employers.

Teacher candidates become primed for unpredictable and changing work conditions, the principal above describes, through their own placements for student teaching as well. Procedures for assigning teacher candidates to mentoring teachers in local schools for their student teaching involve a great deal of unpredictability regarding the specific classroom contexts the candidates will experience. Faye, a teacher candidate, requested that she do her student teaching with a local schoolteacher whom she knew and who told her he would be happy to supervise her. Faye explains how this changed unexpectedly:

> So, you get this email, and it's like, "your placement has been confirmed." It's through the Ed School, it's just like this web service. Type in your little password, and I was like, "Hmm; that doesn't say Smith High School. It says Davis." And so, I was like, "Oh, bummer." And then the next day I emailed Mr. Quincy [the mentor teacher who had agreed to supervise her], and was like, "I won't be able to student teach with you; I've got my placement in Davis"; I said, "I'll be teaching world history—I didn't know I would be teaching that—can I stop by in the fall for some resources; thank you for all your help." On my regular student teaching request form, I requested Smith High School and Mr. Quincy. I requested him. I emailed the Ed School, and said, "I was just curious, about this placement; I was wondering why I didn't get it." And they were like, "Well, you didn't request it in the right form." But that doesn't really make sense because I requested it—and they were like, "Well, we didn't get that form." That was it. I mean, I was bummed out, and I wish I were—But at the same time . . . It is what it is, so . . . I didn't feel like there were any options for me to work around it.

Placement for student teaching is beyond teacher candidates' control and renders uncertain exactly what type of students and mentor teacher they will experience at this important stage of their training. Not only did Faye not get to work with the mentor she had requested, but she was assigned to teach a curriculum she did not expect. Experiences like Faye's were common among teacher candidates, and many had their student teaching placement changed without their input, even when they had made arrangements with supervising teachers whom they knew. For those who worked with supervisors they knew and liked, the transition was easier because they could plan ahead, as Faye had tried to do. But such experiences depend largely on the initiative of mentor teachers, which is largely voluntary and in no way uniform. Moreover, as Faye experienced in a large school of education, several hundred teacher candidates are placed each semester in a wide variety of local schools, and changes have to be made for various reasons (e.g., a teacher or principal backs out at the last minute or there is an administrative miscommunication). Consequently, it is difficult for teacher candidates, or education faculty, to anticipate or plan for prospective classroom conditions. The consistent message to develop an ability to adapt teaching strategies emerges out of necessity, as teacher candidates are unable to know in advance exactly what strategies will be appropriate for their future training and work experience.

While adaptation in practice is central to the perspectives all teacher candidates in this study developed, some were offered more consistent and structured strategies than others. Elementary teacher candidates, for instance, were trained in more specific and consistent pedagogical strategies than secondary teacher candidates in many cases. The following exchange during a methods course for elementary education shows the specific strategies they learned as well as how to adapt them. I provide this rather lengthy excerpt to show the combination of pedagogy, curriculum standards, and student characteristics that this faculty member is trying to help teacher candidates balance in their future work.

> Thinking about this as teachers, what else could we talk about here? [Todd, the faculty member teaching the course, repeats student responses.] Trade, transportation, geography, consumerism; that's a big one. The economics you probably wouldn't use with 1st-graders, but definitely with intermediate grades. You could show how there are multiple jobs at each stage of the setup. . . . You've got human resources, capital resources. . . . You want to summarize the steps again . . . health and nutrition as well. So, this attaches to so many different standards. It's a process of investigation to new knowledge. . . . These [holding bananas] are plastic bananas so the younger kids have something to touch, feel, and manipulate. . . .
>
> I'm going to hand out a sheet, and I want you to critique the lesson and resources . . . like the books available, the pros and cons with those. For example, what would you do with younger learners and emergent readers . . . need to use more visuals. These are the books that I'm going to hand out; there are True Books [publisher label] on every topic. . . . Some feel structured, but you can adapt them to your own creative things. . . . Think of ways you can use with K–1st grade, those of you placed in primary, even 3rd graders; you'll want to use similar things because they're right on the border of intermediate. . . . Somebody note your ideas, and then we'll share with the class.

> . . . I'll start the music again [begins Southern Culture on the Skids' "Banana Pudding"].

[Group work for 5 minutes; sporadic discussion. Todd had some individual conversations during this, but my notes are unclear on their content and context.]

> *Todd:* [Resumes whole-class discussion.] There was a lot here, . . . You could pick one specific area and dig into that, like Costa Rica, get into the people, the language. . . . What's a source for inquiry? Nutrition, okay . . . endangered, environmental issues. . . . You could use comparison; a banana doesn't have an opposite, but you could do like an apples/oranges comparison as part of an Idea teach. . . . You have artifacts for these lessons; you don't have to do both, but that's just one way to do it. . . . Make sure you sum up; if you don't it's not engaging. You can't just give them a stack of books, a stack of pictures. Those are the days when you're not prepared, and you're just in survival mode. That will happen, but you can plan units that are creative. . . .
>
> What was my hook? . . . The lunch pail, right. And the setup as you walked in; you are asking, "What the hell is he going to make me do today?" What other hooks could you use? . . . [A teacher candidate describes having students put pictures of the process by which bananas are transported to the grocery store in order on their own]. That's a great idea. You could have them put the setup in order on their own; or you could have pictures of these things and they put them in their own order; that's another way. . . . I'm giving you plenty of stuff. . . . I want you to make your own statements as an "anticipation guide." [Gives each table a book and each one comes to get a sheet of paper and markers.] "I want you to get used to actually doing this yourself. . . . Don't reinvent the wheel, but make your own statements from the books you have. . . . We'll share, these will be useful for discussion and debate.

Todd walks them through the process of developing specific lessons based on four core instructional strategies that guided this methods course. These four strategies, referred to as Inquiry Teach, Idea Teach, History Mystery, and Supermarket, were the same in all sections of this methods course, no matter which faculty member taught the course. Certainly, we still see the injunction to adapt at work here; Todd talks explicitly of modifications to these plans they would need to make depending on the grade level and literacy skills of the students they may be teaching. But such potential adaptation remains within the overall framework of these four strategies. Moreover, he discusses with them ways of adapting the "anticipation guide," which was a specific technique for initiating the lesson. As they develop these plans, he also discusses how these strategies "attach to so many different standards," modeling how they can use these strategies to cover their standardized curriculum. All teacher candidates in elementary education were trained in these pedagogical strategies for teaching social studies. Indeed, I observed Dennis and Nicole—who took different sections of this methods course—both use Inquiry Teach in their student teaching the following semester. Despite their adapting the strategy to students in different grades and different schools, the overall instructional strategy informed both of them in future teaching.

While the adaptation perspective emerged as a commonality among all teacher candidates in this study, the degree to which it supersedes the coordination of knowledge and practice was also influenced by subject-matter and grade-level differences. This finding reflects both the organizational conditions of their teacher education program and those of their future work environment in schools. Teacher candidates are grouped by their grade-level and subject-matter specialties. However, all elementary teacher candidates are trained by faculty in the department of curriculum and instruction and the department of language education, whereas secondary teacher candidates are trained and supervised in subject-matter departments that are largely independent in their course content and curriculum (e.g., a math education department versus a language education department). It makes sense, then, that knowledge and practice is less coordinated among secondary versus elementary teacher candidates. But the emphasis on adaptation in practice is also shaped by prospective work conditions in which teacher candidates know that they will be working largely individually in their own classrooms. Teacher candidates are primed for this through their coursework, but this priming continues through their mentoring relationships with supervising teachers upon their transition into student teaching.

Mentoring in the Classroom

A key element of teacher candidates' training is the mentoring they receive from their supervising teachers during their student teaching placements. While mentoring style and strategies vary quite a bit among individual teachers, a consistent finding is that teacher candidates are encouraged by their supervisors to develop their own preferred practices to teach their content. Supervisors often offered ideas and options for teacher candidates to attempt on their own, but rarely were supervising teachers prescriptive in their advice on how teacher candidates should perform instruction. Teacher candidates responded to this type of mentoring by borrowing ideas from their supervisors, but appropriating them in ways to make them their own while also bringing in practices and activities completely different from those of their supervisors. Through such mentoring interactions, teacher candidates became further primed to adapt instructional strategies of their own that they believe work best for them and their students.

A teacher candidate describes his perspective on how he adapted his own practices vis-à-vis his supervising teacher. The following excerpt is from an interview with Frank, who was trained in secondary language arts and did his student teaching in a middle school.

> *Judson:* How much did you borrow from Mr. Chambers [supervising teacher] versus how much you tried to come up with on your own?
>
> *Frank:* I think I had a good balance of both. He would give me, for like the speeches, he gave me his expectations of it, like these are things we're going to do by these dates and these are the topics we're gonna cover, and then I took that, kind of adjusted it a little bit, got it a little more specific. And then, he gave me the rubric, so that kind of gave me a guideline. The rest of it, I brought in outlines of my own, and came up with the activities on my own, but he gave me like a framework, I guess, to go with, and then I just made it my own.

Much like their education faculty who taught their methods coursework, supervising teachers often supported teacher candidates by offering them options for practices to select and adapt for themselves. We see here how Frank followed a general "guideline" for this particular unit he taught on speeches, but he "adjusted it a little bit" and the actual instructional activities he used were his own. His supervising teacher, Mr. Chambers, supported and encouraged Frank to teach in his own way. In fact, he also believed that Frank would become a better teacher when he could do more of his own independent teaching in his future work.

Such mentoring experiences were common for teacher candidates across grade-level and subject-matter distinctions. Mr. Chambers was actually one of the more hands-off mentors in the sample, but the overall message to adapt was shared by the supervising teachers who hovered over their teacher candidates. Ms. Evans supervised Dennis in his student teaching in elementary education. She was much more present in the classroom when Dennis taught, and turned over full teaching responsibilities to

Dennis much more gradually than most other supervising teachers in the study. However, she still subscribed to the same overall mentoring strategy to help Dennis develop his own arsenal of teaching practices, unique from hers. She describes how Dennis has improved his teaching in this way over the course of his student teaching:

> *Judson:* What have been some key ways that Dennis has improved over the course of his student teaching?
>
> *Ms. Evans:* I think finding more resources, digging in a little bit deeper to the content. How can he take some of his knowledge and interests, and I said, "You know, you shouldn't be me. You have to be you, and take your experiences, your loves and passions, and bring them into the classroom." So, I think he's been much better in bringing in resources. Like using things online; he did Paul Revere's Ride, and they got to do a virtual tour of his travels. So those kinds of things; I think he's spending a little more time digging into the content.

Ms. Evans emphasizes the need for Dennis to draw upon his individual interests and experiences to inform his teaching and the way that he addresses curriculum. Rather than duplicate the way she teaches, she warns him against this type of mimicry in instruction. Prioritizing individual adaptation in practice within teachers' own classrooms was common in teacher candidates' mentoring relationships. As such, in the ways that they indoctrinate newcomers into their ranks, teachers themselves limit the degree to which they coordinate their instructional practices. In fact, they view their own individual styles, developed within the confines of their own classrooms, as a key to teaching effectiveness. We see them priming teacher candidates for this perspective through their mentoring relationships.

During the transitions through their training, teacher candidates become primed to adapt instruction, and this perspective is shaped by multiple and overlapping conditions of the process: They are offered a range of effective strategies for instruction in their coursework that they must learn to adapt to different groups of students, their future work conditions can change unexpectedly in ways beyond their control, the amount of shared knowledge they possess differs depending on their grade-level and subject-matter specialties, and their mentoring relationships with teachers often encourage individuality in teaching style. Teacher candidates make sense of these training conditions through their collective routines and develop perspectives about their future work roles. They share the perspective that teaching is necessarily unpredictable and dynamic work that requires ongoing adaptation to changing classroom conditions and heterogeneous groups of students. While their practices are often ruled by individual adaptation, teacher candidates define priorities in their future work that are widely shared. In the next section, I discuss findings that foreground the ways teacher candidates develop strongly held goals of positively influencing their students over all other work goals.

The Primacy of Students

To be sure, people initially drawn to teaching already care for the well-being of children (Lortie, 1975). But through their collective training routines, teacher candidates develop perspectives that prioritize positively influencing their students' overall development in ways only loosely tied to academic performance or subject matter. This perspective includes a concern for students' academic achievement, but it is neither limited nor beholden to it. During their coursework, education faculty emphasize students as the chief priority for teacher candidates, as Todd tells his class:

> This is your last chance before student teaching to say, "I can do this." You can't just cruise through stuff and always be in survival mode. I had to survive on occasion, but some teachers do it for the entire year because they have no conscience. I remember once when I had not slept for 2–3 days straight, but I came to work anyway and got through it. On those days when I would just survive, I had those kids in front of me, and I felt guilty. You know, in some other jobs, people can come in and log their hours, and that's it because no one's holding you accountable, but we can't do that as teachers. You gotta be genuine, you gotta be real . . . and that comes from your preparation, your emotion for the topic, and the research allows you to do that. Teaching is not an easy job; it's not a fallback; it's not a safety net.

Appealing to teacher candidates' morality and service ethic to children was a common strategy among education faculty for motivating teacher candidates. Here, Todd is giving the class of teacher candidates a bit of a lecture about their effort on the lesson plans they have been developing. To this point, Todd did not feel that many of them were sufficiently prepared with enough background knowledge on their topics, nor did he feel they were effectively applying the instructional strategies he had taught them in their own plans. He tries to convince them that good planning and background knowledge are the means by which they must accomplish their chief goal of helping their future students. He uses himself and other teachers as examples, saying that when he was less than fully prepared he "felt guilty" because he "had those kids in front of me." Even more forcefully, he characterizes teachers who are chronically underprepared in their lessons as having "no conscience." He explicitly ties their capacity to be "genuine" with kids to their "preparation." While his goal is to convince them to use the practices they have discussed in class, he reinforces the message that benefiting children should be the fundamental motivating factor for teacher candidates' work.

Indeed, goals of positively influencing children are widely shared among teacher candidates. Such idealistic goals were common among the teacher candidates in this study. In learning how to adapt to different students and choosing from different instructional strategies, teacher candidates also have reaffirmed the notion that students' overall well-being is most important to their job. In this interview with Faye, who was in secondary social studies, she had been describing how much trouble she had keeping up with the pace of the amount of required curriculum she had to teach. She had just given the example that since she was teaching world history, she had just finished a lesson on feudal systems in medieval Europe and charters. I asked her whether, despite her frustrations, anything really rewarding happened, and she responded:

> The best things have happened the past two days. Um, yesterday after third period, this girl came in. And she's one of the sweetest girls, and she's done a lot of extra credit, taken a definite interest in the class. Anyway, she's like the last one to go, and she's like, "Can I . . . can I . . . " and she just burst into tears. And so we sat and talked, and she just had like so many things going on. And, um, that was just—I don't know. I felt—You know, at the end she's like, "I feel so much better!" You know, that was like—I don't know, she just burst into tears, and then she felt better. And, you know, that's what I'm there for. Regardless of what they, I mean, in the big scheme of things, I don't really care if they know what a charter is or not. I care that they're interested in education, and that they know that there are people in education interested in them. That's why, that's what it comes down to. And so, that was really cool.

The most rewarding part of the experience for Faye was the ability to feel that she helped a student deal with a personal problem. Similar to her counterparts in other subject matters and grade levels, she felt that ultimately having such an impact is her chief goal. While teacher candidates develop this perspective prior to student teaching, interactions with students within the classrooms they enter as student teachers reinforce it. Also, while she has a subject matter to teach, the content of her courses is secondary to her priority of helping students work through problems and feel as though "people in education are interested in them." In fact, she explicitly disregards the importance of her subject matter relative to her role in fostering the well-being of her students. More important, though teacher candidates often bring elements of this perspective with them to teacher education, it gets reinforced through the priming they experience in their training.

While the goal of positively influencing students is widely shared among teacher candidates, they also develop different strategies for how to accomplish it. Much like they believe that there are a range of good teaching practices from which they must choose, they come to believe that there are multiple paths to positively influencing their students. Moreover, they become primed to believe that such differences among teachers in how they relate to students are actually beneficial for students' education. An example comes from an interview with Nellie's supervising teacher, Mr. Bower:

> The only thing I would say that I do better than Nellie is the discipline, but I've done it for 10 years so that's to be expected. I take control of the classroom probably a little better than she did. But at the same time, to give her credit, she probably was a little more patient with the kids than I am. She had that patience to work with them and wanted to spend that one-on-one time with them, where I want them to be more independent. So that was the only thing we had to work through was she liked to coddle kids, which is okay! Which is fine! She likes to pull them back to her desk and let them hover around her and she'll work through stuff with them, which is probably great for their education. But I don't do that, because I want them to be more independent. So that's a difference in our philosophies, but there's nothing wrong with either one.

Both Nellie and Mr. Bower share the goal to positively influence their students' behavior and performance, but as Mr. Bower describes, they prioritize slightly different values for their students. Mr. Bower prioritizes teaching his students to be independent, and he interprets Nellie's approach as "coddling" students and emphasizing more personal attention than he does. Yet he acknowledges that "there's nothing wrong with either one" of these ways of working with students, and both are effective in benefiting their students' development. While the primacy of students emerges in teacher candidates' perspectives, exactly how to positively influence them can mean different things for individual teachers and their students.

Not only do teacher candidates get mentored in ways that encourage the perspective that prioritizes students' needs, they are rewarded when their supervisors perceive that they have accomplished this goal, especially with difficult students. Positively and effectively influencing students with behavioral, emotional, and social problems earns high praise for teacher candidates as they learn to perform their work roles. In the eyes of both her supervising teacher and university supervisor, Nicole (called Ms. Harris in the following example) achieved this goal with her class of 3rd graders in her student teaching, and the following is an excerpt from her supervisor's formal evaluation letter:

> This class consisted of one of the most challenging groups of students I have encountered in more than 30 years as an educator. Ms. Harris embraced this class with compassion, discipline, and commitment to providing a high standard of education for each student.
>
> Possessing a sound knowledge of the relevant content and the state standards governing the 3rd-grade curriculum, Ms. Harris used a wide variety of resources to plan and present lessons that were engaging and challenging. . . . Personalizing instruction is a difficult task for any teacher, especially one with little classroom experience. The unique makeup of students in this class made it necessary for Ms. Harris to do this early and often. She started a file of instructional strategies and ideas to help students with various learning and behavioral needs. She also kept a journal to record which of these proved effective with which students. Her lessons were creative and engaging and were presented by using a wide variety of instructional strategies. Despite the many behavioral and emotional issues of her students, Ms. Harris developed a strong and productive learning relationship with each of them. Nicole Harris successfully completed a student teaching assignment that would have scared off many inexperienced teachers. With additional experience, she will become an outstanding teacher.

Nicole did, indeed, have a challenging group of students to teach. Behavioral disruptions and absenteeism were frequent problems for many of the students in the class. Nicole adapted to this environment and the needs of her students with a "wide variety of instructional strategies" and therefore "successfully completed a student teaching assignment that would have scared off many inexperienced teachers." Her supervisor notes that she has good command of her standardized curriculum, but Nicole receives the most praise for her ability to adapt to her classroom situation in a way that positively influenced a difficult group of students. Both teacher candidates and their supervisors viewed teaching students with a wide range of behaviors, skills, and needs as inherent to the job, and those who demonstrated in their student teaching that they could adapt and succeed were held up as the most promising teachers.

CONCLUSION

I now summarize and situate these findings in a broader context for understanding the occupational status of teaching and discuss policy implications. First, the patterns in new teachers' perspectives include viewing teaching as necessarily unpredictable and dynamic work, viewing adaptation in teaching practice as a fundamental responsibility of the job, and prioritizing students' overall well-being as the chief goal of their work. We can more clearly see the ways new teachers develop these perspectives with analysis of teacher education as a long-term process of social transition that is driven by collective routines and priming events. Contrary to a lot of prior research on teacher education, my findings show that going through this process *does* influence the ways new teachers come to understand their work, how they should perform it, and with what goals in mind. In addition, teacher candidates *do* listen to the content of their training, but they actively interpret and appropriate the content of their training. The analysis in this study helps to identify priming as a key social mechanism through which teacher candidates make sense of their prospective work. Moreover, these findings foreground the agency that teacher candidates exercise in interpreting the conditions of their training and defining future work roles.

Yet we also see certain ways that teacher training is constrained by the broader context of public education in the United States. Indeed, findings of this study reveal competing logics at work in educational institutions that shape how teachers prepare for their future work roles. On the one hand, we see concretely the ways that the logic of standardization in ensuring teacher quality—bound up in the No Child Left Behind Act—is brought to bear on teacher preparation. New teachers develop perspectives that closely align their work goals with curriculum standards, for example. On the other hand, though, we also see this injunction to adapt among new teachers, which reflects another organizational imperative at play in public education, that of addressing enormous heterogeneity among students, most notably in the form of inequality in U.S. school districts and the households they serve. Faced with prospective work in such diverse environments and uncertain what types of school conditions they will work under, new teachers become primed to adapt to a wide range of possibilities. This perspective emerges over time through their collective routines in their coursework and becomes reinforced through their guided classroom practice upon the transition into schools for student teaching. Also, it is important to note that many of the prospective contingencies new teachers face are beyond their control, as well as the control of the teacher education programs that train them. The structure of these experiences shape new teachers' perspectives about their work, and NCLB standards fail to factor in the importance of adaptation to local conditions when defining "quality" teaching.

We also see that new teachers view adaptation in practice as a key means to meeting their work goals of positively influencing students. Initially, we might interpret this finding as a sign of idealism among teacher candidates with little concrete educational benefit for many of their students. However, evidence from additional research on teachers suggests that the primacy of students' overall development among incoming teachers may be more important to students' educational success than is acknowledged by current accountability policies. Hallinan (2008), for example, finds that "teachers who support their students by caring about them and by respecting them and praising them satisfy students' needs, and in so doing, increase students' attachment to school" (p. 282). We know from additional studies that students with relatively high feelings of attachment to school perform better academically, are less likely to drop out, and have higher graduation rates (Marcus & Sanders-Reio, 2001; Muller, 2001).

My findings show that teacher candidates make sense of their training experiences in ways that prioritize precisely these types of relationships with students and, therefore, are primed to have such an impact on students at the point of entry to their jobs. As Hallinan (2008) also points out, however, current accountability measures of teacher quality exclude assessments that would take into account these types of influence teachers have on students, relying almost solely on student performance on standardized tests. As such, accountability mandates under NCLB further serve to deprofessionalize teachers by ignoring a key element of teacher quality, which is shaped in part by a widely shared and strongly held professional ethic that teacher candidates develop in teacher education. In other words, teacher education fosters a service ethic among new teachers that likely increases their competency as an occupational group. Unfortunately, current systems of accountability in public education fail to take into account these phenomena at work in the training and credentialing of new teachers. Consequently, under NCLB mandates governing teachers and teacher education programs, we simultaneously set unattainable expectations for their performance and deny them credit where it is due.

NOTE

1. For a more detailed account of the sample and research design, see Everitt, 2009.

REFERENCES

Becker, H. S., Geer, B., Hughes, E. C., & Strauss, A. L. (1961). *Boys in white: Student culture in medical school*. Chicago: University of Chicago Press.

Britzman, D. P. (1991). *Practice makes practice: A critical study of learning to teach.* Albany: State University of New York Press.

Calderhead, J., & Shorrock, S. B. (1997). *Understanding teacher education: Case studies in the professional development of beginning teachers.* London: Falmer Press.

Corsaro,W. A., & Molinari, L. (2000). Priming events and Italian children's transition from preschool to elementary school: Representations and action. *Social Psychology Quarterly, 63*, 16-33.

Corsaro, W. A., & Molinari, L. (2005). *I compagni: Understanding children's transition from preschool to elementary school.* New York: Teachers College Press.

Elder, G. H., Jr. (1994). Time, human agency, and social change: Perspectives of the life course. *Social Psychology Quarterly, 57*, 4–15.

Entwisle D. R., & Alexander, K. L. (1999). Early schooling and social stratification. In R. C. Pianta and M. J. Cox (Eds.), *The transition to kindergarten* (pp. 13–38). Baltimore: P. H. Brookes.

Everitt, J. G. (2009). *Preparing for the work of teaching: professional socialization and the construction of work perspectives among pre-service teachers.* Unpublished doctoral dissertation, Department of Sociology, Indiana University, Bloomington. Retrieved from ProQuest Dissertations and Theses Database, publication number AAT 3378346.

Furstenberg, F., Cook, T. D., Eccles, J., & Elder, G. (2000). *Managing to make it: Urban families and adolescent success*. Chicago: University of Chicago Press.

Garnier, M. (1973). Power and ideological conformity: A case study. *American Journal of Sociology, 79*, 343–363.

Hallinan, M. (2008). Teacher influences on students' attachment to school. *Sociology of Education, 81*, 271–283.

Hargreaves, A., & Jacka, N. (1995). Induction of seduction: Postmodern patterns of preparing to teach. *Peabody Journal of Education, 70*, 41–63.

Johnson, S. P. (2011, January 24). What if we treated doctors like we treat teachers? *The Huffington Post*. Retrieved from http://www.huffingtonpost.com/shaun-johnson/treating-doctors-like-teachers_b_812096.html

Labaree, D. F. (2004). *The trouble with ED schools*. New Haven, CT: Yale University Press.

Lareau, A. (2003). *Unequal childhoods: Class, race, and family life*. Berkeley: University of California Press.

Levine, A. (2006). *Educating school teachers*. Washington, DC: The Education Schools Project.

Liston, D. P., & Zeichner, K. M. (1991). *Teacher education and the social conditions of schooling*. London: Routledge.

Lortie, D. C. (1975). *Schoolteacher: A sociological study*. Chicago: University of Chicago Press.

Marcus, R. F., & Sanders-Reio, J. (2001). The influence of attraction on school completion. *School Psychology Quarterly, 16*, 427–444.

Merton, R. K. (1968). *Social theory and social structure*. New York: Free Press.

Merton, R. K., Reader, G. G., & Kendall, P. L. (Eds.). (1957). *The student physician: Introductory studies in the sociology of medical education*. Cambridge: Harvard University Press.

Muller, C. (2001). The role of caring in the teacher-student relationship for at-risk students. *Sociological Inquiry, 71*, 241–255.

Schleef, D. (2006). *Managing elites: Professional socialization in law and business schools.* Lanham, MD: Rowman and Littlefield.

U.S. Department of Education, Office of Postsecondary Education. (2006). *The secretary's fifth annual report on teacher quality: A highly qualified teacher in every classroom.* Washington, DC: Author.

CHAPTER 8

The Role of Mentors and Colleagues in Beginning Teachers' Language Arts Instruction

Peter Youngs
Kenneth A. Frank
Ben Pogodzinski

Schools and districts face many challenges with regard to the quality of beginning teachers' reading and writing instruction. At the elementary level, many novice teachers struggle to integrate instruction in phonics, phonemic awareness, and other basic reading skills with strategies that promote reading for comprehension and other forms of higher-order thinking (Phelps & Schilling, 2004; Pressley, Duke, & Boling, 2004). At the middle school level, beginning teachers similarly confront challenges to successfully develop and refine students' higher-order reading and writing skills, for example, through structured process approaches to writing instruction (Hillocks, 2006) and discussion-based approaches to reading instruction (Applebee, Langer, Nystrand, & Gamoran, 2003). In response to concerns about instructional quality, many districts and states have implemented induction programs for novice teachers (Education Week, 2010). These programs typically feature formally assigned mentors, orientation sessions, and workshops and seminars. Further, many districts offer professional development for beginning and experienced teachers that addresses curriculum, instruction, and assessment in reading and writing.

The emphasis on mentoring and professional development for individual teachers is consistent with the underlying logic of the current accountability movement, which focuses primarily on identifying "effective teachers," providing instructional support to less effective teachers, and getting rid of those teachers who fail to improve their practice. Thus, with increased attention under the federal Race to the Top legislation to teachers' instructional practices and student performance, researchers and policy makers are strongly interested in how mentoring and professional development influence novice teachers' reading and writing instruction. A number of recent qualitative studies have suggested ways that formal mentors can promote beginning teacher learning (Achinstein & Barrett, 2004; Achinstein, Ogawa, & Speiglman, 2004; Athanases & Achinstein, 2003; Feiman-Nemser, 2001; Youngs, 2007). In our view, while these studies have advanced the field, they have failed to acknowledge that when novices arrive at a new school, they join a group of teachers with their own norms about reading and writing instruction. That is, if we assume that beginning teachers are only affected by formal mentors, then we are likely to miss a number of other salient influences on their work.

What factors affect the instructional practices of beginning teachers? In this chapter, we argue that beginning teachers are accountable to other teachers in their schools and that their language arts instruction can be influenced by (a) professional interactions with formal mentors, (b) professional interactions with other teachers (i.e., colleagues) at their schools (Coburn & Russell, 2008), and (c) exposure to norms for instruction represented by mentors' and colleagues' language arts practices (Frank et al., 2008; Pogodzinski, Youngs, Frank, & Belman, under review). Based on an empirical study of more than 180 beginning elementary and middle school teachers, we examine how novices' language arts instruction is affected by the content and frequency of their interactions with mentors and other close colleagues or, less directly, by exposure to the language arts instruction of their mentors and other colleagues.

Our analyses reveal that novices look to mentors for models of higher-order comprehension instruction while their basic skills instruction is more likely to be affected by their interactions with other colleagues. Beyond formal pedagogical discussions between mentors and novices, the nature of mentors' language arts instruction had no effect on beginning teachers' instruction, while the language arts practices of novices' colleagues did influence the novices' basic skills instruction. These findings have important implications for efforts by policy makers and school administrators to improve beginning teacher quality; in particular, they suggest a need for greater attention to how novices' language arts teaching is affected by instructional norms in their schools as well as interactions with other colleagues (in addition to their formal mentors).

The first section of this chapter reviews research on the role of mentors and colleagues in beginning teacher induction. In the second section, we present our theoretical framework, which draws on recent research to hypothesize ways that mentors and colleagues can affect beginning teachers' language arts instruction. The third section introduces the Michigan

Indiana Early Career Teacher study, an innovative examination of beginning teachers, their mentors and colleagues, and changes in their language arts instruction. Fourth, we present findings regarding how mentors and colleagues influenced novices' reading instruction. Finally, the fifth section concludes by considering implications of this analysis for future research.

RESEARCH ON MENTORS, COLLEAGUES, AND BEGINNING TEACHERS

While several studies have examined ways in which formal mentors can support teacher learning, recent research indicates that intensive mentoring may have limited effects on beginning teachers' language arts instruction (Glazerman et al., 2010). At the same time, several studies have investigated how other forms of mentoring as well as school-based colleagues can shape novices' language arts teaching.

Research on Formal Mentoring

A number of qualitative studies suggest ways that mentors can promote beginning teacher learning. For example, Feiman-Nemser (2001) examined how one mentor used several strategies to promote novices' development; the strategies included finding openings that could lead to productive conversation, pinpointing specific problems, probing novices' thinking, noticing signs of their growth, focusing on students, reinforcing the use of theory, demonstrating teaching techniques, and modeling reflective teaching. Athanases and Achinstein (2003) considered two beginning elementary teacher-mentor pairs from a 2-year study of 20 such pairs. The researchers concluded that the mentors in the study used two main strategies to focus novices on student learning. First, the mentors drew on knowledge of content standards, curricular alignment, and student assessment to help beginning teachers make connections among instructional content, assessment strategies, and student learning. Second, the mentors helped beginning teachers enact and refine pedagogical strategies based on their accumulated knowledge of students' learning styles and needs. When mentors addressed such knowledge and strategies in their interactions with novices, the novices, in turn, were more able to use scaffolding and grouping strategies to meet their students' learning needs (Athanases & Achinstein, 2003).

In a third study, Achinstein and Barrett (2004) collected data on three mentor-novice pairs and found that the mentors promoted reframing as a way to interpret experiences, address problems, and expose the underlying values held by teachers. Along those lines, they used student observations, analyses of student work, and teacher-student transcripts to help beginning teachers focus on students' needs. By reframing novices' views, mentors were able to help make hidden or ignored dynamics affecting student learning more apparent (Achinstein & Barrett, 2004). A fourth study, by Achinstein et al. (2004), examined how two beginning elementary teachers' induction experiences were shaped by mentoring and district curricular policies. One of the teachers, Liz, focused more with her mentor on issues related to classroom management and parents than on instruction. With regard to possible influences from colleagues and district policy, the expectations placed on Liz by her colleagues and district policy were to follow routines, curricula, and assessments designed by the state and district. In contrast, Sam met weekly with his mentor to co-plan instruction, and he benefited from grade-team collaboration, working with a district instructional coach, and participating in an action research group. In addition, he enjoyed numerous professional development activities that emphasized inquiry (Achinstein et al., 2004).

The studies by Feiman-Nemser, Achinstein, and others provide some insight into effective mentoring practices. In particular, they suggest that mentors can promote student-centered instruction and attention to learners' needs by probing novices' thinking, focusing on students, reframing beginning teachers' views, drawing on knowledge of assessment, and analyzing student learning. The emphasis in these studies on one-to-one mentoring is consistent with the current accountability movement, which concentrates on the effectiveness of individual teachers. At the same time, it is less clear from these studies whether or how particular mentoring practices are associated with changes in novice teachers' actual literacy instruction.

In some ways, a recent study by researchers at Mathematica (Glazerman et al., 2010) challenges findings of other research on mentoring and induction. This study used random assignment to compare a group of novice elementary school teachers who experienced "comprehensive" induction with an equivalent group exposed to their districts' conventional induction activities. The teachers in the treatment group participated in comprehensive induction programs from either Educational Testing Service (ETS) or the New Teacher Center (NTC) at the University of California–Santa Cruz. These programs featured full-time, trained mentors who were released from teaching, weekly meetings between mentors and mentees, professional development opportunities for mentees, and formative assessments for mentees that featured observations and constructive feedback (Glazerman et al., 2010). In many cases, the mentors had little prior knowledge of or experience in their mentees' schools (i.e., either as a teacher or as a mentor). In contrast, the teachers in the control group were assigned to mentors who taught full time, did not receive release time for mentoring, and did not use formative teacher assessments in their work with them. In addition, the control group teachers had fewer professional development opportunities.

Seventeen districts in 13 states participated in the study, each of which had more than 50% of its students eligible for free or reduced-price lunch. In each district, elementary schools were assigned to either the control group or one of two treatments (selected by the district). In these analyses, teachers who received intensive mentoring through the ETS and NTC programs were considered to be part of one treatment group. Based on data collection in the 1st year of the study, the researchers reported no statistically significant differences between treatment and control group teachers with regard to their performance on any of the three domains of literacy practices on which they focused: lesson implementation, lesson content, and classroom culture (Glazerman et al., 2010). In addition, the lead investigator for this study (Glazerman, personal communication, 2010) indicated that logical next steps for researchers would be to more fully investigate whether or how beginning teachers are influenced by the types of mentors in the control group in the Mathematica study (i.e., full-time teachers who mentor novices in their own schools) as well as other teachers in their schools.

Research on Professional Support from Other Teachers

In contrast to studies that focused on formal mentors, a few studies have considered how other teachers (i.e., other school-based colleagues) can affect beginning teachers' language arts instruction. For example, one study by Valencia, Place, Martin, and Grossman (2006) focused on how the reading practices of four beginning elementary teachers were influenced by reading curricular materials and colleagues in their schools. They reported that teachers' opportunities to learn to teach reading were shaped by a combination of their own knowledge of reading, the curricular materials they encountered, and their interactions with colleagues. Two of the teachers had weak knowledge of reading instruction or more restricted curricular materials, and these individuals were less able to adapt reading instruction to meet their students' needs. In contrast, the other two teachers had stronger knowledge of reading instruction, access to a rich variety of materials, and more comprehensive instructional support in their schools; these individuals had much greater opportunities to learn to teach reading through conversations with colleagues and were more able to adapt instruction to address the learning needs of students (Valencia et al., 2006).

A second study by Grossman and Thompson (2004) from the same research project addressed the induction experiences of two beginning middle school language arts teachers and a novice high school English teacher. One of the middle school teachers, Allison, had access to subject-area colleagues who shared curricular materials with her and helped her plan instruction and make sense of district and state standards and assessments. As a result, she was able to develop student-centered instructional practices that reflected district and state policies as well as the teaching approaches of her mentor and colleagues. In contrast, the other two novices, Frank and Nancy, had infrequent access to English/language arts colleagues. Consequently, they struggled in their efforts to respond to district and state policies and to develop effective instructional practices (Grossman & Thompson, 2004).

In sum, several qualitative studies have explored ways that formal mentors can promote novice teacher development, but recent large-scale research has raised questions about the effects of intensive mentoring on beginning teachers' language arts instruction (Glazerman et al., 2010). At the same time, research suggests that other forms of mentoring and school-based colleagues can affect novices' reading instruction (Achinstein et al., 2004; Feiman-Nemser, 2001; Grossman & Thompson, 2004; Valencia et al., 2006) and their commitment levels.

HOW MENTORS AND COLLEAGUES CAN INFLUENCE NOVICES' LANGUAGE ARTS INSTRUCTION

In this section, we present a theoretical framework that posits that beginning teachers are accountable to other teachers in their schools and, therefore, they are likely to be affected by their professional interactions with formal mentors and other school-based colleagues, and exposure to the norms represented by their mentors' and colleagues' language arts practices. In terms of the former, this section addresses how novice-mentor and novice-colleague interactions related to language arts instruction can shape instruction in basic literacy skills, lower-order comprehension, and higher-order comprehension. With regard to an exposure effect, the framework considers ways in which beginning teachers' exposure to their mentors' and colleagues' language arts practices can affect the novices' practices in the same three areas.

Elementary and middle school language arts teachers teach a range of literacy skills over the course of the year. In this study, we define instruction in basic literacy skills as that which teaches students word analysis (e.g., decoding, word families, sight words), grammar, spelling, phonics, sound segmenting, sound blending, and sight recognition. Such instruction also addresses editing, punctuation, and word use in writing. Instruction in lower-order comprehension is defined as instruction that addresses reading fluency, listening and reading comprehension, written composition, use of context in reading words, activating prior knowledge, making predictions about text, summarizing important details, using concept maps, and answering questions that have answers stated directly in the text. Finally, we define instruction in higher-order comprehension as instruction that involves having students examine literary techniques, identify an author's purpose, write extensive answers to questions, and answer questions that require inferences. Such instruction also involves having students revise their writing by elaborating or reorganizing text (Phelps & Schilling, 2004; Pressley, Duke, & Boling, 2004).

Influence of Interactions with Mentors and Colleagues

How, if at all, do mentors actually influence beginning teachers' language arts instruction? The recent Mathematica study indicates that there is little difference in terms of effects on novices' language arts practices between interactions with full-time, highly trained mentors (who are released from teaching) and interactions with part-time mentors with less training who teach full time (Glazerman et al., 2010). In addition, other research suggests that school-based mentors who are teaching full time in novices' schools can affect novices' language arts teaching (Achinstein et al., 2004; Feiman-Nemser, 2001). Drawing on these findings, we argue that the nature and frequency of novices' interactions with school-based mentors will be associated with changes in novices' language arts instruction.

In particular, we hypothesize that frequent interactions with mentors that address instructional issues will lead to increased frequency of higher-order comprehension instruction by novices and decreased emphasis on basic skills instruction. Given their years of teaching experience, their knowledge of school curriculum, and their expertise, we expect that mentors will be more adept than novices at higher-order comprehension instruction. Further, given the complex nature of such instruction, novices will be more likely to engage in such instruction when they have regular interactions with mentors who, in turn, have greater experience, curricular knowledge, and expertise. Therefore, the first set of hypotheses addressed in this study is as follows:

> *Hypothesis 1a:* When a novice teacher interacts frequently with his or her formally assigned mentor about instructional issues, the frequency at which he or she provides higher-order comprehension instruction will increase.

Hypothesis 1b: When a novice teacher interacts frequently with his or her formally assigned mentor about instructional issues, the frequency at which he or she provides basic skills instruction will decrease.

Along with formal mentors, many beginning teachers typically develop productive relationships with one or more other school-based colleagues (Grossman & Thompson, 2004; Valencia et al., 2006). For elementary teachers, these individuals can include grade-level colleagues, reading specialists, colleagues who have previously taught their language arts curriculum, and peers who are similar in age or years of experience. Likewise, for middle school teachers, these individuals can include subject-area colleagues, department chairs, colleagues who have previously taught their curriculum, and peers who are similar in age or years of experience. We posit that frequent interactions with colleagues that address instructional issues will lead novices to more frequently enact higher-order comprehension instruction and to less frequently focus on basic skills instruction.

As with mentors, we expect that novices' colleagues will generally have more experience, curricular knowledge, and expertise than the novices themselves. In addition, because beginning teachers choose the colleagues with whom they work closely, they are likely to have a common language about teaching with these individuals and their relationships with these colleagues are likely to be characterized by high levels of trust. Again, given the complex nature of higher-order comprehension instruction, novices will be more likely to engage in such instruction when they have frequent interactions with colleagues who, in turn, are likely to have more experience, stronger curricular knowledge, and more expertise. Thus, the second set of hypotheses addressed in this study is as follows:

Hypothesis 2a: When a novice teacher interacts frequently with his or her colleagues about instructional issues, the frequency at which he or she provides higher-order comprehension instruction will increase.

Hypothesis 2b: When a novice teacher interacts frequently with his or her colleagues about instructional issues, the frequency at which he or she provides basic skills instruction will decrease.

Influence of Exposure to Mentors' and Colleagues' Instructional Practices

In addition to possible effects of interactions between novices and their mentors and colleagues, the theoretical framework underlying this study posits that mentors and colleagues can affect novices' instruction through an *exposure* effect (Frank et al., 2008; Pogodzinski et al., under review). In the study reported on here, an exposure effect relates to the level of change in a beginning teacher's language arts instructional practices as a function of the language arts practices of his or her formal mentor or colleagues. As teaching is inherently an uncertain task, beginning teachers often look to mentors and colleagues to model what they should be doing. Thus, effects on teaching practice are not only related to how many people a beginning teacher interacts with, how often he or she interacts with them, and the content of these interactions. According to our framework, changes in novices' language arts instruction are also related to the nature of their mentors' and colleagues' practices in this area.

We hypothesize that novices' language arts practices are likely to be influenced by exposure to the practices of their formal mentors. As mentors are typically assigned to beginning teachers, they represent the formal organization of the school or formal district policy. As a result, novices may feel pressure to conform to the practices of their mentors. Therefore, the third set of hypotheses addressed in this study is as follows:

Hypothesis 3a: When a novice teacher's mentor frequently engages in basic skills instruction, the novice will provide such instruction more frequently.

Hypothesis 3b: When a novice teacher's mentor frequently engages in higher-order comprehension instruction, the novice will provide such instruction more frequently.

Finally, we hypothesize that a beginning teacher's language arts instruction will be closely related to the extent to which they are exposed to close colleagues who address basic skills in literacy, higher-order comprehension, or both. Because of the uncertain nature of teaching, novices are likely to be aware of their close colleagues' approaches to teaching literacy (i.e., the extent to which these individuals emphasize basic skills) and align their practices over time with those of their close colleagues. Thus, the fourth set of hypotheses addressed in this study is as follows:

Hypothesis 4a: When a novice teacher's colleagues frequently engage in basic skills instruction, the novice will provide such instruction more frequently.

Hypothesis 4b: When a novice teacher's colleagues frequently engage in higher-order comprehension instruction, the novice will provide such instruction more frequently.

In sum, the theoretical framework used in this analysis hypothesizes that beginning teachers' language arts instruction is a function of the nature and frequency of their interactions with their formal mentors and other school-based colleagues. In addition, we hypothesize that novices' language arts practices will also be influenced by exposure to the language arts practices of their mentors and colleagues. We discuss our results from testing all of these hypotheses below.

THE MICHIGAN AND INDIANA EARLY CAREER TEACHER STUDY OF BEGINNING TEACHERS AND THEIR MENTORS AND COLLEAGUES

The Districts

The district sample for our study included six Michigan districts and five Indiana districts that were part of a larger study, the Michigan Indiana Early Career Teacher (MIECT) study. These districts varied in size, from 8,000 students to more than 29,000 students; with regard to students' race/ethnicity; and with regard to students' socioeconomic status (i.e., the percentage of students eligible for free and reduced-price lunch). See Table 8.1 for more details about the demographics of the student populations served by these districts.

Table 8.1. 2007–8 Enrollments and Demographic Information for 11 Participating Michigan and Indiana Districts

District	Total Enrollment (approximate)	% Free/Reduced Lunch (approximate)	% Non-White (approximate)
Daus (MI)	18,000	50–55	10–15
Engram (IN)	14,000	60–65	45–50
Greenberg (MI)	21,000	60–65	75–80
Kaline (MI)	9,000	40–45	45–50
Luckman (IN)	16,000	40–45	55–60
Payton (IN)	11,000	45–50	80–85
Sayers (IN)	22,000	60–65	55–60
Underwood (MI)	29,000	10–15	10–15
Wagner (MI)	8.000	35–40	45–50
Whitaker (MI)	12,000	25–30	15–20
Wilson (IN)	13,000	55–60	55–60

The Beginning Teachers

In 2007–08, we administered two surveys (in fall 2007 and spring 2008) to beginning teachers in the 11 districts. The beginning teacher sample for our study included 183 elementary general education teachers and middle school English/language arts teachers in the 11 Michigan and Indiana districts who taught in grades 1–8 and who were in their first 3 years of teaching in public schools as certified teachers. Table 8.2 includes information about key characteristics of the beginning teachers in our study. About 83% of the teachers were female, about 90% were White, about 25% were in their 1st year of teaching, and about 72% were teaching at the elementary level.

The Mentors and Colleagues

In winter 2008, for each beginning teacher in the study, we administered surveys to their formal mentor and up to four of their colleagues who were also classroom teachers. That is, our mentor/colleague samples for novice teachers included those nominated by the novices as mentors and key colleagues and, of these individuals, only those responsible for classroom instruction.

The Measures

To measure language arts instruction, in both the fall and spring surveys, the beginning teachers were asked to indicate the frequency (based on a 6-point scale ranging from "never" to "every day")[1] with which 21 different topics were the primary focus of instruction in reading/language arts. For our analysis, the topics were aggregated into three distinct categories[2]: basic skills (e.g., grammar), lower-order comprehension (e.g., written composition), and higher-order comprehension (e.g., examining literary techniques) (see Figure 8.1 for a full list of topics by category). Table 8.2 provides descriptive information about the frequency at which the beginning teachers provided different types of language arts instruction. For example, a mean of 4.05 for the frequency of basic skills instruction indicates that across the sample of beginning teachers in this study, on average they taught basic literacy skills 1 to 2 times a week in spring 2008.

The novices were asked to indicate their frequency of interaction (based on a 6-point scale ranging from "never" to "every day")[3] with both their formal mentors and other colleagues around reading/language arts curriculum, teaching strategies, and student assessment. We calculated the mean frequency of interaction between novice teachers and their mentor and colleagues (respectively) to form composite measures of interaction around reading/language arts instruction. On average, the novice teachers in this study interacted with their colleagues about language arts instructional issues 1 to 2 times a week in spring 2008 (a mean of 3.88 for the frequency of interactions with colleagues in Table 8.2).

Since we were interested in how mentors and colleagues affected the development of teachers' language arts instruction over the course of the year, we first had to identify teachers' baseline level of instruction in basic skills, lower-order comprehension, and higher-order comprehension. On average, the beginning teachers in the study taught basic skills more than 1 to 2 times a week in fall 2007 (Table 8.2; a mean of 4.26), lower-order comprehension almost 3 to 4 times a week in fall 2007 (Table 8.2; a mean of 4.79), and higher-order comprehension 1 to 2 times a week in fall 2007 (Table 8.2; a mean of 3.91). In sum, the teachers focused relatively more on such activities as reading fluency, reading comprehension, and summarizing important details (i.e., aspects of lower-order comprehension instruction) than such activities as word analysis, grammar, and spelling (i.e., basic skills) or examining literary techniques and answering questions that require inferences (i.e., aspects of higher-order comprehension).

With regard to mentors' and colleagues' language arts instruction, the mentor/colleague survey asked respondents to indicate the frequency with which the same 21 topics were the primary focus of their reading/language arts teaching. The beginning teacher survey and the mentor/colleague survey both asked for additional information such as years of experience, degrees, certification, and university attended.

The Models

We use quasi-experimental regression models (see chapter 2) to assess the influence of mentors and close colleagues on beginning teachers' language arts instruction. Each statistical model uses the regressor variable method (Allison, 1990) to examine changes in teachers' instruction: a basic technique for examining change over time where a teacher's instruction in the spring is predicted by the influence of his or her mentor and other colleagues, a set of control variables related to instruction, as well as the teacher's approach to instruction in the fall. The control variables included prior frequency of instructional practice, as well as teacher, school, and district characteristics. In addition, our models take account of the multilevel nature of the data: teachers nested within schools, nested within districts, a common feature of educational data. Further, our models have several important properties. First, since we examine change over time, these models provide very rigorous estimates of others' influence, which is independent

Table 8.2. Descriptive Information on Instructional Practice, Instructional Interaction, and Background: Measures of Central Tendency and Variability

Variable	Description	Mean	Standard Deviation	Min	Max
Basic skills (t)	Frequency of teaching basic skills in spring	4.05	1.665	1.00	6.00
L.O. comp (t)	Frequency of teaching lower-order comprehension skills in spring	4.71	0.696	2.80	6.00
H.O. comp (t)	Frequency of teaching higher-order comprehension skills in spring	4.01	1.047	1.00	6.00
Mentor interaction	Frequency of novice's interaction with mentor	3.11	1.298	1.00	5.67
Colleague interaction	Frequency of novice's interaction with colleagues	3.88	0.907	1.33	6.00
Teacher-level controls					
Basic skills (t-1)	Frequency of teaching basic skills in fall	4.26	1.549	1.00	6.00
L.O. comp (t-1)	Frequency of teaching lower-order comprehension skills in fall	4.79	0.661	3.09	6.00
H.O. comp (t-1)	Frequency of teaching higher-order comprehension skills in fall	3.91	1.060	1.00	6.00
Efficacy	Teacher self-efficacy	3.14	0.418	2.20	4.00
Female	Female teacher	0.83	0.380	0.00	1.00
White	White teacher	0.90	0.302	0.00	1.00
First year	First-Year Teacher	0.25	0.436	0.00	1.00
Middle school	Teaches middle school	0.28	0.451	0.00	1.00
School-level controls					
Percent White	% White students	0.49	0.279	0.02	0.99
Percent free/reduced lunch	% Students eligible for free/reduced lunch	0.55	0.216	0.02	0.96
District-level controls					
District size	Total district K–12 students Population/1,000	15.62	5.688	7.99	29.62

Figure 8.1. Language Arts Instructional Activities by Topic

Basic skills (7 topics)

Word analysis (e.g., decoding, word families, sight words)
Grammar skills
Spelling
Using phonics-based or letter-sound relationships to read words in sentences
Sound segmenting, such as writing the individual sounds students hear
Sound blending
Sight recognition

Lower-order comprehension (11 topics)

Reading fluency (e.g., repeated reading, guided oral reading)
Listening comprehension
Reading comprehension
Written comprehension
Using context, pictures, or sentence meaning and structure to read words
Activating prior knowledge or making personal connections to text
Making predictions, previewing, or surveying text
Students' generalizing their own questions
Summarizing important or critical details
Using concept maps, story maps, or text structure frames
Answering questions that have answers stated directly in the text

Higher-order comprehension (3 topics)

Examining literary techniques
Identifying the author's purpose
Answering questions that require inferences

of the teacher's initial approach to instruction in the fall. Second, each model allows us to compare the relative importance of two estimates of influence, one for mentors and the other for close colleagues. Third, we examine the effect of professional interactions and exposure to norms of instruction separately, such that the total effect of both forms of influence are represented in our models.

In our analyses, we also included controls for beginning teachers' personal characteristics and school and district demographics. The controls for novice teachers' characteristics included measures of teacher gender, race/ethnicity, year of experience (i.e., 1st year vs. 2nd/3rd year), and school level. The controls for school characteristics included student race/ethnicity (school level) and student socioeconomic status, measured by percentage eligible for free/reduced lunch (school level). Finally, the control for district characteristics included a measure of district size (Table 8.2).[4]

MENTORS AND COLLEAGUES' INFLUENCE ON INSTRUCTION: FINDINGS FROM THE MIECT STUDY

In this chapter, we are primarily interested in the social networks within schools that influence instruction. Indeed, we did not find large school-to-school differences in overall patterns of instruction. Instead, the majority of variation in all three categories of instruction (i.e., basic skills, lower-order comprehension, and higher-order comprehension) was among individual teachers as opposed to between schools. This indicates that within a given school, beginning teachers' language arts instruction can vary significantly based on a variety of factors.

Effects of Instructional Interaction with Mentors and Colleagues

Table 8.3 reports the regression coefficients from a series of 3-level models that focused on associations between novices' language arts instruction and some of the focal independent variables of interest. In Model 1, we included the variables for frequency of interaction with mentor and frequency of interaction with colleagues about basic skills instruction (in language arts) as the outcome variable. In Model 2, we included the variables for frequency of interaction with mentor and frequency of interaction with colleagues about lower-order comprehension instruction as the outcome variable. In Model 3, we included the variables for frequency of interaction with mentor and frequency of interaction with colleagues with higher-order comprehension instruction as the outcome variable.

The results from these models indicate that frequent interactions with formal mentors related to reading/language arts curriculum, teaching strategies, and student assessment are associated with novices' increasing the rate at which they teach higher-order comprehension skills (at the $p < .10$ level; a confidence level benchmark appropriate for studies of this size). This suggests that through regular interactions with their mentors, beginning teachers acquire knowledge and skills that enable them to teach higher-order comprehension more often. Similarly, frequent interactions with colleagues related to reading/language arts curriculum, teaching strategies, and student assessment are associated with novices' reducing their frequency of basic skills instruction (at the $p < .10$

Table 8.3. Estimated Effects of ECT Interaction with Mentors and Colleagues on Language Arts Instruction

Level/Variable	(1) Basic Skills	(2) L.O. Comp.	(3) H.O. Comp.
Intercept	1.48 (1.122)	1.11 (0.511)	0.60 (0.829)
Mentor interaction	0.04 (0.064)	0.07 (0.046)	0.08 (0.049)*
Colleague interaction	-0.17 (0.101)*	-0.06 (0.043)	0.00 (0.075)
Instruction (t-1)	0.92 (0.072)**	0.72 (0.074)**	0.60 (0.074)**
Efficacy	-0.34 (0.259)	0.01 (0.112)	0.27 (0.184)
Middle school		-0.28 (0.218)	-0.13 (0.358)
First year	0.19 (0.255)	0.01 (0.112)	-0.02 (0.195)
Female	-0.04 (0.300)	0.07 (0.124)	0.04 (0.208)
White	-0.02 (0.383)	0.23 (0.158)	0.17 (0.272)
School level			
Percent White	-0.22 (0.513)	0.15 (0.222)	0.12 (0.388)
Percent free/reduced lunch	0.06 (0.639)	-0.06 (0.261)	-0.21(0.466)
District level			
District size	0.02 (0.021)	-0.01 (0.008)	-0.01(0.015)

* $p < 0.10$. ** $p < 0.01$.
Standard errors are provided in parentheses.

level). In other words, when beginning teachers have opportunities to talk with their colleagues about instruction, they may start to employ different, more challenging instructional strategies while relying less on basic skills instruction (in grammar, spelling, phonics, phonemic awareness, etc.). These other strategies can include, but are not limited to, lower- and higher-order comprehension.

Indirect Effect of Exposure to Others' Instruction

Table 8.4 reports the regression coefficients from a series of three-level models that focused on how exposure to a) mentor's language arts instruction and b) colleagues' language arts instruction affected the beginning teachers' instruction in basic skills, lower-order comprehension, and higher-order comprehension. The results indicate that when novices' close colleagues teach basic skills with greater frequency, the novice is more likely to then teach basic skills with greater frequency (at the $p < .01$ level). This does not necessarily mean that they teach lower-order comprehension or higher-order comprehension with less frequency though, since they aren't mutually exclusive. For example, a teacher who scores high on rate of basic skills

Table 8.4. Influence of Mentor/Colleague's Language Arts Instruction on Novices' Language Arts Instruction

Variable	MENTOR INFLUENCE			COLLEAGUE INFLUENCE		
	Basic Skills	Lower-Order Comprehension	Higher-Order Comprehension	Basic Skills	Lower-Order Comprehension	Higher-Order Comprehension
Intercept	0.16	1.19*	1.47*	-0.05	0.90*	1.56*
	(0.433)	(0.377)	(0.43)	(0.327)	(0.336)	(0.337)
Influence	0.02	0.00	0.02	0.04*	0.01	0.00
	(0.018)	(0.01)	(0.019)	(0.015)	(0.008)	(0.013)
Prior	0.84*	0.75*	0.62*	0.80*	0.76*	0.64*
	(0.063)	(0.064)	(0.065)	(0.328)	(0.063)	(0.065)
R^2	0.6123	0.5139	0.4166	0.6300	0.5140	0.4138
n	121	142	142	121	142	142

* $p < 0.01$.
Standard errors are provided in parentheses

instruction and on rate of higher-order comprehension instruction is likely to be integrating basic skills with higher-order comprehension instruction, maintaining students' time on task throughout most of their instructional time, or both.

We also found that mentors' language arts practices had a positive, albeit nonsignificant, effect on beginning teachers' practices in the areas of basic skills and higher-order comprehension. In sum, we argue that greater exposure to colleagues who more regularly teach basic skills leads novice teachers on average to also more regularly teach basic skills. This is possibly a result of the norms of the school (associated with the curriculum), expectations placed on teachers, and so on.

CONCLUSION

The analyses presented here indicate that beginning teachers' language arts instruction can be influenced by professional interactions with formal mentors and other school-based colleagues as well as exposure to norms in their schools, represented by their colleagues' language arts practices. These findings have important implications for research and policy related to new teacher mentoring and induction programs and teacher and school accountability. In this section, we first consider the implications of our findings for efforts by schools and districts to provide support to novices as they enter the profession. Next, we distinguish between conceptualizations of instruction as being caused by characteristics of individual teachers versus being caused by normative approaches in schools, and we consider the implications of this distinction for research and policy related to accountability.

In this study, we found that regular interactions with formal mentors concerning reading/language arts curriculum, teaching strategies, and student assessment were related to beginning teachers' increasing the frequency of their higher-order comprehension instruction. This was a particularly robust finding because we controlled for novices' initial levels of higher-order comprehension instruction. This result is consistent with several qualitative studies that have documented ways that formal mentors can promote teacher learning (Achinstein & Barrett, 2004; Achinstein et al., 2004; Athanases & Achinstein, 2003; Feiman-Nemser, 2001; Youngs, 2007). In addition, this finding builds on recent research by Glazerman and colleagues (2010) that found little difference in the effects on novices' language arts instruction of intensive mentoring provided by full-time mentors who were released from teaching versus mentoring provided by part-time mentors who were teaching full time. The mentors in our study were virtually all full-time teachers working in the same schools as their mentees; in other words, they were very similar to the mentors in the *control* group in the research by Glazerman and colleagues. Thus, while the Mathematica study found few differences between the effects of intensive mentoring and the effects of school-based mentoring, our study suggests that frequent interactions with school-based mentors who are teaching full time can promote increases in novices' enactment of higher-order comprehension instruction.

In our study, we also reported that regular interactions with colleagues related to reading/language arts curriculum, teaching strategies, and student assessment were related to beginning teachers' decreasing the rate of their basic skills instruction. As discussed above, this suggests that the knowledge and skills acquired from colleagues in such interactions can enable novices to rely less on basic skills instruction while enacting different, more challenging pedagogical strategies. In contrast to recent research and policy related to new teacher induction (which has focused almost exclusively on the role of one-to-one mentoring and professional development for individual teachers), this finding suggests that other school-based colleagues (in addition to formal mentors) can serve as key resources to novices. When policy makers, district administrators, and principals assume that beginning teachers are subject to the influence of only formal mentors, they are likely to neglect other key factors that can affect their development and practice.

Finally, this study found that exposure to norms for instruction represented by colleagues' language arts practices can influence novices' language arts instruction. More specifically, when a beginning teacher's colleagues taught basic skills in literacy more frequently, the novice was likely to enact basic skills instruction more often. Again, this was a very robust finding, given that we controlled for beginning teachers' initial levels of basic skills instruction. Further, this finding points to a key difference in the way instruction is conceptualized by current policies related to accountability as compared with sociological studies of instruction that account for school context. The underlying premise of the current accountability movement, as represented by the federal Race to the Top legislation, is that effective instruction is primarily the result of individual teacher characteristics. That is, these policies assume that "effective teachers" can be readily identified, instructional support can be provided to less effective teachers (in the form of mentoring and professional development), and teachers who fail to improve their practice should be removed.

But these policies do not fully account for the role of school organizational context, including norms for instruction in schools, in influencing teachers' language arts instruction (Bryk & Schneider, 2002; Newmann,

King, & Youngs, 2000). In the case of beginning teachers, when they enter the profession, they also typically enter an existing school with a group of faculty with their own norms about reading and writing instruction. As we have shown, these individuals can influence novices' practices through their interactions with them as well as the norms represented by their language arts teaching. When policy makers, district leaders, and school leaders do not take account of school context, including novices' colleagues, they may neglect or ignore salient factors that can shape and ultimately increase or constrain novices' opportunities to improve their instruction and, ultimately, teach more effectively.

NOTES

1. The levels of frequency in the survey were as follows: (1) never, (2) less than once a month, (3) 1–3 times a month, (4) 1–2 times per week, (5) 3–4 times per week, and (6) every day.

2. The English/language arts topics and categories were derived from the Study of Instructional Improvement (SSI).

3. The scale of frequency in the survey were as follows: (1) never, (2) less than once a month, (3) 1–3 times a month, (4) 1–2 times per week, (5) 3–4 times per week, and (6) every day.

4. In this study, there were missing data for key independent variables and to a lesser extent other control measures. There was no missing data on the mentor and colleague interaction variables, but missing data on the exposure measures ranged from 41 to 107 responses. Control variables had fewer than 10 missing responses and in many cases no missing data. Following Cohen and Cohen (1983), missing data was coded to a value of 0 and a flag was included in the models to indicate missing data.

REFERENCES

Achinstein, B., & Barrett, A. (2004). How new teachers and mentors view diverse learners and challenges of practice. *Teacher College Record, 106*, 716–746.

Achinstein, B., Ogawa, R. T., & Speiglman, A. (2004). Are we creating separate and unequal tracks of teachers? The impact of state policy, local conditions, and teacher characteristics on new teacher socialization. *American Educational Research Journal, 41*, 557–603.

Allison, P. D. (1990). Change scores as dependent variables in regression analysis. *Sociological Methodology, 20*, 93–114.

Applebee, A., Langer, J. A., Nystrand, M., & Gamoran, A. (2003). Discussion-based approaches to developing understanding: Classroom instruction and student performance in middle and high school English. *American Educational Research Journal, 40*, 685–730.

Athanases, S. Z., & Achinstein, B. (2003). Focusing new teachers on individual and low performing students: The centrality of formative assessment in the mentor's repertoire of practice. *Teacher College Record, 105*, 1486–1520.

Bryk, A. S., & Schneider, B. (2002). *Trust in schools: A core resource for improvement*. New York: Russell Sage Foundation.

Coburn, C. E., & Russell, J. (2008). District policy and teachers' social networks. *Educational Evaluation and Policy Analysis, 30*, 203–235.

Cohen, J., & Cohen, B. (1983). Applied multiple regression/correlation analysis for the behavioral sciences. Hillsdale, NJ: Lawrence Erlbaum.

Education Week. (2010). *Fresh course, swift current: Momentum and challenges in the new surge toward common standards. Quality Counts 2010.* Washington, DC: Editorial Projects in Education.

Feiman-Nemser, S. (2001). Helping novices learn to teach: Lessons from an exemplary support teacher. *Journal of Teacher Education, 52*, 17–30.

Frank, K. A., Muller, C., Schiller, K., Crosnoe, R., Riegle-Crumb, C., Strassman-Muller, A., & Pearson J. (2008). The social dynamics of mathematics coursetaking in high school. *American Journal of Sociology, 113*, 1645–1696.

Glazerman, S., Isenberg, E., Dolfin, S., Bleeker, M., Johnson, A., Grider, M., & Jocubus, M. (2010). *Impacts of comprehensive teacher induction: Final results from a randomized controlled study*. Washington, DC: U.S. Department of Education, Institute of Education Sciences.

Grossman, P. L., & Thompson, C. (2004). District policy and beginning teachers: A lens on teacher learning. *Educational Evaluation and Policy Analysis, 26*, 281–301.

Hillocks, G. (2006). Middle and high school composition. In P. Smagorinsky (Ed.), *Research on composition: Multiple perspectives on two decades of change* (pp. 48–77). New York: Teachers College Press.

Newmann, F. M., King, M. B., & Youngs, P. (2000). Professional development that addresses school capacity: Lessons from urban elementary schools. *American Journal of Education, 108*, 259–299.

Phelps, G., & Schilling, S. (2004). Developing measures of content knowledge for teaching reading. *Elementary School Journal, 105*, 31–48.

Pogodzinski, B., Youngs, P., Frank, K., & Belman, D. (under review). The influence of principal-teacher relations on novices' intent to remain teaching.

Pressley, M., Duke, N., & Boling, E. (2004). The educational science and scientifically based instruction we need: Lessons from reading research and policymaking. *Harvard Educational Review, 74*, 30–61.

Valencia, S. W., Place, N. A., Martin, S. D., & Grossman, P. L. (2006). Curriculum materials for elementary reading: Shackles and scaffolds for four beginning teachers. *Elementary School Journal, 107*, 93–120.

Youngs, P. (2007). District induction policy and new teachers' experiences: An examination of local policy implementation in Connecticut. *Teachers College Record, 109*, 797–837.

CHAPTER 9

Teachers' Social Capital and the Implementation of Schoolwide Reforms

William R. Penuel, Kenneth A. Frank, Min Sun, Chong Min Kim

Key goals of current federal policy and foundation investments in teacher quality are to identify and empower effective teachers. Policy makers and foundation leaders justify these policies by drawing attention to studies documenting important variation in teacher effectiveness derived from studies of achievement growth (Rivkin, Hanushek, & Kain, 2005; Sanders & Horn, 1998). Experimental studies show that such effects are not simply effects of selection—that is, more effective teachers being assigned students who learn more readily (Kane & Staiger, 2008). Within-school variability with respect to teaching practices and reform implementation is also often high, so much so that students face what has been called an "instructional lottery" when it comes to what they can expect from the teachers they are assigned (McLaughlin & Talbert, 2001). Variability in the quality of instruction poses a challenge to efforts to improve achievement, since researchers have found that teaching quality is related to teacher effectiveness (Kane, Taylor, Tyler, & Wooten, 2010; Rowan, Correnti, & Miller, 2002).

Current policy recommendations to address these concerns focus on improving processes for selecting, rewarding, and promoting individual teachers who are effective. The premise behind such policies is that by incentivizing individual excellence, schools will improve at dramatically faster rates than could be accomplished by focusing on teacher professional development alone (Bill and Melinda Gates Foundation, 2010; Hanushek, 2009). Yet estimates of individual teachers' effectiveness in promoting achievement gains show that interactions with peers who are more effective can have positive effects on those estimates

(Jackson & Bruegmann, 2009). Most likely, these spillover effects arise from more effective peers' sharing of information about effective instructional practices and about the implementation of instructional reforms they are using with colleagues, to the extent that those practices and reforms are the most proximal causes of student achievement.

In this chapter, we present evidence to support the theory that a teacher's *social capital*, specifically, the expertise that they obtain through interactions with colleagues, partly explains variation in the implementation of reforms. We develop our theory and present an empirical illustration using a sample of 21 schools, each engaged in locally defined schoolwide change efforts. In this illustration, we use analyses of social network dynamics to account for influences on teachers' instructional practices. A multilevel model of teachers nested within subgroups and schools then accounts for interactions within and across subgroup boundaries.

TEACHERS' SOCIAL CAPITAL AND INSTRUCTIONAL CHANGE

A key premise of our theoretical framework is that an understanding of teacher quality requires attention to teachers' social context, a premise supported by a wide range of empirical studies. Using reading and math test score data from upper elementary students in North Carolina, Jackson and Bruegmann (2009) found that students achieve larger gains when their teachers receive help from more effective colleagues (as measured by colleagues' value-added estimates). These spillover effects persist across time, moreover, suggesting a strong, lasting effect of peer interactions on performance. Other studies show that peer interactions can facilitate the implementation of technology (Frank, Zhao, & Borman, 2004) and the development of a shared vision and commitment to action (Penuel, Riel, Krause, & Frank, 2009). Importantly, researchers also find that the degree to which interactions support transformational change in teaching depends on the depth and content of collegial interactions (Coburn & Russell, 2008).

We posit that interactions with colleagues shape teaching and learning outcomes because they are an important source of teachers' *social capital*, defined here as the resources and expertise individuals can obtain through their ties with others (Coleman, 1990; Lin, 2001). Social capital has a network structure (Burt, 2000; Lin, 2001); that is, resources and expertise are embedded within particular positions in a social network and not freely available to anyone in a particular system. Rather, it is through one's ties to others that one gains access to particular expertise and resources by relying on norms of helpfulness and obligation to others that arise among individuals who interact frequently with one another.

Teachers' collegial interactions with one another can help them implement reforms in their classrooms in two key ways that reflect different functions of social capital in shaping individual action. First, interactions may exert *normative pressure* on teachers in schools to adopt particular practices. When individuals who share a tie also share a relationship with a third party, trust and relations of obligation that exist between individuals become "enforceable" by third parties, establishing norms conducive to coordination and cohesion (Coleman, 1990). Second, interactions may provide individuals with access to *new knowledge* needed to implement reforms. Close colleagues may not always be the best source of such knowledge, since knowledge circulates more freely among colleagues who share ties. More important may be the ability to obtain help from people with relevant expertise from outside one's immediate circle (Reagans & McEvily, 2003). For teachers, experts outside their social circles may be located within the school (e.g., an instructional coach or a colleague from another grade-level team) or come from outside the school (e.g., a professional development leader).

These two potential functions of social capital imply that it is important to attend to the concentration of collegial interactions within schools related to help on instructional matters. Where interactions are concentrated, that is, more dense and frequent, the normative function of social capital is likely to shape the extent to which teachers implement reforms their school has adopted, as teachers conform to their colleagues' behavior. Where interactions are less dense and more infrequent, attending to the potential of interactions to support knowledge transfer is likely to shape teachers' implementation of reforms. Since teachers tend to be professionally close and interact with just a few colleagues in the school with whom they may share common beliefs about teaching (Bidwell & Yasumoto, 1997; Yasumoto, Uekawa, & Bidwell, 2001), understanding the composition of subgroups within schools and the expertise that circulates within them is critical to understanding how collegial interactions shape the implementation of reforms.

INTERACTIONS THAT LEAD TO INSTRUCTIONAL CHANGE: A STUDY OF SCHOOLWIDE INITIATIVES

To illustrate how this theory might be applied to studying dynamics in a specific sample of schools, we analyzed how patterns of collegial interaction in 21 schools, each engaged in its own locally defined comprehensive school reform initiative, related to changes in individual teachers' implementation of reforms. The diversity of instructional reforms adopted by the schools in our sample was intended to help show the prevalence of social capital's influence on teachers' practice across a wide variety of settings and reform designs being undertaken by real schools and districts. While by no means representative, the findings here lend important empirical support to the claim that social capital matters for instructional change.

The Measures

We surveyed all staff with responsibilities for classroom teaching in fall 2004 (Time 1) and again in spring 2005 (Time 2) to measure the social ties among faculty at the school, patterns of interaction around instructional matters, and reports about how much the reform had influenced their teaching practice at each time point. We defined two types of interactions through which teachers might be influenced to adopt practices associated with their school's reform. First, teachers may adopt the behaviors of others who were helpful with implementing the reform; we refer to this as direct influence through a network of helpful others. Second, we used data from our questionnaire to construct subgroups composed of teachers who were most likely to report interacting regularly with one another (Frank et al., 2004). Our dependent variable in the study was a measure of the sum of the number of classroom practices teachers reported that reforms had affected, using a scale we adapted from an earlier RAND study of whole-school reform implementation (Bodilly, 1998). In our models, we controlled for teachers' exposure to professional development; their baseline implementation levels of their school's reform; and teacher background characteristics, including their grade-level assignments, number of years experience teaching and teaching in the school, certification (emergency, provisional, clear, National Board Certified), class size, subjects taught, gender, and ethnicity.

The models we fit to the data explored different ways that interactions with colleagues might lead to changes in practice. Influence through any network can occur through norms or transfer of new knowledge. If it is through norms, then a teacher should be influenced by the *mean* prior level of implementation of members of his or her network. Here, the mean represents the normative pressure of the group (e.g., high mean levels of implementation represent widespread agreement about approaches to instruction among members of the subgroup). If it is through knowledge transfer, a teacher might be influenced by the *sum* of expertise, defined by others' prior levels of implementation, to which he or she has access through his or her network. Note then that others' implementation can exert influence through two mechanisms, as a normative effect or as a resource. This is consistent with theories of influence that differentiate between persuasion and informational effects (e.g., Chaiken & Stangor, 1987). Because we did not have an a priori hypothesis about which type of effect would be more significant, in our modeling we explored both of these two basic kinds of network effects on reform implementation and fit different models to the data to explore these potential effects.

The Schools

The sample for our study included elementary and secondary schools that were part of a larger study examining the potential of using social network analysis in educational evaluation (see Penuel, Frank, & Krause, 2006, for more details). That study had the dual purpose of investigating the feasibility of collecting social network data from teachers and of developing general models, such as the one tested here, that link network data to important teaching and learning outcomes. The purpose was not to evaluate a particular reform initiative or to test hypotheses on a representative sample of schools or school communities. Hence, we emphasize that the findings presented here are not a definitive test of our hypotheses but rather are an illustration of how models incorporating network data might be applied to the study of organizational change in schools, specifically, to the problem of reform implementation within schools.

A review of the Comprehensive School Reform database, a database of schools engaged in federally funded school reforms during the 1990s and early 2000s (Southwest Educational Development Laboratory, 2005), shows that most school reform models are "locally defined"; that is, they do not follow specific well-known reform models. Our sample's strength derives from the fact that the most common type of schoolwide reform is the "homegrown" kind that characterized all but one of the schools we studied (Table 9.1). Each of the schools in the sample was engaged in a different kind of reform, and the reform models adopted had been ones developed at the building level. Common to nearly all was a focus on improving *instruction*, that is, practices of teachers in classrooms that could improve student learning. A few schools focused on improving services to students outside school, but even these schools were also engaged in instructional reforms. The most common reforms targeted literacy and the improvement of teacher collaboration about instructional matters.

A number of schools did have some contact with outside organizations in developing their reforms. As Table 9.1 shows, the schools varied with respect to how much teachers interacted with reform intermediary organizations from outside the school. Just one had significant interactions with an outside intermediary organization, and six had some interactions with an intermediary organization. The schools also varied with respect to the maturity of their reform initiatives. Six of the schools were engaged in initiatives that had begun more than four years before the study

Table 9.1. Schools and Their Schoolwide Initiatives

School	Focus of Initiative	Reform Intermediary Involvement	Year Began	Alignment to Standards	Curriculum Enactment	Instructional Strategies	Assessment Tools	Collaboration with Other Teachers
1	Student-centered learning community	None	Before 1999			X	X	X
2	Improving literacy	None	2000–2001	X	X	X	X	X
3	Lesson study	Some	1999–2000				X	X
4	Using data to inform instructional design	None	2002–2003	X	X	X	X	X
5	Improving literacy for English language learners (II/USP)	Some	2002–2003	X	X		X	X
6	Cycle of inquiry into teaching practices	Some	2004–2005	X	X	X	X	X
7	Prevention and intervention with students with learning difficulties	Significant	1999–2000	X		X	X	X
8	Service learning	None	2004–2005	X	X	X	X	X
9	Two-way language immersion	None	Before 1999		X	X	X	X
10	Integrating technology into instruction	None	Before 1999		X	X	X	X

11	Developing standards-aligned classroom assessments	None	2004–2005	X	X		X	X
12	Improving literacy for English language learners (II/USP)	None	1999–2000	X	X	X	X	X
13	Improving alignment of teaching and assessment to standards	None	2004–2005	X	X	X		X
14	Building teacher community	None	2003–2004				X	
15	Use of technology in both instruction and teacher collaboration	None	2003–2004	X		X	X	X
16	Creating a "high-performing school"	Some	2002–2003	X	X	X	X	X
17	Cycle of inquiry into teaching practices	Some	2002–2003			X	X	X
18	Shared leadership	None	2003–2004	X		X	X	X
19	Improving English language development	None	2003–2004	X	X	X	X	X
20	Student advisories	None	2004–2005	X	X	X	X	
21	Integrating technology into instruction	None	2004–2005	X			X	

began, while five began the year the study began. Finally, the schools varied with respect to the specific dimensions of practice targeted, creating the potential for significant variation in the outcome variable of interest, reform implementation. The number of dimensions targeted ranged from two (1 school) to all five listed in the table (6 schools).

The Teachers

The school staff who were faculty members in the schools in the study included all regular faculty members in schools, as well as specialized staff whose chief assigned function in their school was to promote the schoolwide initiative. In our research, furthermore, teachers could and did name any member of the school staff (including the principal) as someone who provided them with expertise or resources to help them implement their school's initiative. Thus, our social network data included "positional" school leaders, though the respondents identified them individually using a roster.

Table 9.2 summarizes key characteristics of faculty members in our sample. About 80% of teachers were female and White, and three-quarters of faculty members held a clear (i.e., not conditional or temporary) teaching certificate. Consistent with the ratio of elementary to secondary schools in the sample, the majority of teachers in the study were elementary-level teachers. In addition, on average, teachers in the sample reported having 13.5 years of experience in classroom teaching (*SD* = 9.8), including 6.5 years (*SD* = 6.6) at their current school. The median class size was 22 students.

FINDINGS FROM THE 21-SCHOOL STUDY OF SCHOOLWIDE REFORMS

Having identified subgroups within each school as described above, we analyzed our data at three levels: individual, subgroup, and school. Because of the nested structure of the data set, we used hierarchical linear modeling (Raudenbush & Bryk, 2002), a family of statistical analyses well suited to educational research. Below, we present an analysis of teachers' changes in reform implementation over time, plus three sets of results investigating the effects of (1) the normative influence of teacher networks, (2) the informational influence of teacher networks, and (3) results showing the combined effect of both normative and informational network effects. For each analysis we report results from "means as outcomes" models, which seek to explain the key factors that lead to instructional change among individual teachers, interacting subgroups of teachers, and the school as a whole.

Table 9.2. Characteristics of Faculty Members in the Sample

Variable	N	Percentage
Gender		
Male	131	19.3
Female	548	80.7
Race/Ethnicity		
White	520	78.2
African American	15	2.3
Hispanic/ Latino	78	11.7
Asian	32	4.8
Native American	2	0.3
Other/ Unknown	18	2.7
Certification Status		
Provisional	101	15.2
Emergency	15	2.3
Clear	501	75.3
National Board	15	2.3
Missing	33	5.0
*Teaching Assignment**		
Pre-K	7	0.8
K	44	5.0
1	76	8.7
2	67	7.7
3	76	8.7
4	40	4.6
5	84	9.6
6	54	6.2
7	21	2.4
8	85	9.7
9	7	0.8
10	16	1.5
11	13	1.5
12	67	7.7
Other	219	25.0

* Some teachers listed multiple assignments

Changes in Teachers' Reform Implementation over Time

In many of the 21 schools we studied, targeted instructional reform efforts were well under way at the time of our observation. Thus, at Time 1, teachers reported more than two-thirds (11.41 of 16) of all dimensions of practice had already been influenced by their school's initiative. These dimensions include both the goals teachers held for student learning and their specific instructional practices. By Time 2, that figure had not changed significantly (11.34), perhaps because we focused on implementation across just one school year. Importantly, individual teachers' adoption of instructional reforms was highly variable; for some teachers virtually every classroom practice was affected, others reported less than half their practices were affected.

Although we would naturally expect some variation between teachers in how much their classroom practices changed during the period of our study, this variation was far from random; it also depended on the individual's subgroup and their school. Subgroups and schools made a difference in reform implementation, and our subsequent analyses sought to explore how.

In order to examine the effects of collegial interaction, and determine whether that influence might be more normative or informational in nature, we first had to assess for each teacher the level of uptake of reform practices among the colleagues they interacted with. The mean and sum of reform practices (representing normative and informational effects, respectively) of colleagues who provided help at Time 1, weighted by the frequency of interaction, is reported in Table 9.3. Since the reform efforts we studied were schoolwide, we find that on average, teachers were exposed to high levels of reform practices in interacting with their colleagues. Yet again though, we find that at both the teacher and subgroup level, exposure to colleagues' reform practices was highly variable.

The Normative Effects of Teacher Networks on Implementation

An important part of our analysis was examining changes in teachers' practice over the course of the school year. In one model we fit to the data (Table 9.4), we tested the effects of teachers' interactions with others as if the influence of interactions were primarily normative. Although teachers' baseline levels of implementation were the strongest predictors of implementation levels the second time we surveyed them, there was also a significant effect of interactions with others. We interpreted the effect as normative, because the mean level of implementation of a person's colleagues had an influence on their practice. In other words, if Sam reported receiving

Table 9.3. Descriptive Statistics for Model Variables: Measures of Central Tendency and Dispersion

Level/Variable	N	Mean	Standard Deviation
Individual Level			
Influence of reform at Time 2 (dependent variable)	476	11.34	4.28
Influence of reform at Time 1	476	11.41	4.59
Teach English	476	0.60	0.49
Class size (Scale 1–5)	476	3.37	1.23
Outside professional development	476	5.53	3.92
Mean implementation of individuals who provided help	476	497.50	551.46
Sum of implementation of individuals who provided help	476	3219.07	4386.81
Emergency credential	476	0.013	0.112
Subgroup			
Mean influence of reform at Time 1	122	11.22	3.13
Sum of implementation of reform at Time 1	122	1197.00	1182.60
Mean of implementation from outside subgroup	122	881.60	961.60
Sum of implementation from outside subgroup	122	844.20	730.80
Subgroup size	122	4.15	2.38
School			
Mean level of implementation of reform	20	11.34	2.42

help from Sandra, Sue, and Shelley, and Sandra, Sue, and Shelley reported consistently high levels of reform implementation at baseline, then Sam was likely to report higher levels of implementation at Time 2. The converse was also true: If a teacher interacted with colleagues who reported low levels of reform implementation at baseline, his or her own level was likely to be low at Time 2, once their baseline implementation had been accounted for.

Several other variables in this model were also significant predictors of teacher change. To reiterate, at the individual level, teachers' implementation at Time 1 predicted the degree to which their school's reform had influenced their practice. In addition, teachers who reported they taught English/

Table 9.4. Hierarchical Linear Model (HLM) Results: Norms as Influences on Practice

Level/Variable	Coefficient	Standard Error
Individual Level		
Mean influence of reform at Time 1	0.45***	0.04
Teach English	0.78*	0.30
Class size (Scale 1–5)	0.33**	0.12
Mean implementation of individuals who provided help	0.0006*	0.0003
Emergency credential	-4.27**	1.35
Subgroup		
Mean influence of reform at Time 1	0.41*	0.08
Mean of implementation from outside subgroup	0.0006**	0.0002
Subgroup size	-0.09	0.07
School		
Intercept	11.55***	0.17
Mean level of implementation of reform	0.34**	0.10

*p < .05, **p < .01, ***p < .001

language arts and who had larger class sizes were significantly more likely to report changes to their practice than teachers who did not teach English or who had smaller classes. Teachers who held an emergency credential were significantly less likely than those who did not hold an emergency credential to report that their school's reform had influenced their practice. There was not a significant effect of subgroup size in this model.

The Informational Effects of Teacher Networks on Implementation

In a second model (Table 9.5), we tested whether the effects of collegial interaction on practice operated primarily through the mechanism of exposing teachers to a greater amount of expertise. If informational effects influenced implementation levels, we would have expected that the sum of expertise to which teachers were exposed through collegial interaction would be related to implementation. In other words, recalling Sam and her colleagues, we would have expected that the sum of her three colleagues' implementation levels would have been related to Sam's Time 2 implementation level. We call these informational effects of interactions because our presumption, supported by our own past

Table 9.5. HLM Results: Level of Expertise as Influences on Practice

Level/Variable	Coefficient	Standard Error
Individual Level		
Mean influence of reform at Time 1	0.41***	0.04
Teach English	1.06**	0.31
Class size (Scale 1–5)	0.34**	0.13
Outside professional development	0.16***	0.04
Sum of implementation of individuals who provided help	0.00	0.00
Emergency credential	-4.45**	1.36
Subgroup		
Sum of implementation of reform at Time 1	0.38[A]	0.21
Sum of implementation from outside subgroup	0.31	0.23
Subgroup size	0.13[A]	0.07
School		
Intercept	11.16***	0.21
Mean level of implementation of reform	0.68***	0.08

[A] $p < .10$, *$p < .05$, **$p < .01$, ***$p < .001$

research (e.g., Frank et al., 2004), is that implementation produces practice knowledge that can be shared with colleagues who may need strategies that could support their own implementation of reforms. Our model results that looked only at informational effects on implementation did not find evidence for these kinds of effects on implementation, however. Results indicated that among the indicators of the amount of expertise to which teachers were exposed, outside professional development was the only statistically significant predictor.

The Combined Effect of Normative and Informational Dimensions of Social Capital

We tested a third model (Table 9.6) that included variables from both models to test the hypothesis that a combination of normative and informational effects could have been related to changes in implementation. In this third and final model, we explored the possibility that both normative pressure and informational effects could have influenced teachers' reported changes to their practice. For individuals, both the mean implementation levels of their colleagues and the sum of their

Table 9.6. HLM Results: Norms and Level of Expertise as Influences on Practice

Level/Variable	Coefficient	Standard Error
Individual Level		
Mean influence of reform at Time 1	0.41***	0.04
Teach English	0.98**	0.30
Class size (Scale 1–5)	0.31*	0.12
Outside professional development	0.16***	0.04
Mean implementation of individuals who provided help	0.0007*	0.0003
Emergency credential	-4.26**	1.32
Subgroup		
Mean influence of reform at Time 1	0.37***	0.08
Sum of implementation from outside subgroup	0.13**	0.04
Subgroup size	-0.20***	0.07
School		
Intercept	11.14***	0.19
Mean level of implementation of reform	0.29*	0.11

*p < .05, **p < .01, ***p < .001

colleagues' levels of implementation were related to teachers' practices at Time 2. In other words, there was evidence of both normative and informational effects on practice. There was also a normative effect that was significant at the subgroup level, suggesting that teachers conformed to the teaching practices of colleagues who were most likely to interact with one another. For subgroups, the total expertise to which they had access through social interactions in the school as a whole mattered as well. Teachers who were exposed—through interactions outside their own subgroup—to teachers in other subgroups inside the school who were implementing reforms at high levels at baseline were more likely to report higher levels of implementation at Time 2, controlling for other factors.

CONCLUSION

The schools in this study were engaged in multiple reforms, and their leaders shared a desire for all teachers to implement whatever their school's reform demanded. As with reforms everywhere, schoolwide implementation could not be presumed ahead of time. Both accountability systems and policies that demand that schools select "research-based" reforms presume that teachers need both new sources of motivation and new resources to improve instruction. Recruitment of new teachers may bring teachers with more motivation and skill into schools, but for teachers in a school, both new and veteran, how does the process of improvement unfold and take place?

For the sample of schools in our study, teachers' interactions with others in their subgroups (i.e., groups of teachers who tended to interact with one another more frequently), outside their subgroups, and outside their school all influenced their adoption of practices aligned with their school's goals for improvement. Of particular importance was access to expertise through direct ties to other teachers implementing reforms. The more help that individuals received from others who are experienced in implementing a reform, the more likely they were to increase their own implementation of the reform. Our investigation also yielded evidence that supported the idea that interactions with colleagues could operate as a normative influence on a teacher. When teachers interact with others about instructional matters, they tend to conform their own practices to those of the colleagues with whom they interact. Last, our findings lend support to the idea that information obtained beyond the subgroup and from professional development can also influence change in practice for teachers. In other words, receiving help from a colleague with whom interaction might have been less frequent (whether because the teacher taught at a different grade level or because he or she was in a different career cohort), affected practice, most likely by providing the teacher with access to new knowledge necessary for implementing a reform.

Because of the limitations of our survey data set, we can only speculate about the specific normative or expertise-related mechanisms that are operating at each school. For example, we do not know whether normative effects are significant because teachers are aligning their attitudes and behaviors to achieve balance in their collegial relationships or for some other reason, such as to conform to an ideal of professionalism. Likewise, we do not know how the expertise obtained by subgroups from other subgroups circulates within that group and how that expertise is similar to or different from the expertise transferred through outside professional development. Answering such questions would require a different type of study, with different data sources (such as shadowing or direct observation of teachers).

Although additional research is needed on the mechanisms that account for the effect of social capital on teachers' interactions, our results demonstrate the potential contribution of network measures of social capital to improving teacher effectiveness. It is widely recognized that "value-added" estimates of teacher effectiveness derived from achievement test score data are insufficient measures of teacher quality; complementary indicators that include observational measures of teaching practice are essential (Kane et al., 2010; Working Group on Teacher Quality, 2007). We posit that network measures of social capital, such as the ones included on our surveys, can be an important part of a system for measuring teacher quality, serving as a kind of early indicator to school and district leaders that a reform is taking hold. Whether or not such measures become part of personnel evaluation, they could be used to support efforts to promote continuous improvement by helping identify sources of variation in school reform implementation, a first step toward effecting coordinated instructional change in schools.

A further extension of this work would be to consider a teacher's "value-added" in terms of the value a teacher adds to his or her colleagues. The findings from the Jackson and Bruegmann (2009) study showing peer effects on value-added estimates that persist over time provide some empirical support for this extension. We posit that peer effects may often be the results of the processes we analyzed in this chapter; that is, they are a function of collegial interactions about practice that result in changes to instruction, which then produce greater learning gains. Thus, a teacher's value-added might be estimated by focusing not only on achievement results but also on how he or she affects his or her colleagues' practice. Such estimates may be particularly useful for providing early feedback on new systems of promotion developed as part of initiatives to reward and empower effective teachers. In this way, our approach represents yet another way that measuring a teacher's social capital and classroom practice can become an integral part of systems for measuring teacher effectiveness.

Policy currents in teacher effectiveness today seem in some cases to imply the truth of the adage "Good teachers are born not made," but a social capital approach takes a different view of instructional improvement. Rather than presuming that estimating a teacher's value-added in student achievement is the best indicator to use in selecting teachers into the profession, a social capital approach views teaching less as a solo practice and more as a practice that evolves within a broader social and organizational context. Those contexts, a social capital approach enjoins us to consider, are important targets for supporting instructional improvement in schools.

REFERENCES

Bidwell, C. E., & Yasumoto, J. Y. (1997). The collegial focus: Teaching fields, colleague relationships, and instructional practice in American high schools. *Sociology of Education, 72*, 234–256.

Bill and Melinda Gates Foundation. (2010). *Empowering effective teachers: Strategies for implementing reforms*. Seattle: Author.

Bodilly, S. J. (1998). *Lessons from New American Schools' scale-up phase.* Santa Monica, CA: RAND.

Burt, R. S. (2000). The network structure of social capital. *Research in Organizational Behavior, 22*, 345–423.

Chaiken, S., & Stangor, C. (1987). Attitudes and attitude change. *Annual Review of Psychology, 38*, 575–630.

Coburn, C. E., & Russell, J. L. (2008). District policy and teachers' social networks. *Educational Evaluation and Policy Analysis, 30*, 203–235.

Coleman, J. S. (1990). *Foundations of social theory.* Cambridge, MA: Harvard University Press.

Frank, K. A., Zhao, Y., & Borman, K. (2004). Social capital and the diffusion of innovations within organizations: Application to the implementation of computer technology in schools. *Sociology of Education, 77*, 148–171.

Hanushek, E. (2009). Teacher deselection. In D. Goldhaber and J. Hannaway (Eds.), *Creating a new teaching profession* (pp. 165–180). Washington, DC: Urban Institute.

Jackson, C. K., & Bruegmann, E. (2009). Teaching students and teaching each other: The importance of peer learning for teachers. *American Economic Journal: Applied Economics, 1*, 85–108.

Kane, T. J., & Staiger, D. (2008). *Estimating teacher impacts on student achievement: An experimental evaluation* (NBER Working Paper No. 14607). Cambridge, MA: National Bureau of Economic Research.

Kane, T. J., Taylor, E. S., Tyler, J. H., & Wooten, A. L. (2010). *Identifying effective classroom practices using student achievement data* (NBER Working Paper No. 15803). Cambridge, MA: National Bureau of Economic Research.

Lin, N. (2001). *Social capital: A theory of social structure and action*. New York: Cambridge University Press.

McLaughlin, M. W., & Talbert, J. E. (2001). *Professional communities and the work of high school teaching*. Chicago: University of Chicago Press.

Penuel, W. R., Frank, K. A., & Krause, A. (2006). The distribution of resources and expertise and the implementation of schoolwide reform initiatives. In S. A. Barab, K. E. Hay, & D. T. Hickey (Eds.), *Proceedings of the 7th International Conference of the Learning Sciences* (pp. 522–526). Mahwah, NJ: Erlbaum.

Penuel, W. R., Riel, M., Krause, A., & Frank, K. A. (2009). Analyzing teachers' professional interactions in a school as social capital: A social network approach. *Teachers College Record, 111*, 124–163.

Raudenbush, S. W., & Bryk, A. S. (2002). *Hierarchical linear models: Applications and data analysis methods*. Thousand Oaks, CA: Sage.

Reagans, R., & McEvily, B. (2003). Network structure and knowledge transfer: The effects of cohesion and range. *Administrative Science Quarterly, 48*, 240–267.

Rivkin, S. G., Hanushek, E. A., & Kain, J. F. (2005). Teachers, schools, and academic achievement. *Econometrica, 73*, 417–458.

Rowan, B., Correnti, R., & Miller, R. J. (2002). What large-scale, survey research tells us about teacher effects on student achievement: Insights from the Prospects Study of Elementary Schools. *Teachers College Record, 104*, 1525–1567.

Sanders, W. L., & Horn, S. P. (1998). Research findings from the Tennessee Value-Added Assessment System (TVAAS) database: Implications for educational evaluation and research. *Journal of Personnel Evaluation in Education, 12*, 247–256.

Southwest Educational Development Laboratory. (2005). *Comprehensive School Reform Awards Database*. Retrieved from http://www.sedl.org/csr/awards.html

Working Group on Teacher Quality. (2007). *Roundtable discussion on value-added analysis of student achievement: A summary of findings*. Washington, DC: Author.

Yasumoto, J. Y., Uekawa, K., & Bidwell, C. (2001). The collegial focus and student achievement: Consequences of high school faculty social organization for students on achievement in mathematics and science. *Sociology of Education, 74*, 181–209.

CHAPTER 10

Improving Teacher Quality

Incentives Are Not Enough

Adam Gamoran

The effort to elevate the quality of classroom teaching is one of the oldest endeavors in research on education (Doyle, 1977; Dreeben, 1994). Early writers tended to focus on teacher characteristics such as personality and intelligence (e.g., Barr, 1929, 1948; Ryans, 1960). Later researchers shifted attention to classroom processes and student outcomes (e.g., Brophy & Good, 1986; Dunkin & Biddle, 1974). Instead of considering the qualities of teach*ers*, this approach centered on the quality of teach*ing*. Building on Carroll's (1963) model of school learning, sociologists such as Barr and Dreeben (1983) and Sørensen and Hallinan (1986) recognized that the effectiveness of teachers' actions depended on a number of other conditions, such as the time available for teaching, the curricular materials used for instruction, and the ability and effort students brought to their learning. While this line of work yielded a compelling conceptualization of the quality of teaching, it was less successful in identifying conditions that strongly and consistently predicted student achievement. As a result, research on the quality of teachers and teaching through the 1980s did not lead to a body of knowledge that could be relied upon to produce effective teachers.

Important developments in data availability and statistical processing have led to new ways of thinking about teacher quality. Value-added models of teacher effects pioneered by Sanders (1998) demonstrated that teachers vary substantially in their annual contributions to student achievement. The same conclusion emerged from work by economists using different statistical models (fixed effects instead of random effects) but the same general logic (e.g., Rivkin, Hanushek, & Kain, 2005). Research on the strengths and limitations of value-added achievement models for assessing the impact of teaching continues amid substantial controversy, as Konstantopoulos (chapter 2), Hamilton (chapter 3), and Jennings and Corcoran (chapter 4) report in this book. Despite the ongoing debate, one cannot dispute that some teachers produce greater gains in student achievement than other teachers.

Now, consider the position of a policy maker reviewing this evidence. On the one hand, little reliable guidance exists about how to select or create a teacher who is substantially more effective than other teachers at promoting student learning. On the other hand, more and less effective teachers can be identified using the data that all states and districts are required to collect. Faced with this dilemma, it should be no surprise that policy makers have chosen to gloss over the long, difficult endeavor to identify the elements of effective teach*ing*, and move straight to an emphasis on effective teach*ers*—leaving what makes some teachers more effective than others as an unsolved mystery. Thus, in contrast to the credentials-based approach to identifying a "highly qualified teacher" in the No Child Left Behind Act (2002), more recent policy pronouncements (e.g., the U.S. Department of Education's Race to the Top initiative)[1] have urged states and districts to reward the most effective teachers and drop the least effective teachers as indicated by the progress of their students on standardized tests of achievement in reading and mathematics.

In contrast to research on instruction, which had strong theory but inconsistent empirical results, research on teacher effects has consistent empirical findings but weak theory. This is evident in results from a prominent new study of incentives to promote high levels of teacher performance (Springer et al., 2010). Researchers at the National Center on Performance Incentives (NCPI) conducted a randomized trial in which they tested the effects of increasing the pay of teachers who produce higher levels of student achievement on subsequent achievement growth. The idea behind this study, based on the literature on teacher effects, was that higher pay would motivate teachers to produce greater achievement gains. These gains might occur because teachers would work harder or make greater use of effective teaching strategies, but the point of the study was not to examine the intervening mechanisms. Rather, the study was aimed at testing the impact of a policy that has been embraced by the U.S. Department of Education[2] and is being increasingly used across states and large districts: "pay for performance," that is, paying teachers more if they produce higher achievement. The randomized design was an important strength of the study. Typically, pay for performance is implemented throughout a district, so it is impossible to tell whether the policy leads to higher achievement overall than would have occurred without the policy. In the NCPI study, middle school teachers of mathematics in Nashville volunteered to participate in a study in which annual salary bonuses of up to $15,000 would be awarded to the highest-performing teachers. The volunteers were then randomly assigned to two groups, one in which teachers were eligible for the bonuses (the experimental group) and one in which teachers were not eligible (the control group). With few exceptions, average achievement of students taught by teachers in the experimental group was no higher than achievement of students whose teachers were in the control group. Teachers continued to vary in the achievement they produced (consistent with the teacher effects literature), but the variation did not correspond to the treatment-control assignment. Thus, the possibility of increased pay for extraordinary performance did not lead teachers to become higher performing.

Why did the incentives theory fail to hold up in this landmark study? The chapters in this book go a long way toward providing answers to that question, as well as offering new ideas about how to improve teacher performance. In short, incentives are not enough. Rather, a system of teacher improvement, which includes incentives but also resources that enable teachers to respond to incentives, is more likely to boost the performance of teachers, particularly those working with our most needy students. In the remainder of this chapter, I elaborate on this claim by synthesizing the arguments presented in this book on what else besides incentives is necessary to elevate the impact of teaching on learning. I identify major challenges to undertaking such an improvement effort, and I also consider promising new opportunities for research aimed at improving teacher quality.

BEYOND INCENTIVES

None of the authors in this book reject the notion that educators should be held accountable for their performance. Moreover, most recognize the potential for incentives to motivate teachers to act. However, several authors point out that the rewards and sanctions found in current accountability systems can lead to negative as well as positive consequences, and their notions for improving teacher quality involve ways to enhance the positive and minimize the negative effects. In addition, the chapter authors have identified a number of conditions that could elevate the chances that accountability measures would pay off in improved achievement. Finally, several writers point to new directions in emerging research that could overcome past obstacles to identifying elements of effective teaching.

The Upside and Downside of Incentives

The rationale behind paying teachers more if their students achieve at higher levels is based on a simple theory of motivation: Because teachers value increased pay, they will work differently (harder or more effectively) to produce higher achievement among their students if their compensation is tied to achievement gains. In practice, however, the link from financial rewards to classroom instruction is not so simple. The relation between incentives and performance is complicated by an imbalance between control and accountability in our current approach to assessing teacher and school performance, and by a system of assessments that does not effectively capture the full range of teachers' instructional goals.

Imbalance Between Accountability and Control. As Harris (2010) explains in a new book on value-added assessment, the first rule of an effective accountability system is to hold persons accountable only for what they can control, and not for what is out of their control. According to this rule, accountability for student performance should not focus on achievement at a single point in time, because teachers and schools cannot control the achievement levels of students before they enter school. Instead, meaningful accountability must focus on achievement *growth*, which is the only aspect of achievement that educators can influence. Under No Child Left Behind (NCLB), schools and districts are held accountable for bringing students to specific achievement targets without much attention to students' different starting points. Yet educators have no control over where students started in their achievement trajectories. In this book, Cann (chapter 6) explores a particular manifestation of this problem in which teachers compete for the opportunity to instruct high-achieving students, so that differences between teachers in the achievement of their students reveal more about teachers' abilities to secure desirable class assignments than about their capacities to get the most out of their students.

Ingersoll (chapter 5) draws out another aspect of this issue in his discussion of teacher autonomy. Despite the relatively decentralized system of education in the United States, teachers have little control over many conditions that affect their teaching. In contrast to most other professions, for example, teachers cannot choose their clients. Teachers also have little influence over schoolwide decisions such as the curriculum for their grade level and who teaches which classes. Even inside their own classrooms, teachers often lack much say over which textbook to use, the number of students in their classes, and the availability of funds for additional materials. Because teachers cannot control the conditions that would allow them to be more effective, attaching rewards and sanctions to increased productivity is bound to have little impact. Indeed, such "carrots and sticks" may even be counterproductive.

Ingersoll provides another reason to explain why performance-based compensation may have negative rather than positive effects. Whereas the notion of performance pay suggests that teachers are not sufficiently motivated to achieve their maximum success, Ingersoll's research indicates that on the whole, teachers are highly committed to their profession. Since they are already highly committed, increased pay is unlikely to boost their motivation for success. On the contrary, in Ingersoll's view the emphasis on test-based accountability may undermine teachers' commitment rather than enhance it.

To address these challenges, Ingersoll does not propose to abandon the idea of rewarding teachers for promoting high achievement. Instead, he advocates a better balance between accountability and control, that is, giving teachers greater control over their working conditions so they can meet accountability demands. How could schools improve this balance? Several chapters in this book point to teacher collaboration as one answer to this question. Penuel, Frank, Sun, and Kim (chapter 9), for example, explain the value of collegial interactions among teachers for introducing instructional reforms. Such interactions provide two benefits that may help counter the imbalance between control and accountability identified by Ingersoll. First, collegial interactions foster norms of behavior that encourage colleagues to work together to adopt new approaches to teaching. Second, collegial interactions in a professional network offer a mechanism for the diffusion of information among teachers, increasing the likelihood of a coordinated approach to improving student outcomes. This flow of information need not be limited to teachers in a school, but also provides an avenue for external information to reach teachers within a school, so that outside expertise has a better chance to penetrate teachers' work practices. Penuel and his colleagues demonstrate the empirical validity of these claims by showing that teachers' professional networks promoted the implementation of reforms through both normative pressures and information flows. Whether implementation of reforms advanced student achievement was not addressed in this study, so the empirical assessment does not fully establish the claim that collegial interaction provides a context in which incentives may enhance productivity. A different approach to incentives may better support accountability while also promoting collaboration: a system of collective rather than individual incentives or, as Hamilton (chapter 3) proposes, a combination of collective and individual incentives. Other examples of the benefits of teacher collaboration are found in the chapters by Cann (chapter 6) and Youngs, Frank, and Pogodzinski (chapter 8), but in all these cases, the link to student achievement remains to be established.

Assessments That Do Not Capture Teachers' Goals. Numerous writers have commented on problems of perverse incentives attached to test-based accountability, such as the inducement to cheating, the narrowing of the curriculum to tested content, the focus on students just below the passing threshold at the expense of other students, and so on (e.g., McNeil, 2000; Nichols & Berliner, 2007). Jennings (Booher-Jennings, 2005; Booher-Jennings & Beveridge, 2007; Jennings & Beveridge, 2009) has been one of the most prominent voices on this topic, identifying negative side effects of high-stakes accountability. In this volume, Jennings and Corcoran (chapter 4) not only elaborate on these concerns, but also raise the additional possibility of negative side effects for other educational outcomes as a consequence of incentives that focus exclusively on test scores. They demonstrate that teachers who are effective on a high-stakes test are not necessarily judged effective on a low-stakes test (see also Harris and Sass, 2009). It seems likely that the correlation of effectiveness measures would be even lower if nonacademic measures such as children's psychological development were examined.

Based on these findings, one may argue that incentives would have more power to improve teacher productivity if they promoted a broader range of schooling outcomes. Hamilton makes this case in chapter 3 in this volume. She proposes broadening accountability measures in two directions: creating richer assessments of content for students, and extending the accountability criteria to include desirable teacher practices such as student assignments with high cognitive demand. Hamilton's call for better assessments is consistent with the direction that federal policy has moved under the Barack Obama administration. Although NCLB remains unchanged as of 2011 (and probably will not be reauthorized until after 2012), several federal programs have encouraged states to adopt more meaningful assessments than have been used for accountability under NCLB. For example, to be eligible to compete in the Race to the Top competition, a program that distributed $4 billion in onetime money to reform-minded states, states were required to join a consortium promoting common standards. Over 40 states have joined the Common Core State Standards Initiative.[3] Following the release of common standards in reading and mathematics, two groups won federal awards to develop broader and deeper assessments for states to use to measure students' progress toward these standards. In addition, the National Research Council has developed a new framework for standards in science and will work with Achieve, Inc. to develop standards and assessments based on this framework. These new standards and assessments may increase the upside and mitigate the downside of incentives for teacher productivity by rewarding teachers for what they enjoy most about teaching—building relationships with students and promoting students' long-term development—instead of what they enjoy least: drilling students on fragmented bits of information in preparation for standardized tests.

Incentives and Teacher Learning

In setting the stage for subsequent chapters, Kelly (chapter 1) argues that teacher improvement is not constrained by a lack of incentives. On the contrary, teachers are already motivated to perform well (as Hamilton and Ingersoll demonstrate in chapters 3 and 5, respectively). From Kelly's perspective, the limiting factor is not motivation, but rather working conditions that prevent teachers from translating motivation into action. It is unproductive to provide compensation incentives to teachers, according to this view, unless they have the resources they need to capitalize on motivation by improving instruction. Like Ingersoll in chapter 5, Kelly argues that test-based accountability for teachers and schools may be counterproductive if poor working conditions prevent teachers from responding to incentives. Key elements of a more supportive system of teacher working conditions include opportunities for collaboration as already noted, as well as preservice and in-service training experiences that provide teachers with the tools they need to succeed.

Everitt (chapter 7) reveals that teacher education candidates come to understand effective teaching as an ability to respond or "adapt" to the particular needs of their students and unique conditions of their schools. This understanding may be at odds with a notion of effective teaching as evidenced by an ability to promote high levels of achievement on standardized tests. Whereas Everitt defends teacher preparation programs in schools of education as focusing on what matters for students in the long run, this approach does not orient teachers for the narrower, more focused expectations of test-based accountability. In Everitt's view it is not university-based teacher training that is problematic, but rather an accountability system that fails to recognize important aspects of teachers' work, such as their capacities to be responsive to students rather than pursuing a prescribed agenda irrespective of students' different needs. Although adaptiveness may help teachers to respond to classroom contingencies, other research supports a system in which teachers are receptive to a framework of instructional goals and strive to implement best practices (e.g., Borman, Hewes, Overman, & Brown, 2003; Rowan, Camburn, & Barnes, 2004). Reflecting on Everitt's findings, one may propose two new directions that could help teachers respond to standards as they adapt to classroom contingencies. First, more selective admissions into teacher education might elevate the initial capacities of teachers to enhance both their students' overall well-being and their test performance. Second, a preparation program that focused more systematically on strategies for promoting cognitive gains could also provide tools that would help teachers succeed in an accountability-driven education system.

Mentoring of novices by veteran teachers, both in preservice preparation as described by Everitt (chapter 7) and as a component of inservice training as discussed by Youngs, Frank, and Pogodzinski (chapter 8), may also play a role in promoting effective teaching. Everitt explains that teachers in training are encouraged by their supervising teachers to develop their own approaches to teaching, using their mentors as models but adapting to the uncertainties and contingencies that emerge, often unexpectedly, in the classroom. While this approach may help teachers focus on student needs, it does not emphasize the standards for which teachers are held accountable, so it may leave them without the strategies and practices they need to respond to accountability demands. Interestingly, Youngs, Frank, and Pogodzinski find that novice teachers look to their school-based mentors for help with strategies to pursue higher-order cognitive aspects of literacy instruction, whereas colleagues who are not in formal mentoring roles provide advice about instruction in basic skills. These authors conclude that instructional activities within a school exert normative pressure on new teachers to follow the practices of their peers. However, the role of mentors in affecting higher-order practices takes on new significance in light of the current emphasis on richer and deeper assessments. If higher-order thinking becomes more prominent in the new assessments, mentoring may be a strategy for providing teachers with the skills they need to succeed.

New Directions for Research on Teacher Quality

In addition to identifying conditions under which incentives for better teaching could be beneficial instead of counterproductive, the chapters in this book also point toward new directions for research that could yield ideas and approaches that will foster better teaching and greater student learning. Perhaps the greatest need for new research lies in a field that researchers have been plowing for decades: the relation between instructional practice and student performance. As I noted at the outset, research in this area has failed to identify conditions and practices that consistently make teachers successful, and this failure has led policy makers to abandon evaluations of teachers based on what they do and to focus instead on what teachers produce. In light of this history, why should policy makers support continued efforts to document the elements of effective teaching? Konstantopoulos takes up this issue in chapter 2. He calls for new efforts: observations and interviews with teachers judged to be effective to create a profile of an effective teacher that others can emulate, and new large-scale studies of effective classroom instruction that yield reliable data on effective practices. Both these approaches are reflected in new national research initiatives.

In addition, Hamilton (chapter 3) argues that neither researchers nor educators have sufficiently exploited the knowledge to be gained from large-scale data systems that are now available in every state, and that promising developments are on the horizon in the form of better data systems.

Emerging Evidence on Effective Teaching. The National Research Center on Scaling Up Effective Schools is a new effort funded by the Institute of Education Sciences at the U.S. Department of Education to pursue the first approach that Konstantopoulos advocates (although at the school rather than the teacher level).[4] Researchers at this center, which is headquartered at Vanderbilt University, will use value-added achievement models to identify effective schools. Then, the researchers will use interviews, surveys, and observations to determine what is occurring at these unusually effective schools that may be contributing to their successes. In contrast to such "outlier" studies of the past (for a critical review, see Hoffman & Rutherford, 1984), identifying the practices of effective schools is just the first step in this research agenda. Subsequently, in collaboration with school participants, the research team will design an intervention intended to help less effective schools adopt the practices identified as characteristic of more effective schools. Finally, the researchers will test whether adoption of such practices in a new set of schools elevates student performance over time. By carefully considering school social processes and testing whether the practices found in effective schools can help make other schools more effective, this research offers a more rigorous approach to identifying feasible pathways toward raising the quality of schools and teachers than have past studies of this type.

Konstantopoulos's second recommendation favors new large-scale studies of teaching and learning. A prominent example of this approach is the Gates Foundation's new project on Measures of Effective Teaching (MET).[5] Like the research of earlier decades (e.g., Brophy & Good, 1986), the MET links observed measures of teaching with student learning gains. Four conditions, however, set this research well apart from past studies. First is the sheer scope of the study. Nearly 3,000 teachers in school districts across the country are participating in the study, and over 20,000 lessons have been observed and coded. Second, the study takes advantage of the new state data sets to capture achievement trends for students over multiple years. Importantly, the research team will also administer supplemental assessments in the participating classes to better gauge student performance on tasks that require higher-order cognitive skills. Third, the study relies on new technologies that allow teachers to operate video cameras in their classrooms. All observed lessons are videotaped, which means they can be coded on multiple schemes for rating the quality of instruction. Fourth, the study applies recent advances in research on teaching and learning to the observed lessons and teacher surveys, gauging such conditions as the quality of the classroom environment (Pianta, La Paro, Payne, Cox, & Bradley, 2002) and teachers' content knowledge for teaching (Hill, Rowan, & Ball, 2005). With these advantages, the study holds promise for a leap forward in our understanding of what qualities of teachers and elements of teaching are most essential for promoting high levels of student achievement on basic and higher-order skills.

New Uses of Data Systems. In case studies of three states, Hamilton and her colleagues (2007) have shown that teachers often respond to test-based accountability measures by seeking new ways to improve their teaching. In chapter 3 in this volume, however, Hamilton notes that districts and schools typically have not used evidence of effective teaching to help teachers understand and learn from their instructional strengths and weaknesses. Until very recently, most schools did not have such data available. This is no longer the case, as nearly all states have systems of data that link students and schools across years, and in most cases student achievement trajectories can also be linked to their teachers. While many states are beginning to use these data for teacher evaluation, Hamilton's point is that there are other, perhaps more productive uses of such data systems. Evidence about student achievement growth linked to teachers not only is valuable for evaluating teacher performance, but also could inform the design of instruction. This will be possible, however, only if assessments are rich and broad enough to draw implications for instruction and if the results are accessible to teachers in a timely fashion. Hamilton reports substantial diversity across three states in whether state test results provide useful instruction, with substantial influence of state tests in Georgia, less in California, and the lowest levels in Pennsylvania (see chapter 3, Table 3.4). This pattern is interesting in light of a Pennsylvania natural experiment conducted by McCaffrey and Hamilton (2007) that found that providing value-added achievement results to teachers made little difference to teachers' instructional practice. On the one hand, it may be that the use of data for instruction is less common in Pennsylvania than in other states. On the other hand, it seems likely that using data for instruction will require more than simply providing teachers with their value-added results. Rather, data use will probably need to be embedded in a program of professional learning to become consequential for teaching.

In addition, to be truly useful to teachers, it is not enough to know about the average achievement growth among their students. Hamilton calls for analyses of differential effects that allow for the possibility that teachers have different effects for students with different characteristics. For example, some teachers may be effective with high-achieving students but less so with low achievers, and vice versa. Such information would be useful to teachers as they plan their instruction, and to principals who assign students to classes. The calculation of differential value-added effects is extremely complex, but recent innovations in statistical computations for differential value-added may open up this possibility (Lockwood & McCaffrey, 2007; Meyer & Dokumaci, 2010; see also Gamoran, 2011).

CONCLUSION

Research on the quality of teachers and teaching has shifted in focus over the years, from traits to behavior to student outcomes. While researchers have not lost sight of classrooms, the place of classroom events in teacher evaluations has diminished as student test performance has taken center stage. The chapters in this book provide an important corrective to the current trend in the study of teacher effects, making the case that one cannot understand teacher effects without looking inside schools and classrooms.

Because teachers, for the most part, are already highly committed to their work, incentives for raising student test scores do not provide leverage that is sufficient to improve outcomes. As a complement to incentives, school systems must provide teachers with conditions that are conducive to success, such as time for collaboration, constructive mentoring, opportunities for professional learning, and access to data systems. Better selection and preparation of teachers could also enhance teacher effects.

It is ironic that of all the conditions that may magnify teacher effects, the most difficult to identify is that which is most directly involved: the activities and materials of classroom instruction. Researchers have pursued answers to questions about effective teaching for more than half a century, but precise answers are available only in narrowly defined areas of teaching. New directions in research, such as national efforts directed at finding effective schools and teachers and identifying what they do, may open a new vista on elements of effective teaching. If this line of work succeeds, it will be possible to bring together new knowledge about effective practice with the instructional support systems advocated by the authors of this book. Surely that would provide the leverage needed to transform teaching and enhance learning.

NOTES

1. See http://www2.ed.gov/programs/racetothetop/index.html.

2. For example, the U.S. Department of Education's Teacher Incentive Fund allocates money to school districts to support performance pay compensation systems for teachers and principals; see http://www2.ed.gov/programs/teacherincentive/index.html.

3. See http://www.corestandards.org/.

4. I am a member of the national advisory board for this center. See http://peabody.vanderbilt.edu/Faculty_and_Research/Peabody_Research_Office/About_Peabody_Research/Funded_Projects/National_Center_on_Scaling_Up_Effective_Schools_Project_Home.xml.

5. I have also served as an advisor for this project. See http://www.metproject.org/.

REFERENCES

Barr, A. S. (1929). *Characteristic differences of good and poor teachers.* Bloomington, IL: Public School.

Barr, A. S. (1948). The measurement and prediction of teaching efficiency. *Journal of Experimental Education, 16,* 203–283.

Barr, R., & Dreeben, R. (1983). *How schools work.* Chicago: University of Chicago Press.

Booher-Jennings, J. (2005). Below the bubble: "Educational triage" and the Texas accountability system. *American Educational Research Journal, 42,* 231–268.

Booher-Jennings, J., & Beveridge, A. A. (2007). Who counts for accountability? High-stakes test exemptions in a large urban school district. In A. Sadovnik, J. O'Day, G. Bohrnstedt, & K. Borman (Eds.), *No Child Left Behind and the reduction of the achievement gap: Sociological perspectives on federal education policy* (pp. 77–95). New York: Routledge.

Borman, G. D., Hewes, G. M., Overman, L. T., & Brown, S. (2003). Comprehensive school reform and achievement: A meta-analysis. *Review of Educational Research, 73,* 125–230.

Brophy, J., & Good, T. (1986). Teacher behavior and student achievement. In M. Wittrock (Ed.), *Handbook of research on teaching* (3rd ed.) (pp. 328–375). New York: Macmillan.

Carroll, J. (1963). A model of school learning. *Teachers College Record, 64,* 723–733.

Doyle, W. (1977). Paradigms for research on teacher effectiveness. *Review of Research in Education, 5,* 163–198.

Dreeben, R. (1994). The sociology of education: Its development in the United States. *Research in Sociology of Education and Socialization, 10,* 7–52.

Dunkin, M., & Biddle, B. J. (1974). *The study of teaching.* New York: Holt, Rinehart, & Winston.

Gamoran, A. (2011). Designing instruction and grouping students to enhance the learning of all: New hope or false promise? In M. Hallinan (Ed.), *Frontiers in sociology of education* (pp. 111–126). New York: Springer.

Hamilton, L. S., Stecher, B. M., Marsh, J. A., McCombs, J. S., Robyn, A., Russell, J. L., Naftel, S., & Barney, H. (2007). *Standards-based accountability under No Child Left Behind: Experiences of teachers and administrators in three states*. Santa Monica, CA: RAND.

Harris, D. N. (2010). *Value-added measures in education: What every educator needs to know*. Cambridge, MA: Harvard Education Press.

Harris, D., & Sass, T. (2009). *The effects of NBPTS-certified teachers on student achievement*. Journal of Policy Analysis and Management, 28(1), 55–80.

Hill, H. C., Rowan, B., & Ball, D. L. (2005). Effects of teachers' mathematical knowledge for teaching on student achievement. *American Educational Research Journal, 42*, 371–406.

Hoffman, J. V., & Rutherford, W. L. (1984). Effective reading programs: A critical review of outlier studies. *Reading Research Quarterly, 20*, 79–92.

Jennings, J. L., & Beveridge, A. A. (2009). How does test exemption affect schools' and students' academic performance? *Educational Evaluation and Policy Analysis, 31*, 153–175.

Lockwood, J. R., & McCaffrey, D. F. (2007). Exploring student-teacher interactions in longitudinal achievement data. *Education Finance and Policy, 2*, 439–467.

McCaffrey, D. F., & Hamilton, L. S. (2007). *Value-added assessment in practice: Lessons from the Pennsylvania Value-Added Assessment System Pilot Project*. Santa Monica, CA: RAND. Retrieved from http://www.rand.org/pubs/technical_reports/TR506

McNeil, L. (2000). *Contradictions of reform: Educational costs of standardized testing*. New York: Routledge.

Meyer, R. H., & Dokumaci, E. (2010). *Value-added models and the next generation of assessments*. Princeton, NJ: Educational Testing Service.

Nichols, S. N., & Berliner, D. C. (2007). *Collateral damage: How high-stakes testing corrupts America's schools*. Cambridge, MA: Harvard Education Press.

No Child Left Behind Act of 2001, Pub. L. No. 107–110, 115 Stat. 1425. (2002). Retrieved from http://www2.ed.gov/policy/elsec/leg/esea02/107–110.pdf

Pianta, R. C., La Paro, K. M., Payne, C., Cox, M. J., & Bradley, R. (2002). The relation of kindergarten classroom environment to teacher, family, and school characteristics and child outcomes. *The Elementary School Journal, 102*, 225–238.

Rivkin, S. G., Hanushek, E. A., & Kain, J. F. (2005). Teachers, schools, and academic achievement. *Econometrica, 73*, 417–458.

Rowan, B., Camburn, E., & Barnes, C. (2004). Benefiting from comprehensive school reform: A review of research on CSR implementation. In C. Cross (Ed.), *Putting the pieces together: Lessons from comprehensive school reform research* (pp. 1–52). Washington, DC: National Clearinghouse for Comprehensive School Reform.

Ryans, D. G. (1960). *Characteristics of teachers*. Washington, DC: American Council on Education.

Sanders, W. (1998). Value-added assessment. *The School Administrator, 15*, 24–32.

Sørensen, A. B., & Hallinan, M. T. (1986). Effects of ability grouping on growth in academic achievement. *American Educational Research Journal, 23*, 519–542.

Springer, M. G., Ballou, D., Hamilton, L., Le, V. N., Lockwood, J. R., McCaffrey, D., et al. (2010). *Teacher pay for performance: Experimental evidence from the project on incentives in teaching*. Nashville, TN: National Center on Performance Incentives, Vanderbilt University. Retrieved from http://www.rand.org/content/dam/rand/pubs/reprints/2010/RAND_RP1416.pdf

About the Contributors

Colette Cann is assistant professor of education and Africana studies at Vassar College, where she teaches and mentors preservice undergraduate students. She also serves as the co–faculty director of the Urban Education Initiative, partnering with the local K–12 educational community. Prior to joining the education department at Vassar, Colette taught high school mathematics after graduating with a BA from Stanford University. She received her MA in policy, organization, measurement, and evaluation and PhD in social and cultural studies from the Graduate School of Education at UC Berkeley. Dr. Cann completed her postdoctoral research at Stanford University as an Institute of Educational Sciences (U.S. Department of Education) scholar.

Sean P. Corcoran is associate professor of educational economics at New York University's Steinhardt School of Culture, Education, and Human Development; an affiliated faculty of the Robert F. Wagner Graduate School of Public Service; and a research fellow at the Institute for Education and Social Policy. He has been a research associate of the Economic Policy Institute in Washington, DC, since 2004 and was selected to be a resident visiting scholar at the Russell Sage Foundation in 2005–6. In addition to being a member of the board of directors of the Association for Education Finance and Policy (formerly the American Education Finance Association), he serves on the editorial board of the journal *Education Finance and Policy*.

Judson G. Everitt is known for his innovative research on beginning teachers' critical first experiences working with students. An award-winning teacher himself, Dr. Everitt is currently an instructor in the department of sociology at Loyola University of Chicago. Dr. Everitt received his PhD in sociology from Indiana University, where he was a research assistant through the Spencer Foundation's Discipline-Based Scholarship in Education Program. His research addresses various issues in teachers' work lives, including teacher education and professional socialization, career stage and its development among teachers, the role of teachers in shaping moral socialization messages in schools, and forms of gender inequality within the teaching profession.

Kenneth A. Frank is professor of counseling, educational psychology, and special education at Michigan State University. His research interests focus on how teachers' social networks affect reform implementation and how students' social networks influence opportunity to learn. In particular, he uses social network analysis to study network effects on teachers and students. Recent publications have appeared in *American Journal of Sociology*, *Educational Evaluation and Policy Analysis*, and *Sociology of Education*.

Adam Gamoran is the MacArthur Professor of Sociology and Educational Policy Studies and director of the Wisconsin Center for Education Research at the University of Wisconsin–Madison. A nationally renowned scholar for his work on tracking, instructional improvement, and school reform, he was elected to the National Academy of Education in 2001. His current projects include a study of the effects of teacher development for sustained, inquiry-based instruction in elementary science on student achievement. The study is a randomized trial involving 40 treatment and 40 control schools in Los Angeles. He is the editor of *Standards-Based Reform and the Poverty Gap: Lessons for No Child Left Behind* (Brookings Institution Press, 2007). In 2010, he was appointed by President Obama to serve on the National Board for Education Sciences.

Laura S. Hamilton is a senior behavioral scientist at the RAND Corporation and adjunct associate professor in the University of Pittsburgh's Learning Sciences and Policy program. Her research focuses on educational assessment, accountability, and the measurement and evaluation of instruction and leadership practices. She is currently evaluating several reform efforts that involve changes to teacher and principal evaluation and compensation systems. She has served on a number of national panels, including the APA/AERA/NCME Joint Committee to Revise the Standards for Educational and Psychological Testing and the Center on Education Policy's Panel on Student Achievement under NCLB. She recently chaired a panel on data-driven decision making for the What Works Clearinghouse and serves on the editorial boards for *Educational Evaluation and Policy Analysis* and the *Journal for Research in Mathematics Education*. She received a PhD in educational psychology and an MS in statistics from Stanford University.

Richard M. Ingersoll taught in both public and private schools for a number of years. He is now professor of education and sociology at the University of Pennsylvania. His research on the character of elementary and secondary schools as workplaces, teachers as employees, and teaching as a job is nationally recognized. Dr. Ingersoll received the 2004 Outstanding Writing Award from the American Association of Colleges for Teacher Education for his book *Who Controls Teachers' Work? Power and Accountability in America's Schools*, published by Harvard University Press. He has conducted numerous briefings of local, state, and federal policy makers and been invited to present his research before many groups, including the Aspen Institute's 2007 Education Policy Program for Members of Congress.

Jennifer L. Jennings is assistant professor of Sociology at New York University. Her research focuses on the effects of accountability systems on racial, gender, and socioeconomic inequality in educational outcomes, teacher and school effects on noncognitive skills such as motivation and self-control, and the effects of noncognitive skills on cognitive outcomes. Her recent work has asked whether increases in achievement and reductions in inequality observed on high-stakes tests generalize to other measures of achievement and attainment, such as low-stakes tests and college attendance.

Sean Kelly is a visiting assistant professor in the department of Educational Administration at Michigan State University. He has published over 25 scholarly articles and book chapters on the social organization of schools, student engagement, classroom instruction, educational policy, and the work lives of teachers. He holds a PhD in sociology from the University of Wisconsin–Madison and is a recipient of the Spencer Foundation's Exemplary Dissertation Award. Before coming to Michigan State University, Dr. Kelly was an assistant professor and faculty researcher at the University of Notre Dame's Center for Research on Educational Opportunity. Prior to receiving his PhD, he was a survey research specialist at the Research Triangle Institute and the UW Survey Center, and a statistician at the National Research Center on English Learning and Achievement.

Chong Min Kim, PhD, is a postdoctoral researcher at Northwestern University's School of Education and Social Policy. His research interests include social network theory and analysis, casual inferences, value-added models, distributed leadership, and school reform. He holds a BA and an MA from Yonsei University, South Korea, and a PhD in measurement and quantitative methods from Michigan State University.

Spyros Konstantopoulos is a leading expert on how to identify the impact of schools and teachers on student achievement growth. Dr. Konstantopoulos teaches courses on educational measurement and quantitative methods in the department of counseling, educational psychology, and special education at Michigan State University, where he is an associate professor in the College of Education. He received his doctoral degree from the University of Chicago in research methodology. His methodological work involves applications of multilevel models in the design of experimental or nonexperimental studies and focuses on power analysis in designs with complicated nested structures. Konstantopoulos's substantive work encompasses research on the effects of educational interventions such as class size, school and teacher effects, and the social distribution of academic achievement.

William R. Penuel is professor of educational psychology and learning sciences in the School of Education at the University of Colorado at Boulder and a senior researcher for the National Science Foundation-funded center Learning in Informal and Formal Environments. His expertise is in the areas of technology-supported classroom-based assessment, program evaluation, and science and technology education policy. His research projects, which have been funded by the National Science Foundation and the U.S. Department of Education, have examined the effects of networked handheld computers on science and mathematics learning, the relationship between professional development activities and curriculum implementation in science, and the effects of intra-organizational dynamics on reform implementation. His research has appeared in the *American Educational Research Journal*, *Teachers College Record*, *American Journal of Evaluation*, *Science Education*, and *Educational Studies of Mathematics*.

Ben Pogodzinski is assistant professor of educational leadership at Wayne State University. His research interests focus on how teacher unions and labor-management relations influence teacher quality. A recent publication appeared in *Teacher Assessment and Teacher Quality: A Handbook.*

Min Sun is a doctoral candidate in educational policy and measurement and quantitative methods at Michigan State University and has a dual research interest in exploring questions of import for educational policy and applying cutting-edge quantitative methods and developing new methods. Her research seeks to understand the development of instructional leadership and how intra-organizational mechanisms may mediate the impact of external interventions on improving teaching and learning. Methodologically, she is interested in causal inference in both experimental and quasi-experimental studies, program theory-driven evaluation, and social network analysis.

Peter Youngs is associate professor of educational policy at Michigan State University. His research interests focus on education policy effects on teaching and learning in the core academic subjects. In particular, his work concentrates on state and district policy related to teacher preparation, induction, and professional development in the United States and their effects on teachers' instructional practices, commitment to teaching, and retention in the teaching profession. Recent publications have appeared in *Teachers College Record*, *Elementary School Journal*, and *Teacher Assessment and Teacher Quality: A Handbook.*

Index